African American War Heroes

AFRICAN AMERICAN WAR HEROES

James B. Martin, Editor

ABC-CLIO

Santa Barbara, California • Denver, Colorado • Oxford, England

Library of Congress Cataloging-in-Publication Data

African American war heroes / James B. Martin, editor.
     pages cm
   Includes bibliographical references and index.
   ISBN 978-1-61069-365-3 (hardcopy : alk. paper) — ISBN 978-1-61069-366-0 (e-book)   1. United States—Armed Forces—African Americans—Biography—Encyclopedias.   2. African American soldiers—Biography—Encyclopedias. I. Martin, James B., 1953–, editor.

   U52.A42   2014
   355.0092'397073—dc23   2013045811

ISBN: 978-1-61069-365-3
EISBN: 978-1-61069-366-0

18   17   16   15   14   1   2   3   4   5

This book is also available on the World Wide Web as an eBook.
Visit www.abc-clio.com for details.

ABC-CLIO, LLC
130 Cremona Drive, P.O. Box 1911
Santa Barbara, California 93116-1911

This book is printed on acid-free paper ∞

Manufactured in the United States of America

This book is dedicated to all the African American soldiers, sailors, airmen, and marines who have served this nation with courage and honor.

This book is also dedicated to RA, my best friend and constant companion.

CONTENTS

LIST OF ENTRIES

PREFACE

On July 25, 1992, General Colin Powell, chairman of the Joint Chiefs of Staff, presided over the dedication of the Buffalo Soldier Monument at Ft. Leavenworth, Kansas. He was the first African American to occupy America's most senior military position and certainly is a hero to us all. His comments at this same spot two years earlier, during the groundbreaking ceremony for the monument, reflect the reasons this encyclopedia has been written. Powell told the crowd assembled at the western fort where the 10th Cavalry Regiment was raised that "since 1641 there has never been a time in this country when blacks were unwilling to serve and sacrifice for America, but for most of that time blacks served without recognition or reward for the contribution they made for our freedom, for the freedom they did not enjoy here in their own beloved native land." Many of the rewards that military personnel receive are intangible, but a well-known practice for providing such reward is the awarding of commendations or medals recognizing courage, valor, and self-sacrifice. This volume provides recognition to some of these African Americans, who served and sacrificed, eventually to be honored for their courage as war heroes.

Most cultures love heroes, and America is no exception. Whether these heroes come from the world of sports, entertainment, politics, or the military, there is a special place in this country for our heroes. The opportunities for the African American community to celebrate its military heroes have been restricted over the 237 years since the Revolutionary War. African American soldiers, sailors, airmen, and marines often experienced just as much prejudice in the service of their country as in the civilian populace from which they came. Time and time again, African American soldiers proved their worth in wartime, only to have their capacity to serve questioned once again when the danger had passed. Restricted to segregated units until 1948, with many of those units being restricted to noncombat roles, in many instances African American warriors were denied the opportunity to become war heroes. While the truck drivers and stevedores in World War II still served, African American soldiers wanted the opportunity to prove that they could protect their country in combat with its enemies. Most of them were denied this opportunity, either because of an inaccurate perception of their capability by the white leaders of the military or because of overt racism.

This encyclopedia is a tribute to a group of African Americans who were truly war heroes. Some of them received the Medal of Honor or other medals for valor. Three individuals profiled here received no medal or commendation, but their actions as a militiaman, spy, or scout in the service of their country predated our medal system and still qualified them as true war heroes. For many African Americans in the 19th century, the road to success led to the Buffalo Soldiers and the first African American professional soldiers in America's history. They were the forerunners of the African American military heroes of today. African Americans have served with distinction in every conflict America has been in since the founding of the nation and they have done so with a courage and loyalty far surpassing the loyalty their country showed to them. They fought for a nation that treated them poorly at its best and almost inhumanely at its worst.

The 80 men and women featured in this encyclopedia are not the only war heroes from the African American community; they are a small selection intended to serve as an example of all those who fought with them. Certainly, General Powell is considered a hero and America's great African American military leaders might be expected to be included here, but rather than retell the stories of these great men and women, we have chosen to recognize specific combat actions that resulted in recognition for heroism. These 80 are all African American heroes, but they are also heroes for all Americans. They fought not just for the African American community but also for what America could be and what it still can be.

INTRODUCTION

The history of African Americans in the American military tradition is a mix of prejudice, frustration, and glory. Through American history, the lot of the African American soldier has closely mirrored that of the overall African American community. Racism and prejudice strangled their ability to succeed in and out of the military, especially during peacetime. While African Americans were successful in combat throughout our history, they were inevitably returned to a restrictive, segregated life upon returning to a peacetime status. Throughout these troubling problems, African American military men and women have proven themselves to be capable of great deeds under the stress of war. In every major conflict America has fought since the time of the Revolution, African Americans have performed with courage and often have been rewarded for that courage with prestigious medals. This volume examines 80 such heroes and the courageous acts that they performed.

While the individuals represented in this encyclopedia collectively received at least 46 Medals of Honor, 3 Distinguished Service Crosses, 4 Navy Crosses, 1 Air Force Cross, 9 Silver Stars, 20 Distinguished Flying Crosses, 4 Bronze Stars with Valor Devices, and 4 Croix de Guerre (from the French Army in World War I), these awards for valor were much harder to come by for African Americans warriors than for their white counterparts. No African Americans were awarded the Medal of Honor during either World War I or World War II, though this was remedied in the 1990s when eight soldiers from these wars either had their previous awards upgraded to America's highest award for valor or their recommendations were finally addressed. The four French medals came from segregated African American units that were attached to the French Army during World War I. The French were quicker to honor these soldiers than their own government and, more than once, pushed the American Army to follow their lead and recognize the valor of the African American soldiers.

The reason for this lethargy or outright aversion in recognizing the valor of African Americans is obvious in American culture. Such recognition brought with it an admission that African Americans were capable of feats of bravery and self-sacrifice that did not fit the image of their race for many senior white officers or civilian leaders. Each time a soldier in one of the segregated units was awarded a medal from what has been called the "pyramid of honor" (Medal of Honor, Distinguished Service Cross [after World War I, including the Navy and Air Force Cross], Distinguished Service Medal, and Silver Star), the brick wall which represented the argument against their abilities based on their race lost another brick.

At the outset of the Civil War, the vice president of the Confederacy, Alexander Stephens, gave a speech that has often been referred to as the Cornerstone Speech. In it, he specified the foundation or cornerstone of the Confederate government, which he said was "the great truth that the negro is not equal to the white man." This "great truth" is the unacknowledged mortar in the brick wall of racism that has existed in America since its founding. A second Civil War leader from the south provided yet another quote that bears on this discussion of African Americans as soldiers and war heroes. General Howell Cobb, a prominent Georgian and senior officer in the Army of Northern Virginia, answered the call to enlist slaves into the Confederate Army by stating, "If slaves will make good soldiers, then our whole theory of slavery is wrong." Cobb's dichotomy of the negative racial view of African Americans and the problem of logic it created for him if they could perform well as soldiers speaks directly to the issues and problems associated with African American heroism being recognized in American military history.

In a democracy like the United States, the pinnacle representations of citizenship are voting and protecting the democracy itself from tyranny. While the U.S. Congress acted to provide African American men the right to vote in the years after the Civil War, the question of African Americans' ability to protect their country was still being fought by many white leaders. Segregated units were created to keep African Americans from being placed in positions of authority over whites, and medals for valor were scrutinized or ignored by white leadership at every level in the military. For this reason, the number of African Americans who received recognition as a percentage of their participation in war has been far less than whites. This was true not only for African American soldiers, as Asian Americans suffered from the same prejudice in World War II and Medals of Honor were only approved belatedly after reconsideration over 50 years later. With this historical backdrop, each of the medals for valor that African Americans received in service to America meant more to their community than was true for soldiers from the white majority. After the Korean War and the end of segregated units in the U.S. military, this trend began to wane. African American soldiers serving next to white soldiers, often saving the lives of their white comrades by sacrificing themselves, were rewarded for their actions with far less regard to skin color. General Colin Powell attributed his opportunity to succeed in the military to the African Americans who came before him in defending America. The 80 heroes selected for this encyclopedia are a representative sample of those individuals who, in Powell's words, "went before me and . . . shed their blood and made their sacrifices so that I could sit where I sit today."

The Revolutionary War was fought by relatively small numbers of soldiers by modern standards. During this initial conflict in U.S. history, it is estimated that as many as 5,000 African Americans contributed to the war effort in the militia or in some other way. Three African American men are featured in this volume as representatives of this small group. Two were militiamen and one a spy, serving the Continental Army at Bunker Hill and behind enemy lines to gather badly needed information. The only award for valor created during this period was the Badge of Military Merit, which was represented by a cloth purple heart. It was awarded to precious few individuals, possibly as few as three, and is the antecedent of the Purple Heart medal provided today to military personnel who are wounded in combat. Today, we have added the outline of its original creator, George Washington, inside of the purple heart itself.

The Civil War saw the creation of the Medal of Honor, initially in the navy, but eventually extending to all branches of service. It was the only award for valor that existed and, predictably, this period represents the largest number of Medal of Honor recipients among African Americans of any conflict in American history. Out of the nearly 3,500 Medals of Honor awarded since its inception, 87 African Americans have received the Medal, with one individual receiving two. Of these, nine of the Medals were received for peacetime service, something no longer allowed. African American service during the Civil War took the form of segregated units in state militias, such as the famous 54th Massachusetts Volunteer Infantry Regiment, or segregated national forces created outside the regular army, such as the United States Colored Troops. In all, close to 179,000 African American troops, roughly 10 percent of all Union forces, fought for their freedom during the war. Of these soldiers, 25 received the Medal of Honor for their courage and valor. Over one-half of these Medals came late in the war at the Battle of New Market Heights. This is explained by the fact that for the first time, African American units were put in the front of the Union forces instead of being held out or used in support of white units. General Benjamin Butler believed his regiments from the United States Colored Troops could storm the fortifications at New Market Heights outside of Richmond in the spring of 1864, and they proved his confidence warranted by taking the position and opening the way to Richmond.

After the Civil War, the United States Colored Troops and state militias were mustered out, leaving no African American soldiers in the regular army. Responding to criticism from the African American community, the government created segregated African American regiments for service in the regular army, situating them mainly on the frontier away from most of the white population. Eventually these regiments settled into two cavalry and two infantry regiments, the 9th and

10th Cavalry and 24th and 25th Infantry, respectively. These units would be the first to be called Buffalo Soldiers, a name that apparently started with the 10th Cavalry Regiment and soon came to refer to all four regiments. It is the members of these segregated units, with African American soldiers and white officers, that Colin Powell dedicated the statue to at Ft. Leavenworth. These four regiments fought during the Indian Wars from 1865 to 1890 and then again during the Spanish-America War and Philippine Insurrection in 1898 and 1899. By this time, there were two separate awards that could be received: the Medal of Honor for acts of valor and courage and the Certificate of Merit that was largely focused on saving a life. The certificate was often given to a soldier who had performed an act that might be recognized by a second Medal of Honor, because unlike the Medal it brought with it a two dollar a month raise in pay. Buffalo Soldiers made up a relatively small percentage of the force that policed the frontier, and historians estimate they were engaged in 11 to 13 percent of the combat against the Indians. With these relatively small numbers, just four regiments worth, African Americans still received 18 Medals of Honor (11 in the 9th Cavalry alone) and numerous Certificates of Merit for their actions during the Indian Campaigns.

On the heels of the Indian Wars, trouble broke out with the Spanish in Cuba and the Philippines. A very small regular army created the need to raise militia units and the four African American regiments were deployed to Cuba largely because it was believed they would handle the heat and tropical diseases better than white soldiers. Fighting alongside white regulars and volunteer militia units, the African American regiments performed well in some of the fiercest fighting of the war. Six African Americans, five from the 10th Cavalry Regiment and one from the U.S. Navy, received Medals of Honor for their actions in Cuba. This included Sergeant Major Edward L. Baker, who received the Medal of Honor for his actions at Kettle Hill and San Juan Hill, as he led his unit up the same ground that soon-to-be President Teddy Roosevelt and his Rough Riders climbed. Most early histories only discussed or depicted the Rough Riders, but the 9th and 10th Cavalry Regiments were on line with them at the famous charge.

By World War I, additional awards for valor had been created and the number of Medals of Honor began to be greatly restricted. The Distinguished Service Cross was created to recognize valor at a level below the pinnacle award and the Silver Star Citation was created to honor at a step lower. The Silver Star Citation, as created in 1918, was originally represented by a small star device affixed to the appropriate campaign ribbon. This was changed in 1932 to create a separate medal, the Silver Star, and all Citation Stars were converted to the Silver Star. No African Americans received the Medal of Honor during World War I, though the recommendation written in 1918 for Corporal Freddie Stowers's heroism was finally authorized in April 1991. He fought with the French "Red Hand" Division as part of the 371st Infantry Regiment and the original file recommending him for the Medal of Honor was lost for 70 years before it was acted upon. Other African American heroes were recognized during World War I with the Distinguished Service Cross and the Silver Star Citation. Such awards were rare and the French units to which a number of the segregated African American units were attached sought to reward them for their valor with medals of their own, such as the Croix de Guerre with Golden Palm, France's highest decoration for valor, or the Medaille Militaire.

World War II continued the American policy of segregated units in the army and a renewal of the question as to whether or not African Americans could perform well in combat. Most African Americans serving in units in Europe were restricted to support jobs such as truck drivers on the Red Ball Express or stevedores at the ports. A few segregated army combat units, such as the Tuskegee Airmen, the 761st Tank Destroyer Battalion, and the 555th Parachute Infantry Regiment, fought in Europe and gained significant fame. At the beginning of World War II, the navy only opened billets as cooks or mess attendants to African Americans and the Marine Corps refused to accept African Americans. One of the first heroes of World War II was Doris (Dorie) Miller, a cook who earned the Navy Cross at Pearl Harbor on December 7, 1941. By 1942, the Marine Corps was forced to include African Americans and opened up a training center at Camp Lejeune, North Carolina. The men who trained there were called the Montford Point Marines, named after the site of their segregated training camp, and were the first in a long line of African American marines to serve their country. A large number of these soldiers, sailors, airmen, and marines performed with courage during the war and were rewarded with medals for valor. Not a single African American received the Medal of Honor during World War II, a statistic that brought into question the continuing existence of the brick wall of racism. Decades after the war, the secretary of the army established a separate commission to investigate whether this was based on racism or a lack of heroic acts. The independent commission found 10 individuals they believed to have been denied the Medal based on racism, and the army board of senior officers finally agreed with them on seven of the men. These Medals of Honor were authorized in 1997, with the only surviving member of the group, Vernon Baker, on hand to receive his Medal.

The Korean War was the last conflict in which African Americans participated in segregated units. The 24th Infantry Regiment was a segregated unit that received much attention for its conduct during the early stages of the war, with historians split as to whether the problems were caused by low-quality African American soldiers or poorly qualified white leaders. At least twice, when new regimental commanders fired large numbers of white officers for incompetence and replaced them, the regiment's performance improved dramatically. The 24th fought in some of the worst combat during the war, over tough terrain and in bad weather, alongside other combat units of varying quality. Two members of the regiment received Medals of Honor posthumously, and one Silver Star recipient claimed that his commander openly told him that he had not received the Medal of Honor because the army could not afford to give the African American community a living hero. Regardless of the veracity of this claim, the record of the regiment and its treatment by official army historians is fodder for significant controversy.

The Vietnam War marked the first major conflict the military fought with totally integrated units. The number of awards for valor received by African Americans rose, partly because of an increase in their participation in combat roles and partly because they were now serving side by side with fellow soldiers of other races. Twenty African American soldiers and marines received the Medal of Honor for their actions during the Vietnam War, 14 of them presented posthumously. In addition to those who won the highest award their country had to offer, many more distinguished themselves through heroism in combat and were recognized by their commanders. Some of these heroes performed these acts repeatedly and were honored more than once. In the spring of 1972, Captain Ronald Radcliffe received the Distinguished Service Cross and Silver Star for actions that occurred less than two months apart. It was in Vietnam that the brick wall of racism seemly began to break down when it came to recognizing African American war heroes. While the racial conditions were still poor, African Americans were given significantly more recognition for their courage and self-sacrifice on the battlefield.

The initial war in the Middle East, Desert Storm, was of such short duration and so one-sided, that a list of African American war heroes is hard to identify. In Operation Iraqi Freedom, however, two individuals from the Department of the Navy are perfect representations of the continuing tradition of courage by African American service members. Navy crosses were received by two African American marines for actions occurring in this conflict, providing additional living examples of the courage and sacrifice we expect from our heroes.

This work has been an eye-opening experience for a career soldier and historian. The gaps in the available Silver Star citations have certainly caused the exclusion of worthy heroes who have earned the third highest award given strictly for valor. The names of the heroes included in this encyclopedia demonstrate the depth of heroism attributable to the African Americans who have served this country since 1776. Many more exist in the shadows or were excluded because there simply was not adequate space. In many cases, these African American heroes went back to their communities and represented the future possibilities to the young men and women who met them.

During the research for this project, it became apparent that one of the heroes represented here, career Buffalo Soldier and Medal of Honor recipient Sergeant Major William McBryar, had lived in close proximity to another African American hero. Lieutenant Robert L. Campbell served in World War I with a segregated African American unit. He earned the Distinguished Service Cross for his heroism in France and returned to his native North Carolina after the war. He started the

Reserve Officers' Training Program at North Carolina State A&T in Greensboro, and the building that houses the program today bears his name. A comparison of Campbell's address and that of William McBryar's after his retirement put these two heroes living on opposite sides of what is now called North Carolina Agricultural and Technical State University, a mere mile apart after World War I. The African American community in Greensboro had two of their own war heroes in their midst, one from the Indian Wars and one from World War I. It creates a mental image of them spending time together and with community members over coffee, on the campus, or at their church. While some senior military or civilian officials may have sought to deny the African American community their own living war heroes well into the 20th century, in Greensboro, North Carolina, after World War I they were simply too late.

Anderson, James, Jr.

Born: January 22, 1947
Died: February 28, 1967
Home State: California
Service: Marine Corps
Conflict: Vietnam War
Age at Time of Award: 20

James Anderson Jr. was born on January 22, 1947, in Los Angeles, California. He attended Carver Elementary School and Willowbrook Junior High School before moving to Centennial Senior High School in Compton, California. After graduating from Centennial, he attended Los Angeles Harbor Junior College for a year and a half. He left college in 1966 and joined the Marine Corps, enlisting on February 7 of that year.

Anderson was assigned to the 1st Recruit Training Battalion, Marine Corps Recruit Depot, San Diego, California, for recruit training and, upon graduation in August 1966, was promoted to private first class. After graduation, he was transferred to Camp Pendleton, California, to receive advanced training with the 2nd Battalion, 2nd Infantry Training Regiment. Private First Class Anderson was deployed to the Republic of Vietnam in December 1966, joining the 2nd Platoon, Company F of the 2nd Battalion, 3rd Marine Regiment, 3rd Marine Division and fought with this unit until his death on February 28, 1967.

On that fateful day, Anderson's company was dispatched to the support of a reconnaissance patrol operating in the Quảng Trị Province that had come under heavy enemy fire and was badly in need of reinforcement. The company was airlifted into a nearby landing zone and began the movement toward the beleaguered unit. The 2nd Platoon was in the lead position in the company movement and had advanced just a short distance from the landing zone when they came under intense enemy fire from positions in very close proximity. Amid machine gun and small arms fire, the platoon deployed into a makeshift line of battle, badly bunched together because of the small amount of space in which they had to operate in so close to the enemy positions.

In what must have seemed to be just moments, the platoon was tightly packed together no more than 20 meters from the enemy ambush and began to take casualties at a high rate. The fire fight continued unabated for some time, with things worsening for the Marine unit who were outnumbered and trapped in a kill zone. With no real warning, an enemy grenade landed just in front of Private First Class

Anderson's position and rolled within arm's reach of his head. With the unit so tightly packed together, the blast from this one grenade would have done immense damage to the unit and Anderson instinctively reacted. He reached out and grabbed the hand grenade, pulling it toward his body and shielding his comrades from the explosion and resulting shrapnel. Anderson's body took the brunt of the damage from the grenade, though some members of the platoon were hit by shrapnel from the blast. Anderson had made the ultimate sacrifice, knowingly giving up his life for those in the unit around him.

For the heroic actions detailed in his award citation, Private First Class James Anderson Jr. received the Medal of Honor posthumously. Not only was he the first African American marine to receive his nation's highest military award during the Vietnam War but he was also the first African American marine recipient in the history of the U.S. Marine Corps, largely because of the Corps' policy of not recruiting African Americans until forced to by President Franklin Roosevelt in 1941. In a ceremony held on August 21, 1968, Secretary of the Navy Paul R. Ignatius, acting on behalf of President Lyndon B. Johnson, presented Private First Class Anderson's Medal of Honor to his parents, Mr. and Mrs. James Anderson Sr. The Medal of Honor citation was read by the commandant of the U.S. Marine Corps, General Leonard F. Chapman Jr. Private First Class Anderson was laid to rest in Lincoln Memorial Park in Carson, California.

Over the years, the Marine Corps, navy, and civilian organizations have honored Private First Class Anderson in a variety of ways. In 1970, the Marine Corps named a barracks for him at Quantico, Virginia. In honor of Anderson, the USNS *PFC James Anderson Jr.*, a maritime pre-positioning ship of some 49,500 tons, was brought into service in 1985. The ship was stationed at Diego Garcia and carried equipment to support U.S. Marine Corps operations. It was retired from service in August 2009. The city of Carson, California, also honored him with the creation of PFC James Anderson Jr. Memorial Park. Private First Class Anderson is honored on the Vietnam Veterans Memorial on Panel 15E, Row 112.

James B. Martin and Jonathan D. Sutherland

Further Reading

Greene, Robert Ewell. *Black Defenders of America, 1775–1973*. Chicago: Johnson, 1974.

Reef, Catherine. *African Americans in the Military*. New York: Infobase Publishing, 2004.

"U.S. Gives First Medal of Honor to a Negro Marine." *New York Times*, August 22, 1968, p. 3.

Westheider, James E. *The African American Experience in Vietnam: Brothers in Arms*. Lanham, MD: Rowman & Littlefield, 2008.

Westheider, James E. *Fighting on Two Fronts: African Americans and the Vietnam War*. New York: New York University Press, 1997.

Anderson, Webster

Born: July 15, 1933
Died: August 30, 2003
Home State: South Carolina
Service: Army
Conflict: Korean War, Vietnam War
Age at Time of Award: 34

Webster Anderson was born in Winnsboro, South Carolina, on July 15, 1933, and joined the army in 1953. A career soldier, Anderson served in the Korean War and continued his service after that conflict ended. He was deployed to Vietnam as a section chief with Battery A, 2nd Battalion, 320th Field Artillery, 101st Airborne Division (Airmobile). Staff Sergeant Anderson's unit came under attack at Tam Kỳ on October 15, 1967.

Staff Sergeant Anderson's battery was engaged in fire missions when their firing position was attacked in the early morning hours of October 15. The North Vietnamese Army unit facing Battery A fired on the unit with a variety of weapons, to deadly effect. Heavy mortars, rocket-propelled grenades, recoilless rifles, and automatic weapons fire were used to rake the position and create a gap which allowed the initial attack to breach the firing position's defensive perimeter. Staff Sergeant Anderson moved into the breach and began to orchestrate the battery's response to the attack. Exposing himself to enemy fire on the earthworks around the battery, he directed the gunners to use the howitzers in the direct fire mode and blunted the initial assault. In order to provide the direction necessary to accomplish this task, Staff Sergeant consistently exposed himself to enemy fire and became a primary target for the North Vietnamese infantrymen. He used his rifle and the hand grenades he had available to hold off individual attacks, while directing the main gun firing. During this combat sequence, Anderson was injured when two enemy hand grenades went off in close proximity to his position and severely wounded him in both legs. While these wounds should have prompted his evacuation, Staff Sergeant Anderson continued to fight by propping himself up and returned to directing the fire of the howitzers against the onrushing enemy now that he could not stand and fire his own weapon. Sitting near a gun pit, he observed an enemy hand grenade land near a fellow soldier and immediately reacted, regardless of his earlier injuries. He grabbed the hand grenade and attempted to throw it back at the North Vietnamese. As he was throwing the hand grenade out of the pit, it exploded and further injured him in the right hand and upper torso. Staff Sergeant Anderson continued to refuse medical evacuation and stayed with his battery to motivate his comrades and ensure that the unit held its defensive position. His actions resulted in the North Vietnamese force being repelled and his battery and section firing positions being secured. His sacrifice and willingness to put the safety of his men before his own was in the tradition of all Medal of Honor recipients.

Staff Sergeant Anderson's actions cost him both of his legs and his right hand. Interestingly, the pilot of the medevac helicopter that lifted him out of Tam Kỳ is often reported to have been Patrick Brady, who himself would later receive the Medal of Honor. Anderson eventually recovered from his wounds and was medically retired with the rank of sergeant first class. He received his Medal of Honor on November 24, 1969, from President Richard Nixon. Of the 20 African Americans to earn the Medal of Honor during the Vietnam War, Webster Anderson was among the only five who lived to receive the award.

After retirement, Anderson moved back to his hometown of Winnsboro, South Carolina, as one of two African American native sons born in the Palmetto State to have received the Medal of Honor in Vietnam. He lived in Winnsboro until his death from colon cancer on August 30, 2003. He was buried with full military honors at Blackjack Baptist Church Cemetery in Winnsboro.

James B. Martin and Jonathan D. Sutherland

Further Reading

Greene, Robert Ewell. *Black Defenders of America, 1775–1973.* Chicago: Johnson, 1974.

Westheider, James E. *The African American Experience in Vietnam: Brothers in Arms.* New York: Rowman & Littlefield, 2008.

Westheider, James E. *Fighting on Two Fronts: African Americans and the Vietnam War.* New York: New York University Press, 1997.

Archer, Lee "Buddy," Jr.

Born: September 6, 1919
Died: January 27, 2010
Home State: New York
Service: Army Air Corps, Air Force
Conflict: World War II
Age at Time of Award: 25

Lee "Buddy" Archer was born in Yonkers, New York, on September 6, 1919. After graduation from high school, Archer enrolled at New York University to study international relations. In early 1941, he applied for pilot training with the U.S. Army Air Corps. Although he passed the necessary entrance tests, he was refused on the grounds that the U.S. Army Air Corps did not admit African Americans. He left the

Lee Archer was an original Tuskegee Airman and decorated pilot, receiving the Distinguished Flying Cross for valor during combat over Italy in World War II. (AP Photo/Alastair Grant)

university and joined the U.S. Army and, by May 1942, he had become an instructor at Camp Wheeler, Georgia.

Archer then heard that African Americans were being accepted into pilot training at Tuskegee, and he made an immediate application. Archer graduated in the first class of 1943 and became a second lieutenant, assigned to the 302nd Fighter Squadron (332nd Fighter Group) that flew Curtiss P-40 Warhawks.

In January 1944, Archer retrained with Bell P-39 Airacobras, and his unit was transferred to Italy to fly a variety of missions, including escort and ground attack missions (e.g., Anzio). In March 1944, the squadron was transferred to the 306th Fighter Wing and based at Ramitelli Air Base flying Republic P-47 Thunderbolts, although he would eventually be flying in North American P-51 Mustangs. On October 12, 1944, while escorting bombers bound for Blechhammer, Germany, Archer's squadron encountered multiple enemy aircraft and spotted others taking off from nearby airfields. During the ensuing air combat, Archer had three confirmed kills to add to an earlier Me109 he had shot down. There has long been some controversy as to whether Archer should have been credited with yet a fifth aircraft shot down, as he and another pilot both fired on the same aircraft. While Archer was not considered an ace during World War II, he was later made an honorary member of the American Fighter Aces Association. For his actions on October 12, 1944, Lee Archer was awarded the Distinguished Flying Cross.

Archer flew some 169 combat missions during the war and had at least four confirmed enemy kills. After the war, he returned to the United States and was assigned to the Tuskegee Army Air Field as chief of the Instrument Instructor School. Archer was later granted a regular commission and completed his studies at the University of California at Los Angeles.

Throughout his long and distinguished career, Archer held a variety of posts, including the chief of protocol for the French Liaison Office, Supreme Headquarters Allied Powers Europe, White House Air Force-France project officer; and chief of staff and executive officer of three international military organizations, including the SHAPE Liaison Office, 36th North American Air Defense Division, and HQ USAF Southern Command, Panama.

To accompany his Distinguished Flying Cross, Archer received citations from Presidents Eisenhower, Kennedy, and Johnson, in addition to the director of the CIA. Archer retired in 1970 with the rank of lieutenant colonel after 29 years in the military. In 2007, Archer and the other members of the Tuskegee Airmen were awarded the Congressional Gold Medal for their service to the United States.

In retirement, Archer continued the aggressive and loyal approach that had proven successful as a fighter pilot. He was one of the most successful of the Tuskegee Airmen in civilian life, becoming a vice president at General Foods and then opening his own venture capital firm, Archer Asset Management. In October 2005, accompanied by former Tuskegee Airmen George Watson Sr. and James A. Shepherd, Archer visited the 332nd Air Expeditionary Wing at Balad Air Base in Iraq. The 332nd is the historical successor to the 332nd Fighter Group with whom Archer fought in World War II. The *Associated Press* reported on his comments concerning how America had changed, based on what he saw of the racial and ethnic diversity of the unit in its current state. Archer died on January 27, 2010, at Cornell University Medical Center in New York City. At his funeral in Riverside Church, comedian Bill Cosby provided a eulogy.

A P-51C NA Mustang is painted to represent "INA the Macon Belle" flown by Lt. Lee "Buddy" Archer of the 302nd Fighter Squadron, 332nd Fighter Group, 15th U.S. Air Force and is on display at the Duxford Air Museum in England as a tribute to him.

Jonathan D. Sutherland

Further Reading

Francis, Charles E. *The Tuskegee Airmen*. Boston: Branden, 1988.

Homan, Lynn M., and Thomas Reilly. *Black Knights: The Story of the Tuskegee Airmen*. Gretna, LA: Pelican, 2001.

Jakeman, Robert J. *The Divided Skies: Establishing Segregated Flight Training at Tuskegee, Alabama, 1934–1942*. Tuscaloosa: University of Alabama Press, 1992.

Moye, J. Todd. *Freedom Flyers: The Tuskegee Airmen of World War II*. New York: Oxford University Press, 2010.

Osur, Alan M. *Blacks in the Army Air Forces during World War II: The Problem of Race Relations.* Washington, DC: Office of Air Force History, 1977.

Rose, Robert A. *Lonely Eagles: The Story of America's Black Air Force in World War II.* Los Angeles: Tuskegee Airmen Western Region, 1976.

Sandler, Stanley. *Segregated Skies: All-Black Combat Squadrons of WWII.* Washington, DC: Smithsonian Institution Press, 1992.

Ashley, Eugene, Jr.

Born: October 12, 1930
Died: February 6, 1968
Home State: North Carolina
Service: Army
Conflict: Korean War, Vietnam War
Age at Time of Award: 37

Eugene Ashley Jr. was born on October 12, 1930, in Wilmington, North Carolina. His parents, Eugene Sr. and Cornelia, moved the family to New York City shortly after Eugene's birth. He grew up in the city and attended Alexander Hamilton High School before joining the U.S. Army.

Sergeant First Class Ashley, a member of Company C, 5th Special Forces Group (Airborne), one of the few African American Special Forces troops in combat during the Vietnam War, died in combat near Lang Vei in Vietnam. Sergeant Ashley showed conspicuous gallantry as the senior Special Forces adviser detailed to organize a rescue mission to extract trapped U.S. advisers at Camp Lang Vei. Ashley supported the camp with explosives and illumination mortar rounds during the North Vietnamese attack. He lost communications with the camp and personally directed artillery support and air strikes.

Ashley organized and equipped a group of local pro-American Vietnamese into an assault group. The sergeant led them in multiple attacks on the enemy positions, although he and his forces were exposed to heavy machine gun and automatic weapon fire. As the senior noncommissioned officer, he led five assaults against dug-in enemy positions, contending with numerous suicide attacks on his bunkers by enemy troops laden with satchel charges. In his fifth and final assault to clear the enemy and gain contact with the camp, he ordered air strikes within his own positions to clear the enemy troops barring his approach. The enemy was forced to withdraw, and Ashley's command successfully captured a key hill summit. Despite being badly wounded, Ashley continued to direct his men and carry out his mission without any regard for his own safety. Eventually, the sergeant lost consciousness due to his machine gun wounds and was carried from the summit by his men. Unfortunately, an artillery round landed on his bearers, and Ashley was fatally wounded.

The North Vietnamese deployed seven tanks in the battle, the first time they had done so in the war. Despite the lack of antitank weapons, five of the seven enemy tanks were destroyed.

Sergeant First Class Ashley received the Medal of Honor posthumously for his actions on February 6–7, 1968, as part of Detachment A–101 Company C, 5th Special Forces Group (Airborne), 1st Special Forces. His body was buried at Rockfish Memorial Cemetery, Fayetteville, North Carolina. His Medal of Honor was presented to his family at the White House on December 2, 1969, by Vice President Spiro T. Agnew. His hometown of Wilmington, North Carolina, named the Eugene Ashley High School in his honor. He is honored on the Vietnam Veterans Memorial on Panel 37E, Row 77.

Jonathan D. Sutherland

Further Reading

Phillips, William R., and William C. Westmoreland. *Night of the Silver Stars: The Battle of Lang Vei.* Washington, DC: U.S. Naval Institute, 1997.

Westheider, James E. *The African American Experience in Vietnam: Brothers in Arms.* New York: Rowman & Littlefield, 2008.

Westheider, James E. *Fighting on Two Fronts: African Americans and the Vietnam War.* New York: New York University Press, 1997.

Austin, Oscar Palmer

Born: January 15, 1948
Died: February 23, 1969
Home State: Arizona
Service: Marine Corps
Conflict: Vietnam War
Age at Time of Award: 21

Oscar Austin was born in Nacogdoches, Texas, on January 15, 1948, to Mildred and Frank Austin. The family moved to Phoenix, Arizona, where Oscar graduated from Phoenix High School in 1967. He joined the Marine Corps at Phoenix, Arizona, in April 1968, and reported for recruit training at Marine Corps Recruit Depot in San Diego, California. Completing recruit training in July 1968, Oscar moved to Camp Pendleton, California, and went through individual combat training as part of Company T, 3rd Battalion, 2nd Infantry Training Regiment and graduated in August 1968. Promoted to private first class after completing all of his training requirements, Austin was deployed to the Republic of Vietnam to join Company E, 2nd Battalion, 7th Marines, 1st Marine Division near Da Nang as an assistant machine gunner.

On February 23, 1969, Austin was with his unit west of Da Nang when it came under attack from a significant North Vietnamese force. Austin would find himself faced with a dangerous position when he observed a wounded comrade and chose to try and save him.

Private First Class Austin was assigned to an observation post forward of his unit's main lines when the North Vietnamese Army sent a large force toward his position. The enemy employed hand grenades, automatic weapons, and other explosives in an attempt to dislodge Company E. Austin was engaged in fierce combat when he observed that one of his fellow marines had been wounded and was lying unconscious and exposed to withering enemy fire. Unable to stay in his protected firing position and leave a marine in such danger, Private First Class Austin left his position and moved to rescue his comrade. He moved swiftly to the side of the marine, although he was under intense fire the entire time. As he neared the wounded marine, an enemy hand grenade landed close by and he jumped to place his body between the explosion and the wounded man. Private First Class Austin was seriously wounded from the blast and shrapnel of the grenade but moved forward to examine his comrade and care for him. As he did so, he spotted another North Vietnamese soldier aiming his weapon at his comrade and put his body between the wounded man and danger again. Again, Austin was able to save the marine, but his wound was mortal and he died beside his comrade.

Austin's parents received his posthumous Medal of Honor from Vice President Spiro Agnew at the White House on April 20, 1970. In honor of Austin, an Arleigh Burke-class destroyer, the USS *Oscar Austin* (DDG-79), was commissioned on August 19, 2000, with Austin's mother, Mildred, serving as the matron of honor. Its motto is "honor and sacrifice" and it continues to serve today with recent tours in support of Operation Iraqi Freedom. The ship's motto is fitting in that it epitomizes the actions of Austin in Vietnam in 1969. In Austin's hometown of Nacogdoches, Texas, a memorial to Private First Class Austin has been erected outside of Memorial Hospital.

Private First Class Austin was buried in Greenwood Memorial Lawn Cemetery in Phoenix. His service is memorialized on the Vietnam Veterans Memorial at Panel 32W, Row 88. In a Vietnam Veterans Memorial Fund Web site posting dated August 9, 2000, an individual who identifies himself as the comrade that Private First Class Austin saved that day west of Da Nang memorialized his friend when he wrote, "I will be in Norfolk, VA, to commission the ship they named after you. It will be a bittersweet trip. I am so proud they finally got around to honoring you my friend and I am so saddened even 30+ years later that it is in death that you will be honored. You gave your life for me dear friend, it is a debt I can never repay in this life. Our association and our deep friendship was all too brief."

James B. Martin and Jonathan D. Sutherland

Further Reading

Greene, Robert Ewell. *Black Defenders of America, 1775–1973*. Chicago: Johnson, 1974.

http://www.vvmf.org/thewall/anClip=23337, posted August 9, 2000 (accessed November 24, 2012).

Shaw, Henry I. Jr., and Ralph W. Donnelly. *Blacks in the Marine Corps*. Washington DC: History and Museum Division, Headquarters United States Marine Corps, 1975.

Westheider, James E. *The African American Experience in Vietnam: Brothers in Arms*. New York: Rowman & Littlefield, 2008.

Westheider, James E. *Fighting on Two Fronts: African Americans and the Vietnam War*. New York: New York University Press, 1997.

Baker, Edward L., Jr.

Born: December 28, 1865
Died: August 26, 1913
Home State: Wyoming
Service: Army
Conflict: Indian Wars, Spanish-American War, Philippine Insurrection
Age at Time of Award: 32

Edward L. Baker Jr. was born near Ft. Laramie, Wyoming, on December 28, 1865. The son of a French father and an African American mother, he is reported to have been born in the back of a wagon as his parents traveled west to find a new home. He grew up in Wyoming and became an accomplished horseman and learned to love the outdoors. He also learned to love education and at one point could claim proficiency in four different foreign languages: Spanish, French, Russian, and Chinese. In 1882, prior to his 17th birthday, he left home to join the 9th Cavalry Regiment of the famed Buffalo Soldiers.

After serving with the 9th Cavalry for five years, Baker was transferred to its sister regiment, the 10th Cavalry and stayed with the 10th until after the Spanish-American War in 1898. He rose through the ranks at the 10th Cavalry, eventually becoming the senior enlisted member of the entire regiment when he was appointed to the position and rank of regimental sergeant major. Unlike most Buffalo Soldiers, Baker chose to take a wife early in his military career and it served as a point of friction for him throughout his life. It was simply too difficult to match up a military career and a family as an African American soldier in this period of history. Baker was a unique soldier for his time and was one of the determined African Americans who sought to attain the status of a commissioned officer throughout their career, leading him at one point to seek admission to the French Cavalry School—an unheard idea for an African American noncommissioned officer when he sought the appointment in 1896–1897.

Regimental Sergeant Major Edward Baker deployed with his regiment to Cuba as part of the American invasion force under Major General William Shafter in June 1898. The 10th Cavalry was part of the force encircling Santiago, Cuba, a city protected by a ring of hills, including some which would become famous during the war. At El Caney, Kettle Hill, and San Juan Hill, Buffalo Soldiers fought bravely under Shafter and many received honors for valor. Among this group was Edward Baker. The 10th Cavalry was part of a force given the mission to attack and seize Kettle and San Juan Hills, high ground rising above the San Juan River. The 10th Cavalry was on the far right of line of troops that included the 9th Cavalry and the 1st Volunteer Cavalry, often referred to as the Rough Riders. The troopers of the 10th had moved into position just short of the San Juan River, situated at the base of Kettle Hill. They were seeking concealment in the high grass next to the river, but an observation balloon with two occupants had been raised above their position by the signal corps and it began to attract significant fire from the Spanish positions.

Baker and his regimental commander were constantly moving across in front of their men's positions, ensuring that everything was prepared for their attack, ignoring the enemy fire that was all around them. At one point, an exploding shell blew off his hat and severely wounded his horse, requiring him to seek the cover of the grass with his regiment. Observing one of the privates from his regiment struggling to avoid drowning in the river to his front, he left the grass in order to rescue him. He was constantly under direct fire from Kettle Hill and amazingly made it back to the relative safety of the grass with the private. As he waited to lead the men forward up Kettle Hill, he was wounded in the side and arm by shrapnel. Regardless, he led the men through the barbed wire entanglements the Spanish had laid in front of the position and was in the front of the regiment as it swarmed over the top of Kettle and San Juan Hills with the other American units. The army recognized Edward Baker for his bravery at Kettle Hill and he received the Medal of Honor in July 1902. As the senior enlisted man in his regiment, he had led by example and saved the life of at least one member of the 10th Cavalry under heavy enemy fire.

Like at least one other Medal of Honor recipient from the Buffalo Soldiers, Edward Baker sought life as a commissioned officer after the Spanish-American War. He received a commission as a first lieutenant in the 10th Volunteer Infantry for occupation duty in Cuba. The army believed, incorrectly, that African Americans were immune to tropical diseases and chose to form special units to police Cuba during the occupation period. This volunteer unit mustered out and Baker returned to his regiment in his former capacity as sergeant major. He still sought a commission and, in October 1899, joined the 49th Volunteer Infantry for duty in the Philippines. Baker spent 18 months in the Philippines, thriving as a captain of volunteers and continuing to seek a regular army commission. Though many individuals received commissions during the next three-and-a-half years, only two were African Americans: John E. Green and Benjamin O. Davis. Davis would go on to become the first African American general officer in the U.S. Army and father of Benjamin O. Davis Jr., who commanded the Tuskegee Airmen during World War II.

Edward Baker continued to serve as a volunteer officer and eventually as an officer in the Philippine Scouts, a force made up of Filipinos and commanded by African American officers, until 1909. By this time, his health had deteriorated and his emotional and mental state was questionable. He had not been able to get his family to join him in the Philippines and for the first time he apparently experienced an alcohol problem. In 1908, a board of officers in the Philippines recommended that he not be promoted nor reappointed when his commission expired in 1910. This recommendation made it as far as the adjutant general of the army, who threw the recommendation out and directed that he be promoted to captain. Though the years had not been kind to Edward Baker, senior leadership in the army knew him as a man of character and a hero. They refused to see him tossed aside, as so many African American soldiers had been over the years, and arranged for him to return to duty as a quartermaster sergeant in Los Angeles with an African American unit and then immediately file for retirement. The adjutant general specifically directed the authorities in Los Angeles, California, to ignore "any disqualification that may be found in this case" and cleared the way for the decorated Buffalo Soldier to retire on January 12, 1910.

Baker did not live long after his retirement. His 28 years of service, much of it in tropical climates, had been hard on him physically and he died at Letterman Army Hospital on the Presidio of San Francisco on August 26, 1913. Edward Baker was buried in Los Angeles, where his wife now lived, in Angelus-Rosedale Cemetery. His marker can be found at Section 3, Lot 130, Grave 2SE. He was initially buried with a plain headstone inscribed only with his name and the phrase "Phil. Scouts." In 2008, an historian seeking the final resting places of Medal of Honor recipients identified his grave and sought a more appropriate marker for one of America's heroes. In a final honor to his memory, courage, and self-sacrifice, his headstone now bears the rank of Capt. 10 U.S. Cavalry, marking his final resting spot with the commission he doggedly sought and the regiment in which he so proudly served.

James B. Martin

Further Reading

Leckie, William H. *The Buffalo Soldiers: A Narrative of the Negro Cavalry in the West.* Norman: University of Oklahoma Press, 1967.

Pool, Bob. "Bringing a Buffalo Soldier Back to Life." *Los Angeles Times.* http://articles.latimes.com/2008/sep/26/local/me-honor26, posted, September 26, 2008 (accessed September 1, 2013).

Schubert, Frank N. *Black Valor: Buffalo Soldiers and the Medal of Honor, 1870–1898.* Wilmington, DE: Scholarly Resources, 1997.

Schubert, Frank N. "Buffalo Soldiers at San Juan Hill." 1998 Conference of Army Historians. http://www.history.army.mil/documents/spanam/BSSJH/Shbrt-BSSJH.htm (accessed September 1, 2013).

Utley, Robert M. *Frontier Regulars: The United States Army and the Indian, 1866–1890.* New York: Macmillan, 1973.

Baker, Vernon

Born: December 17, 1919
Died: July 13, 2010
Home State: Wyoming
Service: Army
Conflict: World War II
Age at Time of Award: 26

Vernon Joseph Baker was born on December 17, 1919, in Cheyenne, Wyoming. Orphaned at a young age, he and his two older sisters were raised by their maternal grandparents in Cheyenne. Despite being a high school graduate—no small accomplishment for an African American during the Great Depression—he could not find any good jobs. After working as a shoeshine boy, menial laborer, and porter for the Union Pacific Railroad, he enlisted in the U.S. Army in June 1941. Baker had hoped to serve in the Quartermaster Corps because he had heard that they had the easiest job, but the recruiter signed him up for the infantry.

After his initial training at Camp Wolters, Texas, Baker was transferred to the 25th Infantry Regiment at Ft. Huachuca, Arizona. Since he

Lieutenant Vernon Baker was the only living representative of the seven African American soldiers to receive the Medal of Honor for valor during World War II when, in 1997, he received the award from President Clinton. (U.S. Army)

could read, write, and type, Baker became a company clerk and corporal and soon thereafter a supply sergeant. After the attack on Pearl Harbor, Hawaii, on December 7, 1941, he was promoted again to staff sergeant. Baker's rapid rise caused anger among long-serving troops, white and black, who might have been privates or privates first class for almost 20 years in the army. Not long after being physically assaulted by three white corporals who resented his status (the corporals were never apprehended or court-martialed for their crime), Baker's regimental commander recommended him for Officer Candidate School (OCS). After graduating from the infantry OCS at Ft. Benning, Georgia, Baker was commissioned a second lieutenant on January 11, 1943.

After serving as an airbase security officer at Camp Rucker, Alabama, Baker was transferred to Company C, 370th Infantry Regiment, 92nd Infantry Division. The 92nd Infantry Division was made up of African American enlisted men and noncommissioned officers (NCOs) with some African American junior officers. The majority of officers, however, were white, mostly of Southern extraction, because the army believed that Southerners knew how to "handle" African Americans. Unfortunately, African American units not only received predominantly white Southern officers but also generally received the worst of these officers (based on standardized army training and testing), as the better officers were sent to white units.

The 370th Infantry Regiment arrived in Italy on July 24, 1944, a full three months before the rest of the division, and was temporarily attached to the 1st Armored Division. When the remainder of the division arrived, the division took its place in the Allied lines.

On April 5 and 6, 1945, near Viareggio, Italy, Baker's company was part of a divisional assault on the German strongpoint of Castle Aghinolfi in the mountainous and heavily defended hills of Italy. In the predawn hours of April 5, Baker and his weapons platoon led the company advance, despite losing his mortars to American artillery fire. During this advance, Baker personally destroyed three machine gun nests and an artillery observation position, as well as cutting German communication wire in more than a dozen places. Once the seriously depleted company established a position within 100 yards of the castle, they were hit by a heavy German mortar barrage. During the barrage, Baker's white company commander led the company's wounded executive officer to safety, leaving the company leaderless. Despite desperate calls for artillery support and reinforcements to the regimental headquarters, no help arrived. Because his original 26-man platoon was reduced to fewer than 10, Baker had no choice but to retreat. During the retreat, Baker destroyed three machine gun positions that had been missed during the initial advance. When he finally reached the American lines, only six men from the original 26 remained alive. The next day, Baker was ordered to guide the lead company of the 473rd Infantry Regiment back to the forward-most position his platoon had occupied the day before. Recommended for the Medal of Honor by his battalion commander for his actions, Baker's award was downgraded to the Distinguished Service Cross (DSC), the army's second highest award for valor.

Remaining in the army after the war, Baker lost his commission in 1947 because he did not have a college education. As a master sergeant, he worked as a signal corps photographer for several years. During the Korean War, Baker became a first lieutenant again and volunteered for combat. As one of the few African Americans with the DSC, he was not allowed to return to combat. Instead, Baker was given command of a company in the 11th Airborne Division at Ft. Campbell, Kentucky. After the Korean War, he again reverted to NCO status and served until his retirement in 1968 with 28 years of active service. After retiring from the army, Baker worked for the American Red Cross for 19 years, serving a tour in Vietnam, before retiring to northern Idaho.

In 1993, the U.S. Army commissioned a study to determine why no African Americans had been awarded the Medal of Honor during World War II. The study found widespread racism, and army records revealed a number of Medal of Honor recommendations that had been downgraded to the DSC. On the basis of this evidence, seven African Americans who were awarded the Silver Star or DSC during World War II had their awards upgraded to the Medal of Honor. Only one of them, Baker, was still alive on January 13, 1997, when the medals were presented by President Bill Clinton in a White House ceremony.

In April 1997, Baker was invited by the Italian government to return to Italy on the 52nd anniversary of the battle for Castle Aghinolfi. There, people turned out to honor Baker and celebrate the African American soldiers who freed them from the Nazi occupation.

After a long battle with brain cancer, Vernon Baker died at the age of 90 at his home south of St. Maries, Idaho, on July 13, 2010; he was buried at Arlington National Cemetery.

Alexander M. Bielakowski

AFRICAN AMERICAN SOLDIERS AND THE MEDAL OF HONOR DURING WORLD WAR II

When World War II started for the United States in 1941, African American soldiers had fought bravely in every war since the Civil War. During these conflicts, the Medal of Honor had been received by at least one African American soldier in every war. Particularly during the Indian Wars, this was not unusual due to the percentage of the U.S. Army that African American soldiers represented. While nearly one million African American soldiers served during World War II, not a single African American soldier received the highest award their country can bestow for valor in combat. Statistically, this fact made no sense, and from the perception of the African American community, it was a deliberate decision to exclude soldiers of their race from such honors. This perception simmered throughout the years following the conclusion of World War II and eventually resulted in political pressure to investigate why this occurred and whether the highest award for bravery in the United States had been deliberately withheld from African American soldiers. In 1992, Secretary of the Army John Shannon identified the requirement to create a commission to examine why no African American soldier had been recommended for or received the Medal of Honor. His decision was largely criticized as being one into which he was forced by the possibility of congressional action demanding an accounting for this anomaly. With a sense of distrust of the army pervading the conversation, Secretary Shannon intelligently required that the investigation be conducted by a neutral party that had no connections to the army or the U.S. government. It was determined that the best solution was to use scholars from one of the historically black colleges or universities in the United States. A competition for the contract was held in 1993 and an investigative team from Shaw University in Raleigh, North Carolina, was selected to conduct the study. Led by Dr. Daniel Gibran, a team of five researchers sifted through official records, interviewed veterans, combed through private archives, and eventually produced a document answering Secretary Shannon's questions and making recommendations based on their conclusions. The official report titled "The Medal of Honor and African Americans in the U.S. Army during World War II" was later published as a book and provided wonderful detail on the exclusion of these African American soldiers and the actions taken to correct the situation.

In all previous conflicts from the Civil War onward, African American soldiers had been organized into combat units from the outset of the conflict. Coming out of the interwar period between World War I and World War II, the U.S. Army had restricted African American soldiers to support units based on problems with racism in American society generally and in the U.S. Military specifically. The U.S. Army was not the only service with this issue, as the U.S. Marine Corps was not recruiting any African Americans until forced to by President Roosevelt in 1941. American society had retrenched in its position on race relations and segregation was the law in much of the country. Unable to bring themselves to view African Americans in a positive light and reverting to the pre–Civil War mindset that they could not be made into good combat soldiers, the army leadership created segregated support units that served efficiently at the outset of the war in the transportation and ordnance branches. While not initially assigned to combat duties, African American soldiers still found themselves in combat situations while supporting the frontline combat units. This is always true in modern conflict and World War II was no exception. Later in the war, largely because of political pressure, the army created segregated combat units that served in the European and Pacific Theaters with distinction. Out of all of these support and combat soldiers, not one was ever officially recognized as having been recommended for the Medal of Honor. During the Shaw University study, one commanding officer claimed to have personally recommended an African American soldier for the Medal, but no paperwork to back this assertion up was ever found. African American soldiers did earn other lesser awards for valor, including the Distinguished Service Cross and the Silver Star but not America's most prestigious award. The Shaw University study did not find any overt guidance provided by the army to prevent African Americans from receiving the honor but identified an awards process, which had significant holes, that allowed racism to pervasively affect who would receive the Medal of Honor.

During their study, the Shaw University researchers identified African American soldiers who had performed heroically and with the type of distinctive valor that might have led to the recommendation for the Medal of Honor under more fair circumstances. Their report to the secretary of the U.S. Army, through the army's Military Awards and Decorations Branch, recommended that 10 African American soldiers be considered for receipt of the Medal. Nine of these soldiers had previously received the Distinguished Service Cross, the second most valued award for bravery, for their actions in combat and the final soldier had apparently been recommended for the Medal of Honor by his commander as mentioned previously. A special board of senior officers and noncommissioned officers, made up of African American and white members, was convened to take action on the report. The board recommended seven of the ten soldiers for revocation of their Distinguished Service Crosses and receipt of the Medal of Honor for their actions in World War II. The secretaries of the army and defense, respectively, approved the recommendation and forwarded it to President Bill Clinton. The president approved the awards and, after Congress took the required action of waiving the time limitation for award of the Medal, he presented the awards at a ceremony in the East Room of the White House on January 13, 1997. Of the seven African American soldiers, Vernon J. Baker, Edward A. Carter Jr., John R. Fox, Willy F. James Jr., Ruben Rivers, Charles L. Thomas, and George Watson, only Baker was living to receive his Medal of Honor in person. The other African American soldiers who received the Medal were represented by families and friends at the ceremony.

The belated receipt of the Medal of Honor by deserving African American soldiers cannot undo the racism that played such a critical role in denying proper recognition of valor during World War II. It was the proper action by America to honor the African American soldiers who acted heroically in combat and, in some cases, gave their lives in acts of heroic sacrifice. The Shaw University study was unique in American military history and later paved the way for similar honors to be accorded to 22 Asian Americans who it was determined were denied the Medal of Honor because of pervasive racism during World War II.

James B. Martin

Further Reading

Baker, Vernon J., and Ken Olsen. *Lasting Valor*. Columbus, MS: Genesis Press, 1997.

Collier, Peter, and Nick Del Calzo. *Medal of Honor: Portraits of Valor beyond the Call of Duty*. New York: Artisan, 2006.

Kingseed, Cole C. *Old Glory Stories: American Combat Leadership in World War II*. Annapolis, MD: Naval Institute Press, 2006.

Kingseed, Cole C. "The Saga of Vernon J. Baker." *Army Magazine*, February 2008. pp. 37–44.

Mikaelian, Allen, and Mike Wallace. *Medal of Honor: Profiles of America's Military Heroes from the Civil War to the Present*. New York: Hyperion, 2002.

Smith, Larry. *Beyond Glory: Medal of Honor Heroes in Their Own Words—Extraordinary Stories of Courage from WWII to Vietnam*. New York: W. W. Norton, 2003.

Barnes, William H.

Born: 1840
Died: December 24, 1866
Home State: Maryland
Service: Army
Conflict: Civil War
Age at Time of Award: 23

William Henry Barnes was born in St. Mary's County, Maryland, sometime in 1840. He grew up in Maryland and worked as a farmer before the Civil War began. Responding to the Conscription Act of 1863, which allowed African Americans to enlist in the army, Barnes enlisted at Point Lookout, Maryland, on February 11, 1864. He actually entered service at Norfolk, Virginia, and because of this, he has been incorrectly identified as a native of Virginia in a number of sources.

Barnes participated in combat with the 38th United States Colored Troops in Virginia and on September 29, 1864, he was involved in action at the Battle of New Market Heights in Henrico County, Virginia. This action is also referred to as the Battle of Chaffin's Farm and it was a day of horror and honor for Private Barnes and the other soldiers of the 38th USCT. The attacks on the breastworks of the famous Texas Brigade were met with deadly fire and, before the day was finished, over one-half of the soldiers of the 38th USCT were captured, killed, or wounded. Barnes was cited for his gallantry during the attack on the enemy positions and received the Medal of Honor for his efforts. His simple Medal citation indicated that though severely wounded, he was among the first to enter the fortifications. Thirteen other soldiers from the 38th USCT became recipients of the Medal of Honor that day, representing 14 of the total 25 Medals awarded to African Americans during the Civil War.

After the war, Barnes stayed in the 38th USCT and was sent to patrol the Texas frontier near the Rio Grande Valley as part of the Reconstruction efforts. He was promoted to sergeant in July 1865, and performed patrol duties in the areas around Brownsville, Galveston, and Indianola. His short life came to an end on Christmas Eve 1866 when he died of "consumption" or tuberculosis as it is known today.

In 1867, the African American soldiers who had died and been buried in the vicinity of Indianola were exhumed and reburied in a mass grave in the San Antonio National Cemetery. Sergeant William H. Barnes, Medal of Honor recipient, was among those buried in this mass grave, but because of his Medal of Honor he was honored with a headstone identifying him by name and the award he had received for gallantry at Chaffin's Farm.

James B. Martin

Further Reading

Claxton, Melvin, and Mark Puls. *Uncommon Valor: A Story of Race, Patriotism, and Glory in the Final Battles of the Civil War.* Hoboken, NJ: John Wiley and Sons, 2006.

Hanna, Charles W. *African American Recipients of the Medal of Honor: A Biographical Dictionary, Civil War through Vietnam War.* Jefferson, NC: McFarland, 2002.

Work, David. "United States Colored Troops in Texas during Reconstruction, 1865–1867." *The Southwestern Historical Quarterly* 109(3) (January 2006): 337–58.

Beaty, Powhatan

Born: October 8, 1837
Died: December 6, 1916
Home State: Virginia
Service: Army
Conflict: Civil War
Age at Time of Award: 26

Beaty was the first sergeant in Company G, 5th U.S. Colored Infantry during the Civil War, having been raised to this rank in September 1864. He went on to fight with distinction at the Battle of Chaffin's Farm (September 29–30, 1864), earning the Medal of Honor—one of the few African Africans to be awarded this honor during the Civil War.

Beaty was born on October 8, 1837, in Richmond, Virginia, and later moved to Ohio as a farmer. He briefly served in the Black Brigade of Cincinnati (September 2–20, 1862), when Confederate Gen. Kirby Smith threatened the city. The unit constructed fortifications around Cincinnati.

Beaty entered military service on June 7, 1863, in Cincinnati, training at Camp Delaware, where he was

Sergeant Powhatan Beaty was one of 14 African Americans to receive the Medal of Honor for their actions at the Battle of New Market Heights. (Library of Congress)

posted to Company G, 5th U.S. Colored Infantry (127th Ohio Volunteer Infantry). Within two days of his enlistment, Beaty was promoted to sergeant.

After a period of relative inactivity, in 1864, Beaty marched with Maj. Gen. Benjamin Butler's Army of the James to attack Richmond (Ft. Harrison) north of the River James. Beaty participated in the series of battles known as the Battle of Chaffin's Farm.

The assault on New Market Heights was led by Brig. Gen. Charles Paine's 3rd Division of the 18th Corps, U.S. Colored Troops (USCT). The first assault against Gen. John Gregg's Texas Brigade and the 24th Virginia Cavalry was sent in at 5:30 AM. Almost 700 soldiers attacked the position with fixed bayonets and the percussion caps of the muskets removed to prevent accidental firing as the Colored Troops struggled through the Confederate defenses. The attack failed, and 365 men died. Beaty joined the second assault at 6:00 AM. As Maj. Gen. Benjamin Butler reported on October 11, 1864, Beaty took command of Company G after all of the white officers had been killed or wounded: Milton M. Holland, sergeant major, 5th U.S. Colored Troops, commanding Company C; James H. Bronson, first sergeant, commanding Company D; Robert Pinn, first sergeant, commanding Company I, wounded; Powhatan Beaty, first sergeant, commanding Company G, 5th U.S. Colored Troops—all these gallant colored soldiers were left in command, all their company officers being killed or wounded, and led them gallantly and meritoriously through the day. For these services they have most honorable mention, and the commanding general will cause a special medal to be struck in honor of these gallant colored soldiers (quoted in "Holland" 2003).

Beaty and the others mentioned in the dispatch received the Medal of Honor for their actions. Beaty was discharged on April 6, 1865, the day he received his Medal of Honor. Some 3,000 black soldiers were in action during the two-day battle, of which about 1,302 died, or were wounded or missing. Beaty died on December 6, 1916, and was buried at the Union Baptist Cemetery, Cincinnati, Ohio. His life after military service centered around the theatre and an acting career that once saw him perform at Ford's Theatre in Washington, D.C. His legacy during the Civil War is preserved and honored in a variety of ways; a 12-foot portrait of him is on Richmond's floodwall and a bridge on Virginia's Route 5 crossing over interstate Route 895 has been named the Powhatan Beaty Memorial Bridge.

Jonathan D. Sutherland

Further Reading

Brinsfield, John. "The Battle of New Market Heights." http://www.army.mil/soldiers/feb96/p50.html.

"Holland, Milton M." http://www.nps.gov/rich/holland.htm (accessed August 25, 2003).

Bell, Dennis

Born: December 28, 1866
Died: September 25, 1953
Home State: Washington, D.C.
Service: Army
Conflict: Spanish-American War
Age at Time of Award: 31

Bell was born in Washington, D.C., on December 28, 1866. He initially joined the army and served one undistinguished enlistment with the Buffalo Soldiers in Montana, but in 1898, he returned to the army and was assigned to Troop H, 10th Cavalry. He was posted aboard the *S.S. Florida* for the passage to Cuba. He and a number of other Buffalo Soldiers of Troop H were assigned to a mission led by Lieutenant Carter P. Johnson, a former enlisted man with over two decades of experience in the army. The unit was given the task of resupplying and reinforcing Cuban rebels operating behind Spanish lines. After an abortive attempt to land the nearly 400 Cuban insurgents at an initial location, Johnson settled on landing near the small settlement of Tayabacoa. On June 30, 1898, a landing party of 300 insurgents and 28 American troopers attempted to land in the face of a blockhouse at the mouth of the Tayabacoa River. They were met with intense fire, despite supporting fires from a gunboat accompanying the naval landing vessels. The attacking force never seized a beachhead and they were forced to withdraw at night, but lacked the necessary boats to transport everyone, having lost at least two boats to Spanish cannon fire. Two wounded Americans and a number of wounded Cuban insurgents were stranded in the water at the shoreline.

The Cuban insurgent forces attempted to rescue the trapped men, only to have four successive rescue missions fail in the face of Spanish defensive fire. At the urging of his 10th Cavalry Troopers, Johnson eventually agreed to allow one additional attempt to rescue the stranded men. Five Americans, including Dennis Bell, were selected to carry out the rescue. Moving their landing boat through the water as quietly as possible, because the Spanish garrison was still on high alert for such a rescue mission, the five men made it to the wounded men and pulled them into the boat. As the Spanish positions poured fire into the ocean, the party successfully rescued the stranded men and returned to the *Florida* safely. Lieutenant Johnson is quoted as saying that the "rescue was pronounced by all who witnessed it, as a brave and gallant deed, and deserving of reward."

In early 1899, Lieutenant Johnson petitioned the War Department for proper acknowledgment of the heroic actions of the five troopers at Tayabacoa. The War Department made the decision quickly and determined that the four Buffalo Soldiers deserved the Medal of Honor. This is very interesting in hindsight, as these would be the last Medals of Honor awarded to African American soldiers until well after World War II. No African American soldiers received the Medal of Honor during World War I or World War II, apparently due to the pervasive racism in the military during the intervening years. A number of African American soldiers would be belatedly honored in the 1990s for their actions during the two world wars.

Bell continued to serve as part of the Cuban occupation force with duty at Manzanillo. While still serving in Cuba, he received the Medal of Honor for his actions at Tayabacoa, during a ceremony held on June 23, 1899. Bell continued to serve in the 10th Cavalry, with tours in the Philippines and Texas. War Department records show that he lost his medal in 1906 while visiting a former first sergeant in Alexandria, Virginia. The War Department replaced the lost medal and Bell continued to wear it faithfully until his death. He passed away in Pittsburgh, Pennsylvania, on September 25, 1953, at the age of 86. He was buried in Section 31 of the Arlington National Cemetery.

James B. Martin

Further Reading

Hanna, Charles W. *African American Recipients of the Medal of Honor: A Biographical Dictionary, Civil War through Vietnam War.* Jefferson, NC: McFarland, 2002.

Johnson, Edward A. *History of Negro Soldiers in the Spanish-American War and Other Items of Interest.* Raleigh, NC: Capital Printing Company, 1899.

Schubert, Frank N. *Black Valor: Buffalo Soldiers and the Medal of Honor, 1870–1898.* Wilmington, DE: Scholarly Resources, 1997.

Schubert, Frank N. "Buffalo Soldiers at San Juan Hill." 1998 Conference of Army Historians. http://www.history.army.mil/documents/spanam/BSSJH/Shbrt-BSSJH.htm (accessed September 1, 2013).

Blake, Robert

Born: Unknown
Died: Unknown
Home State: South Carolina
Service: Navy
Conflict: Civil War
Age at Time of Award: Unknown

Robert Blake was an African American runaway slave, who signed up with the U.S. Navy in Virginia, on April 16, 1864, and received the Medal of Honor for his Civil War service.

Blake was designated as contraband—a term used to describe runaway slaves behind Union lines—but was initially assigned to serve on the USS *Vermont*, along with about 20 other fellow contrabands. Blake was later transferred to the steam gunboat *Marblehead*, which was a 691-ton gunboat that had been built in Newbury Port, Massachusetts, and commissioned in March 1862. The vessel was on blockade duty off the coasts of Georgia and South Carolina, and Blake had been serving on board for a year before officially enlisting.

On December 25, 1863, the gunboat was engaged on the Stono River against Confederate positions on John's Island. Blake's commanding officer responded to incoming fire from the Confederate guns and Blake is reported to have followed him on deck. Blake quickly moved to the gun positions on the *Marblehead*, only to be injured by an explosion which killed a powder-boy. Though not assigned to combat duties, Blake assumed the young man's position and began to provide powder to the crews of the guns. The *Marblehead* held its own in the conflict and eventually the Confederate guns fell silent. For his actions in this fight, Seaman Blake received the Medal of Honor. In an historical oddity, he became the first African American to receive the Medal of Honor on April 16, 1864, but not the first to perform actions that led to receiving the Medal. That honor went to William Harvey Carney, whose actions that resulted in the Medal occurred earlier than Blake's, but Carney did not receive his Medal until 1900.

Jonathan D. Sutherland

Further Reading

Buckley, Gail. *American Patriots: The Story of Blacks in the Military from the Revolution to Desert Storm.* New York: Random House, 2001.

Cohn, Michael. *Black Men of the Sea.* New York: Dodd Mead, 1978.

Hanna, Charles W. *African American Recipients of the Medal of Honor: A Biographical Dictionary, Civil War through Vietnam War.* Jefferson, NC: McFarland, 2002.

Boyne, Thomas

Born: 1846
Died: April 21, 1896
Home State: Maryland
Service: Army
Conflict: Civil War, Indian Wars
Age at Time of Award: 32 or 33

Thomas Boyne was born in Prince George's County, Maryland, in 1846. In 1864, he joined B Battery of the 2nd Colored Light Artillery and fought at Wilson's Wharf and

City Point (May–June 1864). His regiment was sent west at the end of the Civil War, and he was discharged in March 1866. Boyne adopted the name of Thomas Bowen, and claiming that he came from Norfolk, Virginia, reenlisted, serving in the 40th Infantry and later in the 25th until 1875, when he transferred into the 9th Cavalry. By the time he was sergeant in Company C of the 9th Cavalry during the Apache Wars (1877–1879), he had already had 15 years' experience.

Boyne was part of a detachment sent to intercept Victorio, leader of the Warm Springs Apache, in May 1879. They found him on May 20, with his men deployed behind defense works in a canyon in the Mimbres Mountains, New Mexico. After a failed attempt to parley, both sides opened fire, and during the engagement Boyne displayed exemplary conduct and gallantry. 2nd Lt. Henry H. Wright wrote, "I was engaged in bringing in a wounded man with a few men and was surprised by the Indians, my horse was killed and corralled by hostiles when Sergeant Thomas Boyne commanded a detachment sent to my assistance, flanked and gallantly charged the Indians driving them off."

By the end of September 1879, Boyne had been involved in five engagements with Apaches, and during 1880 he participated in three more. Maj. Albert B. Morrow, senior officer of the 9th Cavalry, wrote of Boyne, "I have seen him repeatedly in action and in every instance he has distinguished himself. If any soldier deserves a Certificate of Merit or Medal of Honor, Sergt. Boyne does and I hope he may be so rewarded."

Boyne received the Medal of Honor on January 6, 1882, for bravery in action at Mimbres Mountain, New Mexico, on May 29, 1879, and at Cuchillo Negro, New Mexico, on September 27, 1879.

During the winter of 1884–1885, he served in the Indian Territory during the army's attempts to prevent settlers from encroaching on the tribal lands. Throughout this period, Boyne was stricken with frostbite. He spent most of January 1885 at Ft. Caldwell, Kansas, in the hospital.

Boyne reenlisted in July 1885 and served with the 25th at Ft. Meade, Dakota, but his long service was beginning to affect his health, and he developed a hernia while at Ft. Missoula, Montana, in October 1888, which prompted the army to discharge him in January 1889. He was granted a disability pension of $8 a month, which increased to $10 in 1893. In 1890, Thomas Boyne was admitted to the U.S. Soldiers' Home in Washington, D.C., where he died of consumption on April 21, 1896. Sergeant Boyne was a decorated career soldier in the U.S. Army, having served for over half of his life, 25 years, from 1864 to 1889.

Jonathan D. Sutherland

Further Reading

Carroll, John M., ed. *The Black Military Experience in the American West.* New York: Liveright, 1969.

Schubert, Frank. *Black Valor.* Wilmington, DE: Scholarly Resources, 1997.

Branch, Buddie

Born: February 14, 1925
Died: January 31, 2011
Home State: Ohio
Service: Army
Conflict: World War II
Age at Time of Award: 19

Buddie Branch was born in Dayton, Ohio, on February 14, 1925. He was the son of Arthur Branch Sr. and his wife, Genevieve. Buddie grew up in Dayton and went to school at Roosevelt High School. Branch was drafted, along with a number of his high school friends, and entered the army in Cincinnati, Ohio, on August 9, 1943.

Following testing at Ft. Thomas, in Covington, Kentucky, Branch was sent to Ft. Knox, Kentucky, to be trained as an armored crewman. Upon completing basic training in November 1943, Branch was stationed at Camp Hood, Texas, and was assigned to Company B, 761st Tank Battalion, an all-black unit which would go on to win significant acclaim during the war. Branch learned all the jobs of an M4 Sherman tank crew while at Camp Hood, as the 761st stressed cross training so that every soldier could perform in any position on the tank.

Branch and his unit were alerted for deployment to the European Theater of Operations in August 1944, landing by ship at Dorset, England, on September 7, 1944. After drawing their new tanks and equipment, the unit crossed the English Channel and landed at Omaha Beach, following in the footsteps of the units that came ashore on D-Day. The 761st was assigned to General George Patton's Third Army and fought across France and Germany with this famous organization. Branch was promoted to corporal and distinguished himself during combat in Germany.

Branch first saw combat in early November 1944, near the town of Morville, France, while his company participated in the Lorraine Campaign. On November 25, 1944, his company was ordered to attack the German village of Honskirch. The orders were questionable, as the terrain restricted the tanks to the hard surfaced roads and made them ideal targets for antitank guns in the wood lines on either side of the road. Though the company commander protested the orders, eventually six tanks and a force of infantry began the assault on the village. Almost immediately, German gunners began firing on the column hitting every other tank. Pinned to the road, with at least half the tanks burning, Branch's tank tried to provide covering fire for his comrades. The tank was struck in the turret by a round and, though it did not catch fire, the turret was locked in a single position and could not be rotated. With the tank commander injured, Branch instructed the driver to seek cover behind a nearby barn. Upon placing his crew in a position to providing suppressive fire, Branch dismounted and began to save comrades from the burning tanks.

Having created a relatively safe location for approximately 17 wounded soldiers, Branch began to run the length of the tank column checking each tank for wounded. Though under enemy fire constantly, Corporal Branch inspected six of the disabled tanks and helped to evacuate seven soldiers who required litters to get them to safety. Each time Branch had to cover nearly 300 yards to the sheltered position carrying the wounded soldiers amid fire from a variety of German weapons ranging from 88mm antitank guns to machine guns and sniper fire. His actions over a period of nearly four-and-a-half hours under fire were instrumental in saving the lives of numerous members of his unit. For his heroism that day, Buddie Branch was awarded the Bronze Star with V device for valor.

Branch continued to serve with the 761st throughout the remainder of the war, participating in combat near Bastogne during the Battle of the Bulge in December 1944. As the war ended, his was among the tanks of the 761st that met up with the Russian Army at the Enns River on May 6, 1945.

The environment in World War II was not receptive to providing black soldiers with recognition for their valorous actions. As with World War I, no Medals of Honor were awarded to black soldiers until many decades after the war. Very few black soldiers were recognized with other medals for valor such as the Silver or Bronze Star. Branch's unit was one of the most decorated in the European Theater, with six Silver Stars and 38 Bronze Stars being awarded to 761st soldiers.

After World War II, Buddie Branch returned to Dayton and finished out his final year of school at Roosevelt High School. He went on to attend the Cincinnati College of Embalming. He spent a 30-year career working for the Air Force at Wright-Patterson Air Force Base in Dayton and then continued to work as a part-time embalmer after his retirement. Evidence abounds that he spent considerable time in his later years participating in the education of young people on the role of black soldiers during the war. He also took part in the Veteran's History Project, sponsored by the Library of Congress. Recordings of his interviews on the history of the 761st can be reviewed on the Project's Web site. He passed away in Dayton, Ohio, on January 31, 2011, at the age of 85.

James B. Martin

Further Reading

Booker, Bryan D. *African Americans in the United States Army in World War II.* Jefferson, NC: McFarland, 2008.

Pfeifer, Kathryn Browne. *The 761st Tank Battalion (African-American Soldiers).* New York: Twenty-First Century Books, 1994.

Wilson, Joe, Jr. *The 761st "Black Panther" Tank Battalion in World War II.* Jefferson, NC: McFarland, 1999.

Brown, Jesse LeRoy

Born: October 13, 1926
Died: December 4, 1950
Home State: Mississippi
Service: Navy
Conflict: Korean War
Age at Time of Award: 24

Jesse Brown was born in Hattiesburg, Mississippi, on October 13, 1926, to John and Julia Brown. His father worked in a variety of jobs and eventually took up sharecropping to support the family. His mother was a teacher. Jesse was a good student and graduated very high in his class at Eureka High School, the segregated school in Hattiesburg, Mississippi. Determined to get a good education and ready to leave the South, Jesse made application to Ohio State University in Columbus, Ohio, and was accepted. Though he was out of the South, Jesse was still a member of a distinct minority within the student body at Ohio State and struggled against overt racism as he majored in architectural engineering. As he had an interest in flying, Jesse applied repeatedly to the university's aviation program but could never gain admission. When he read that the U.S. Navy would be opening a flight program at a number of major universities, he took the entrance examinations and applied for the program at Ohio State University. He enlisted in the U.S. Naval Reserve in July 1946 and became a member of the university's Naval Reserve Officers' Training Corps (ROTC) Flight Program. Of the more than 5,600 Naval ROTC students in 1947, only 14 were black. This obviously meant that Jesse was once again in the minority as he blazed trails for others to follow.

Brown completed all of his basic flight training programs by fall of 1948 and on October 21 of that year he became the first African American to earn the Naval Aviator Badge, the coveted "Wings of Gold." He was initially assigned to Norfolk Naval Air Station, Virginia, and later to the USS *Leyte* with the 32nd Fighter Squadron. He was commissioned an ensign in the U.S. Navy on April 26, 1949. Serving on the *Leyte* during a cruise in the Mediterranean Sea, Brown's unit was diverted to join Task Force 77 off the Korean Peninsula. While performing this mission, Brown and his unit flew repeated missions in support of fighting around the Chosin Reservoir, regularly providing close air support to the Marine Corps. On December 4, 1950, Brown and five other aircraft from Fighter Squadron Thirty-two (VF-32) flew off the USS *Leyte* (CV-32) in support of marines who had been surrounded by Chinese forces.

Ensign Brown's flight aggressively attacked the ground forces surrounding the marines in the face of severe ground fire. He repeatedly rolled in on the advancing enemy troops, blunting their attack and buying time for the embattled unit. With total disregard for his own safety, he braved ground fire and increasing enemy anti-aircraft fire to secure the position of the marines. Eventually, the anti-aircraft fire became too intense and Ensign Brown's aircraft was hit and crashed near the

Chosin Reservoir. For his courage that day, along with numerous similar engagements near Takson, Manp Jin, Linchong, Sinuiju, Kansan, Wonsan, and other locations, he was recommended for and received the Distinguished Flying Cross.

Brown's wingman, Lieutenant J. G. Thomas Hudner, crash-landed his aircraft near Brown's in an attempt to free him from the wreckage but was unable to do so before he was forcibly extracted from the location because of enemy actions. Jesse Brown died in the wreckage of his aircraft, but his body was never recovered, as it was deemed too dangerous to attempt to recover it for fear of additional ambushes. He was the first naval officer to die in the Korean War. For his actions that day, Lieutenant J. G. Hudner received the Medal of Honor.

On February 17, 1973, the USS *Jesse L. Brown*, a Knox class frigate, was named in his honor at Boston Naval Yard, making him the first African American naval officer to have a naval vessel named after him. Its motto "Versatility, Victory, Valor" would probably have resonated with Ensign Brown, as he showed all three during his short life and valorous naval career. Providing a dedication during the commissioning ceremony, his wingman in Korea, Thomas J. Hudner Jr., memorialized Jesse with these words: "He died in the wreckage of his airplane with courage and unfathomable dignity. He willingly gave his life to tear down barriers to freedom of others."

James B. Martin and Jonathan D. Sutherland

Further Reading

Taylor, Theodore. *Flight of Jesse Leroy Brown*. Annapolis, MD: Naval Institute Press, 2007.

Brown, Roscoe C., Jr.

Born: March 9, 1922
Home State: Washington, D.C.
Service: Army Air Corps
Conflict: World War II
Age at Time of Award: 23

Roscoe C. Brown Jr. was born on March 9, 1922, to Roscoe C. Brown Sr. and his wife. His father was a dentist and held critical positions in the U.S. Public Health Service under President Franklin D. Roosevelt. Brown attended Dunbar High School in Washington, D.C. and joins other luminaries such as Judge William H. Hastie, Dr. Charles R. Drew and the Tuskegee Airmen's own Benjamin O. Davis Jr. as distinguished alumni. After graduation from Dunbar, Brown matriculated to Springfield College in Springfield, Massachusetts. He graduated in 1943, reportedly at the top of his class, and soon after joined the Army Air Corps. Discussing his education at Dunbar and how it prepared him for life in a segregated world, Brown is quoted as

Dr. Roscoe Brown Jr., a decorated member of the Tuskegee Airmen who received the Distinguished Flying Cross during World War II, went on to a successful career in education after the war. (AP Photo/Carlo Allegri)

saying, "That's what they taught you at Dunbar High School: that you had to be better to be equal, and that you can be good and you've got a long history and heritage of being good. Every day in my school was Black History Day."

Brown joined the 332nd fighter group at Ramitelli Air Base in Italy in February 1944 and became flight leader of the 100th Fighter Squadron. In May, he began long-range bomber escort duties. In July 1944, the squadron was issued with North American P-51 Mustangs. Lieutenant Brown's aircraft was nicknamed "Bunnie" after his daughter. On a mission flown on March 24, 1945, Brown and his unit encountered three Me262 German fighter jets. Brown was credited with downing one of these three and was among the first 15th Air Force pilots to shoot down a German jet fighter.

A week later, on March 31, 1945, Brown claimed a Focke Wulf 190, one of 13 claims that day. He was promoted to captain and commanded the 100th until he returned to the United States in October 1945. Brown was awarded the Distinguished Flying Cross and an Air Medal (with eight Oak Leaf Clusters), to accompany the 332nd's Distinguished Unit Citation.

Following the war, he earned a PhD in education from New York University and entered the world of higher education. A distinguished career of public service followed and he served as the director of the Institute for African American Affairs at NYU, president of Bronx Community College, director of the City University of New York Graduate Center for Urban Education Policies, chairman of the New York City Regional Educational Center for Economic Development, and a host of other posts.

Along with other members of the Tuskegee Airmen, Brown has been repeatedly honored for their service to the nation as pilots and pioneers who broke down racial stereotypes. In 1973, Brown's alma mater, Springfield College, recognized him with its Distinguished Alumni Award. On March 29, 2007, Roscoe Brown Jr. was one of the former Tuskegee Airmen present when they were awarded the Congressional Gold Medal for their service. Most recently, on November 14, 2012, the National Football Foundation and College Football Hall of Fame (NFF) announced that he was 2012 recipient of the NFF Gold Medal. In citing Dr. Brown's work, the NFF stated that his combat exploits were only the beginning of his service to his nation and that his long and distinguished career as an educator demonstrated the integrity and courage that the Gold Medal represents. These three awards represent only some of the honors he received, including an honorary doctorate.

The 100th Flying Training Squadron was reactivated on September 24, 1999, as part of the U.S. Air Force's Reserves 340th Training Group. Brown was among the 16 former Tuskegee Airmen present at the reactivation ceremony at Randolph Air Force Base, Texas, the squadron's new home. Roscoe C. Brown Jr. continues to live in Riverdale, New York, and is active in educational speaking and the history of the Tuskegee Airmen. Years after the war, when being interviewed for the National Park Service Tuskegee Airmen Oral History Project, Brown shared his opinion of what made the 332nd so successful. "We were a pretty cocky group of people—confident bordering on cocky—but you almost had to be."

Jonathan D. Sutherland

Further Reading

Francis, Charles E., and Adolph Caso. *The Tuskegee Airmen: The Men Who Changed a Nation.* Wellesley, MA: Branden Publishing, 2000.

Homan, Lynn M., and Thomas Reilly. *Black Knights: The Story of the Tuskegee Airmen.* Gretna, LA: Pelican Publishing, 2000.

Moye, J. Todd. *Freedom Flyers: The Tuskegee Airmen of World War II.* New York: Oxford University Press, 2010.

Stentiford, Barry M. *Tuskegee Airmen.* Santa Barbara, CA: Greenwood, 2012.

Bryant, William Maud

Born: February 16, 1933
Died: March 24, 1969
Home State: Georgia
Service: Army

Conflict: Vietnam War
Age at Time of Award: 36

William Maud Bryant was born in Cochran, Georgia, on February 16, 1933. When he was of age, he moved north to escape the segregated conditions of the Deep South. He settled in Detroit, Michigan, and joined the U.S. Army in 1953, at the age of 20. By March 1969, he had achieved the rank of sergeant first class and served in Airborne and Special Forces units. He was assigned in the Republic of Vietnam with Company A, 5th Special Forces Group, 1st Special Forces and was serving as the commanding officer of Civilian Irregular Defense Group Company (CIDG) 321, 2nd Battalion, 3rd Mobile Strike Force in Long Khanh Province, Vietnam. Civilian Irregular Defense Groups were units made up of a combination of a Special Forces A Team and the indigenous population that trained to act as area defensive forces and also participated, by 1969, in some strike operations. On March 24, 1969, Sergeant First Class Bryant and the CIDG engaged a large enemy force in the action that cost him his life.

On March 24, the 2nd Battalion came under attack by elements of three different North Vietnamese regiments and sustained prolonged heavy fire. During a firefight that lasted more than 34 hours with the enemy pressing the attack throughout, the CIDG held its position. Sergeant First Class Bryant exercised command throughout this period, moving from position to position within the company's defensive perimeter. Whether directing fire at crucial stages in the battle, orchestrating the improvement of the unit's defensive positions, redistributing ammunition among his soldiers, or ensuring that the wounded were adequately cared for, he served as an inspiration to all who observed his actions. At one point during the battle, the CIDG desperately needed a resupply of ammunition and a helicopter drop was planned. The boxes of ammunition were scattered across a large area after the drop and Sergeant First Class Bryant ran through intense enemy fire to retrieve the containers and then redistributed it as needed. In need of information about the enemy's dispositions, Bryant led a patrol out of the company area during a brief break in the fighting. During this intelligence-gathering mission, the patrol was attacked and its movement halted. Sergeant First Class Bryant stood his ground and repulsed the initial enemy assault and was then joined by his soldiers, motivated again by his display of courage. Needing intelligence on the enemy positions and strength, Bryant attempted to recover a wounded enemy soldier by crawling to him under heavy fire, but his actions were in vain as the soldier was already dead when he reached him. Returning to his patrol, he moved them back into the company defensive positions and prepared for the next North Vietnamese attack. Sensing the danger of staying in his defensive positions, Sergeant First Class Bryant organized a patrol to attempt a breakthrough to change the dynamics of the battle. Shortly into the attempted breakthrough, the patrol ran into North Vietnamese forces in heavily fortified bunkers and again began receiving heavy fire. Bryant was severely wounded in the initial exchange in this engagement, but continued to lead by example. He called for air support for helicopter gunships and directed the aviators in the placement of suppressive fire on the enemy positions. Once the last gunship had cleared the area, Sergeant First Class Bryant charged an enemy machine gun position by himself, destroying the position and killing the members of the gun crew. While organizing yet another attack on the enemy bunkers, Bryant was hit by the blast for a rocket-propelled grenade and was mortally wounded. Sergeant First Class Bryant's leadership and bravery while in command of CIDG 321 were crucial factors in the success and survival of his unit. His repeated acts of bravery were everything a soldier would ever expect of a hero.

For his bravery on March 24, 1969, Bryant received the Medal of Honor posthumously. In a ceremony held on February 16, 1971, his family was presented the Medal on his behalf.

SFC Bryant has been honored in a variety of ways in recognition of his heroism and sacrifice for his country. The Georgia State Assembly recognized his place of birth by creating the William Maud Bryant Memorial Highway on a stretch of State Road 87 North outside of Cochran, Georgia. The military honored his entry into service in Detroit by naming a child development center after him on Selfridge Air National Guard Base in Detroit, Michigan. Finally, the Special Forces community has honored him by naming the headquarters building of the Special Warfare Center and School at Ft. Bragg, North Carolina, Bryant Hall, after him. This particular honor means that every Special Forces soldier remembers his sacrifice while they attend training at Ft. Bragg. SFC Bryant is memorialized at Panel 28W, Row 24 of the Vietnam Veterans Memorial. SFC Bryant remains the last African American to receive the Medal of Honor. Bryant was buried in Raleigh National Cemetery, Raleigh, North Carolina.

Jonathan D. Sutherland

Further Reading

Morris, Robert V. *Black Faces of War: A Legacy of Honor from the American Revolution to Today.* Minneapolis, MN: Zenith Press, 2011.

Westheider, James E. *The African American Experience in Vietnam: Brothers in Arms.* New York: Rowman & Littlefield, 2008.

Westheider, James E. *Fighting on Two Fronts: African Americans and the Vietnam War.* New York: New York University Press, 1997.

Bullard, Eugene Jacques

Born: 1894
Died: 1961
Home State: Georgia
Service: French Foreign Legion, French Flying Corps

Conflict: World War I
Age at Time of Award: 22

Eugene Bullard was born in 1894. In 1902, at the age of eight, he ran away from home while his father was in hiding from a lynch mob. Bullard had nine siblings and roots reaching back to the slaves of French refugees from Haiti. As a child, he had always been told by his father about France and that men were equal there.

Bullard reached Virginia by 1906 and stowed away on a German ship bound for Aberdeen. He moved first to Glasgow, then to Liverpool, where he became a boxer. After visiting Paris in 1913, he answered the French call for volunteers in August 1914, joining the 3rd Marching Battalion of the Foreign Legion. After five weeks' training, he was sent to the Somme. He fought at Arras and Champagne. He then was posted to Verdun in February 1916, now a member of the 170th Infantry, the Swallows of Death. Here, he earned the nickname, "The Black Swallow of Death," that would last a lifetime. At Verdun, Bullard was wounded twice and was awarded the Croix de Guerre and the Médaille Militaire. While recuperating, he joined the French Flying Corps, gaining his pilot's license on May 5, 1917. In August, he applied to join the U.S. Army Flying Corps and passed the medical test but was never offered a position due to the segregated nature of the American military. In November, the French Flying Corps assigned him to Escadrille Spad 93 and in his first month he shot down a German aircraft. Sergeant Bullard was dismissed from the French Air Force over a racially tinged incident. This incident, which nearly brought a court-martial, occurred in Paris while Bullard was on a 24-hour pass. He climbed on board a troop truck to catch a lift back to his unit, only to be kicked by a French soldier who said to him: "There's no room for your kind." As the second kick came, Bullard grabbed the leg and punched the man in the face. The man was an officer. Bullard was not court-martialed because of his medals, wounds, and record, but he was posted to a service battalion of the 170th.

After the war, the racism of the American military drove Bullard and other African Americans to remain in France as expatriates. He became a boxer, the leader of a jazz band, and the owner of a nightclub. He married in 1924 and with his French wife had two children. In 1939, Bullard was approached by the Deuxième Bureau to spy on Germans in Paris. When the call came for U.S. citizens to leave France in the spring of 1940, Bullard instead joined the 51st Infantry engaged in the defense of Paris. He led a machine gun section until he was wounded in the back. Bullard headed for the American consulate in Bordeaux, where he obtained his first passport. He crossed the French border into Spain, and then left the continent from Lisbon, arriving in New York in July. With the assistance of the French Underground, his daughters joined him in February 1941.

In 1954, Bullard returned to France to relight the flame at the Tomb of the Unknown Soldier and five years later became a Knight of the Legion of Honor. In 1960, at a reception in New York, General Charles de Gaulle embraced Bullard after recognizing his legion uniform and medals. He died in 1961 and was buried at the cemetery of the Federation of French War Veterans at Flushing, New York, with full French military honors.

Jonathan D. Sutherland

Further Reading

Buckley, Gail. *American Patriots*. New York: Random House, 2001.

Carisella, P. J., and James W. Ryan. *Black Swallow of Death*. Boston: Marlborough House, 1972.

Lloyd, Craig. *Eugene Bullard, Black Expatriate in Jazz-Age Paris*. Athens: University of Georgia Press, 2000.

Williams, Chad L. *Torchbearers of Democracy: African American Soldiers in the World War I Era*. Chapel Hill, NC: The University of North Carolina Press, 2010.

Bussey, Charles M.

Born: April 23, 1921
Died: October 26, 2003
Home State: California
Service: Army
Conflict: World War II, Korean War
Age at Time of Award: 29

Charles M. Bussey was born in Bakersfield, California, on April 23, 1921. He was born into a family with a history of service with the 9th and 10th Cavalry and, though his mother discouraged it, grew up hearing tales of the Buffalo Soldiers on the western frontier and in combat during the Spanish-American War. Bussey credited an older Buffalo Soldier, who lived near him in Bakersfield, with being the influence that eventually sent him into the army. During his time at Bakersfield High School, Bussey participated in the Citizens' Military Training Camp, which he regarded as the rough equivalent of Reserve Officers Training Corps for African Americans. In September, 1941, Bussey joined the army, and because of his CMTC experience and his performance in school, he was accepted into aviation cadet training and assigned to the Tuskegee Army Flying School. After flight training in Alabama and unit training at Selfridge Airbase in Michigan, Bussey was deployed to Italy with the 332nd Fighter Group. Bussey flew 70 missions over Germany, Italy, and North Africa, protecting bomber formations as part of the famed Tuskegee Airmen. He was credited with the downing of two enemy aircraft and the damaging of two more. In the spring of 1945, he was reassigned stateside as a flight instructor at Tuskegee. Bussey left the army after the war ended and worked at a number of different jobs in California. Missing the discipline and camaraderie he had encountered in the military, he joined the California National Guard in 1946 and was assigned as an engineer officer. He attended the University of Southern California and San Francisco State University, eventually graduating with a bachelor's degree in political science in 1949. Frustrated in civilian life, he rejoined the active duty army in 1948 and was assigned as an engineer officer at Ft. Campbell, Kentucky. His long-term intent was to spend 18 months in the army and then transfer to the Air Force, where he could once again fly fighter aircraft. This dream did not come to pass, but a career in the army was in his future. In January 1950, Bussey was reassigned to the Army of Occupation in Japan. After an assignment marred by a highly prejudiced battalion commander, Bussey was given command of an engineer company and performed admirably. With the North Korean attack in June 1950, Bussey began to ready his unit for their eventual deployment to Korea. This move into the combat zone came on July 11, 1950, and his 77th Engineer Company was assigned in support of the African American 24th Infantry Regiment in the Pusan Perimeter. Less than two weeks into Bussey's tour in Korea, he encountered action that resulted in him receiving the Silver Star. On July 20, 1950, Bussey was delivering mail to members of his company that were in support of the 3rd Battalion, 24th Infantry Regiment. He observed the infantry battalion's troops and his under fire and saw a large number of individuals dressed in white peasant clothes maneuvering farther down the slope from the battalion. Bussey commandeered some infantrymen from the 3rd Battalion who were nearby and gathered a water-cooled .30 machine gun and a .50 machine gun and all the ammunition the men could carry. He led the makeshift unit up to the high ground and prepared to reinforce the infantry unit if the white-suited individuals attacked. Sensing the Koreans' intentions after firing warning shots, Bussey and his gunners poured fire into the advancing North Koreans. The gunners on the .30 caliber gun were hit by mortar fire now directed at his position and he instructed replacement gunners to occupy the weapon while he fired the .50 caliber. After the replacement gunner on the .30 was wounded, Bussey moved to that gun and continued to place fire on the enemy until no one moved below him. Accounts of the action indicate that Bussey and his men killed 258 enemy soldiers that afternoon, and in the weeks that followed, Major General William B. Kean, the commanding general of the 25th Infantry Division, arrived in the regimental area and pinned the Silver Star on Bussey for his actions at Yechon. While Appleman's *South to the Naktong* questions whether the action at Yechon actually happened, Bussey's own book points out that division commanders rarely award Silver Stars for mythical actions. Bussey continued to command the 77th Engineer Company until May 1951, earning a Bronze Star with V device for another action and a Purple Heart for wounds suffered in that action. These awards were in addition to the Air Medal he earned with the 332nd Fighter Group. He continued to serve in the army until his retirement in 1966 as a lieutenant colonel. He had eventually returned to flying and spent many hours in rotary and fixed-wing aircraft for the army. Bussey credited much of his outlook on the military and his success to his Tuskegee Airmen commander, Benjamin O. Davis. Davis

Lieutenant Colonel Charles Bussey flew with the Tuskegee Airmen in World War II and was awarded the Silver Star for valor while serving with the 24th Infantry Regiment in Korea. (AP Photo)

was a model for him, as for so many African American officers in the period after World War II. Bussey retired in 1966 at his last duty post in San Francisco. He began an African American run company refinishing wooden furniture and provided wooden crates for the shipment of war materials to Vietnam. In 1969, he was appointed to the San Francisco Juvenile Justice Commission and continued his work with urban youths. In the 1970s, he worked for Bechtel Corporation in Alaska and Saudi Arabia until finally settling down in California for good. Charles Bussey had lived with racism in the army during World War II and Korea and wrote a book in 1991 titled *Firefight at Yechon: Courage & Racism in the Korean War.* His book detailed the challenges encountered by African American soldiers during these years and the blatant racism in the military. He spent many years, with the support of numerous political figures, attempting to have his Silver Star upgraded to the Medal of Honor. He long maintained that Major General Kean had indicated that the Silver Star was simply "a down payment on the highest medal" and that his battalion commander had sidetracked the Medal of Honor paperwork because he did not believe the African American community should have a living hero to give them confidence. Lieutenant Colonel (R) Charles M. Bussey passed away on October 26, 2003, in Las Vegas, Nevada. He was buried in Daly City, California.

James B. Martin

Further Reading

Appleman, Roy. *South to Naktong, North to the Yalu.* Washington, DC: U.S. Army Center for Military History, 1961.

Bowers, William T., William M. Hammond, and George L. MacGarrigle. *Black Soldier, White Army: The 24th Infantry Regiment in Korea.* Washington, DC: Center of Military History, U.S. Army, 1996.

Bussey, Charles M. *Firefight at Yechon: Courage & Racism in the Korean War.* Washington, DC: Brassey's, 1991.

Carney, William H.

Born: February 29, 1840
Died: December 8, 1908
Home State: Massachusetts
Service: Army
Conflict: Civil War
Age at Time of Award: 23

Born a slave in Virginia on February 29, 1840, William H. Carney attended a secret school conducted by a local minister and learned to read and write. Later, he was emancipated when his master died. He moved to New Bedford, Massachusetts, and was studying for the ministry when he learned that the first regiment of African American soldiers was being formed to fight for the Union. President Abraham Lincoln had issued the Emancipation Proclamation on January 1, 1863, and, for the first time, African Americans were being encouraged to enlist in the Union Army. Carney joined the 54th Massachusetts Colored Infantry's C Company, saying that he "could best serve my God by serving my Country and my oppressed brothers."

In July of that same year, the 54th Massachusetts spearheaded the assault on Ft. Wagner in South Carolina, the first real test of the young African Americans who had volunteered for service in the Union Army. When the company's flag bearer was fatally shot, 23-year-old Carney threw down his rifle and grabbed the flag before it fell and then carried it throughout the remainder of the battle.

Although he suffered multiple gunshot wounds in the head, chest, legs, and one arm, Carney carried the flag to safety when the 54th was driven back by a Confederate counterattack. Seeing his predicament, a soldier from another regiment offered to take the flag so Carney could seek medical aid. Carney replied, "No one but a member of the 54th should carry the colors!"

Later, Carney miraculously carried the regiment's flag into camp after the battle to the rousing cheers of his battered comrades. He responded, "Boys, I only did my duty. The flag never touched the ground." He then fell to the ground in a dead faint, weak from the wounds he had received. His actions were specifically noted by the acting regimental commander of the 54th, Lieutenant Colonel E. N. Hallowell in his report of the action at Ft. Wagner. For these feats, he became the first African American to perform action in combat that resulted in the awarding of the Medal of Honor, but he would not receive the medal until long after the action at Ft. Wagner.

The following year, Carney was discharged due to the disabilities of his wounds. He returned to New Bedford and worked as a mail carrier and later as a messenger in the Massachusetts legislature in Boston. On May 23, 1900, nearly 40 years after his valor during the Civil War, Carney was awarded the nation's highest honor for heroism, the Medal of Honor. Though by this time several other African Americans had already received the award for heroism during the Civil War and the Indian Campaigns, Sergeant Carney's action at Ft. Wagner was the first to merit the award.

William Carney died at his home in New Bedford on December 8, 1908, and was buried in Oak Grove Cemetery there. His final resting place bears a distinctive stone—an engraved white marble stone with the gold image of the Medal of Honor, a tribute to a courageous soldier and the flag he loved so dearly.

James H. Willbanks

Further Reading

Blatt, Martin H., Thomas J. Brown, and Donald Yacovone. *Hope & Glory: Essays on the Legacy of the Fifty-Fourth Massachusetts Regiment.* Amherst: University of Massachusetts Press, 2001.

Burchard, Peter. *We'll Stand By the Union: Robert Gould Shaw and the Black 54th Massachusetts Regiment.* New York: Facts on File, 1993.

Hanna, Charles W. *African American Recipients of the Medal of Honor: A Biographical Dictionary, Civil War through Vietnam War.* Jefferson, NC: McFarland, 2002.

Owens, Ron. *Medal of Honor: Historical Facts and Figures.* Paducah, KY: Turner Publishing, 2004.

Carter, Edward Allen, Jr.

Born: May 26, 1916
Died: January 30, 1963
Home State: California
Service: Army
Conflict: World War II
Age at Time of Award: 28

Edward Carter Jr. was born in Los Angeles, California, on May 26, 1916. He was the son of Rev. E. A. Carter, a traveling missionary, and Mary Carter, who was from Calcutta, India. He grew up in India and then moved to Shanghai in China, where he attended a military school. Still in his teens, he ran away from home and joined the Chinese Nationalist Army and fought against the Japanese. Carter had risen to the rank of lieutenant when it was discovered that he was only 15 years old. Reluctantly, he reenrolled in a Shanghai Military School and learned Chinese, Hindi, and German.

During the Spanish Civil War, Carter joined the Abraham Lincoln Battalion and fought against Franco's Fascists in Spain. In 1938, he was forced to flee Spain and headed for France and then back to the United States. He married Mildred Hoover in Los Angeles in 1940.

Carter enlisted in the segregated U.S. Army on September 6, 1941, and before the United States entered World War II, he had been promoted to the rank of sergeant. In 1942, the army began to take an interest in Carter because he was believed to be a Communist. On May 18, 1943, an army intelligence officer at Ft. Benning, Georgia, placed Carter under surveillance and began an investigation into his background. From then on, all of his commanding officers were required to send secret reports to Ft. Benning.

In 1944, Carter was sent to Europe and assigned to transport supplies, but in December of that year, when General Eisenhower needed combat replacements and instituted the Ground Force Replacement Command, Carter was one of 4,562 African American soldiers to be attached to white-only infantry and armor regiments. He was a member of a security detachment assigned to protect Gen. George Patton and his staff. Carter finally saw action, but had to accept a demotion to the rank of private as it was not acceptable for African Americans to command white troops. His work within the new unit was soon recognized and he earned his stripes back and became a squad leader. He served for some time in Patton's Mystery Division, the 12th Armored Division, which in March 1945 carried out a secret offensive in which the troops removed their divisional insignia.

On March 23, 1945, while traveling on a tank near Speyer, Germany, the armored column came under German small arms and antitank weapon fire. Volunteering to deal with the situation, he led three other men across an open field to deal with the enemy. Two of the other soldiers were killed and the third wounded, but Carter continued his actions to defeat the enemy gun positions. He was wounded multiple times in the arm and hand, but eventually defeated an enemy machine gun emplacement and silenced a mortar crew that was firing on the column. Lying badly wounded, eight German infantrymen moved to take him prisoner, but Carter killed six of them and captured the other two. He made his way back to his armored column under intense fire, successfully getting the prisoners to his unit and delivering valuable intelligence in addition to his individual heroism. He was recommended for the Medal of Honor, but this was reduced to the Distinguished Service Cross. He recovered from his wounds in less than a month and became a staff sergeant.

By October 1945, he had been awarded the Purple Heart, the American Defense Service Medal, and the Combat Infantry Badge. He left the army shortly after the war, but found his way back into uniform in the segregated units of the California National Guard. He was transferred to Ft. Lewis, Washington, and attempted to reenlist in 1949, but was turned down because of his supposed Communist connections. He died of lung cancer on January 30, 1963, and was quietly buried in his uniform in a cemetery near UCLA.

A Medal of Honor recipient who fought in the Chinese Army, the Spanish Civil War, and World War II, Carter was denied the chance to fight in Korea because the authorities suspected him of being a Communist.

Throughout World War II, African American soldiers performed with the same courage and dedication that was the hallmark of all American soldiers. Unfortunately, due to racial prejudice at both an institutional and individual level, no African American soldiers received the Medal of Honor, although a number were recommended for our nation's highest honor. Following an investigation commissioned by the Department of Defense in 1993, it was determined that a number of African Americans had not received the Medal of Honor for actions during World War II due to their race. In 1996, Congress approved granting the Medal of Honor to seven African American soldiers from World War II. Staff Sergeant Carter was one of these men. On January 13, 1997, more than 50 years after Carter's heroic efforts in Germany, President Bill Clinton presented the Medal of Honor to Carter's son, Edward Allen Carter III, in a White House ceremony honoring the seven African American World War II veterans whose earlier awards had been upgraded. The only one of the seven still living was Vernon Baker.

On January 10, 1997, Carter's body was exhumed and reburied with full military honors four days later at Arlington National Cemetery. By all accounts, Edward Carter was most comfortable in life as a soldier and these final honors now portrayed him as a military hero for generations to come.

Jonathan D. Sutherland

RED BALL EXPRESS

This volume is dedicated to African American war heroes and almost every individual singled out was a combat soldier during his wartime service. Most African American soldiers in World War I and World War II were employed in noncombat units and missions because of racial discrimination and inaccurate stereotypes. Though they may not have engaged in direct combat or closed with the enemy, many of these African American soldiers performed missions that were critical to the soldiers who were involved in combat. One such organization, a task organized force of approximately 140 truck companies, played a major role in making sure that the forward units had what was necessary to successfully fight the German forces.

From the landings in Normandy in June 1944, until the opening of the Port of Antwerp in November 1944, as the First and Third Armies advanced across France, all of their supplies had to come across the Mulberry Harbor at Arromanches or through the distant port of Cherbourg. This greatly increased the distance supplies had to travel, and with 28 allied divisions involved in combat on the continent, the tonnage of supplies and fuel required to keep them combat ready was significant. Estimated at 20,000 tons a day, the ability to move this level of supplies on trucks rated at 5 tons or less required a solid plan and extraordinary execution. The solution was a system called the "Red Ball Express," which organized the operation, creating one-way highways for trucks moving to the combat forces and other one-way highways returning to the ports. This system required nearly 6,000 trucks and thousands of drivers. The majority of these drivers, in fact nearly 75 percent of them, were African American soldiers who drove incessantly on dangerous roads regardless of weather, light conditions, or enemy action to deliver the needed supplies to the front. Few of the trucks were armed and the drivers carried only carbines to protect themselves. They were easy targets for air strikes, but luckily the German Luftwaffe had been so decimated by the summer of 1944 that the threat was not as serious as it could have been.

The 140 truck companies that supplied vehicles and men to the system traveled nearly 400 miles for a round trip and the route was constantly filled with approximately 900 vehicles. They were spaced at 60-meter intervals and initially governed to a speed of 25 miles an hour. As the weeks passed and the divisions moved faster, many of the drivers disabled the speed governors on their vehicles to achieve better pulling power on hills. Moving at night was the most difficult task, as the drivers could not use lights for fear of identifying the convoy to the enemy. Driving with "cat eyes" or blackout drive, the trucks would have to push along at a very slow pace to avoid leaving the road. The route out and back was marked with white posts with a red ball on them, thus the moniker of the "Red Ball Express." This method of marking the route was adopted from express trains in the United States that had previously followed tracks marked in the same way.

The Red Ball Express has long been credited with being the backbone of the logistics system that allowed Lieutenant General George Patton (and the 761st Tank Battalion) to drive across Europe at the high rate of speed that armored warfare demanded. While heroes such as Warren Crecy and Ruben Rivers received medals for valor in that run across Europe, the reason they had the ammunition and fuel necessary to engage the enemy was their fellow African American soldiers who manned the Red Ball Express. In their own way, every one of the soldiers who drove unarmed trucks on those one-way highways 24 hours a day was a hero. The express ran for a total of 82 days, from August 25 to November 16, 1944, until the Port of Antwerp was opened and the supply line distances were greatly reduced. The exact tonnage the trucks of the express carried is difficult to ascertain, but with an average of 12,500 tons per day over an 82-day lifespan, a rough estimate would be around a million tons. This massive mountain of supplies was all carried on trucks much smaller than those used by modern armies today. In the logistics world, this is still considered one of the great feats of support, and it was largely accomplished by African American heroes.

James B. Martin

Further Reading

Booker, Bryan D. *African Americans in the United States Army in World War II.* Jefferson, NC: McFarland, 2008.

Buckley, Gail. *American Patriots.* New York: Random House, 2001.

Carter, Allene G., and Robert L. Allen. *Honoring Sergeant Carter: Redeeming a Black World War II Hero's Legacy.* New York: HarperCollins, 2003.

Moore, Christopher Paul. *Fighting for America: Black Soldiers—The Unsung Heroes of World War II.* New York: Random House, 2005.

Charlton, Cornelius

Born: July 24, 1929
Died: June 2, 1951
Home State: West Virginia
Service: Army
Conflict: Korean War
Age at Time of Award: 22

Cornelius (Connie) Charlton was born on July 24, 1929, in East Gulf, West Virginia, the son of a coal miner. His father moved the family to the Bronx, New York, where Cornelius grew up. After graduating from James Monroe High School, he enlisted in the U.S. Army and began basic training in November 1946. He served in Germany with the occupation force following World War II and then was transferred to Aberdeen Proving Grounds in Maryland. Again, being assigned overseas, Charlton served time with an engineer unit on Okinawa before volunteering for combat duty. He was assigned to Company C, 24th Infantry Regiment, 25th Infantry Division in early 1951. He was initially made a squad leader and by May 1951 had been elevated to serve as a platoon sergeant. His unit was involved in Operation Piledriver in May and June 1951, the operation in which he was involved when he was killed.

On June 2, 1951, Company C was involved in offensive operations against North Korean forces near Chipo-ri, Korea. Sergeant Charlton's platoon was aggressively attacking heavily defended positions on high ground to their front when the platoon leader was wounded and required medical evacuation. Assuming command of the platoon, Charlton renewed the attack on the high ground by leading from the front. Pushing up the steep slopes, Sergeant Charlton eliminated multiple enemy defensive positions and killed six enemy soldiers with his individual weapon and hand grenades. Despite his leadership, the attack bogged down on the steep ground and the platoon became pinned down and exposed. Understanding the danger of staying in the exposed position, Charlton rallied the unit to continue the attack, but they were met with a sustained defensive effort from the North Koreans in the form of automatic weapons fire and large numbers of hand grenades. Sergeant Charlton was wounded during this second attempt on the hill and was slowed by a significant wound to his chest. He refused medical attention, knowing that the unit could survive only by moving forward and taking the terrain feature. Surveying the situation and identifying the key position that was blunting the platoon's assaults, Sergeant Charlton attacked the reverse slope position by himself and was again hit by a hand grenade blast. Though wounded severely a second time, Charlton turned his weapon on the position and killed all of the defenders. His actions cleared the way for the platoon to seize its objective and allowed it to safely consolidate on the hilltop. Sergeant Charlton's actions had saved the day, but his wounds were too significant to allow the medics to save his life. Sergeant Charlton died of the wounds he suffered on the hillside near Chipo-ri. His actions speak loudly as an answer to the white leadership and press that believed that African American soldiers would cut and run at the first sight of intense combat.

His family accepted the Medal of Honor posthumously from the Secretary of the Army Frank Pace, during a March 12, 1952 ceremony at the Pentagon.

Charlton was initially buried in Mercer County, West Virginia, due to what the U.S. Army called an administrative oversight; Charlton's family charged that racism was the reason. In 1989, the army finally offered to move his remains to Arlington Cemetery, but his family rejected the offer. Instead Cornelius Charlton was reburied at the American Legion Cemetery at Beckley on March 10, 1989. The reburial was witnessed by two army generals, a congressman, an assistant secretary of state, and an honor guard from Ft. Knox. Charlton was the only African American among the 251 soldiers buried in the American Legion Cemetery. Nineteen years later, following a national controversy started by an article in *The Los Angeles Times* and a campaign by supporters, Cornelius Charlton's remains were buried in Arlington National Cemetery with many of our nation's other heroes.

Charlton has been honored in a variety of ways. Initially, the army named a ferry boat which operated in New York Harbor after him. West Virginia honored him by naming a bridge after him on Interstate 77. In 1993, the U.S. Forces Korea honored a hero who had given his life in that country by naming a new barracks building for Sergeant Charlton. The USNS *Charlton*, a Watson-class vehicle cargo ship, was built in San Diego, California, and was named after Sgt. Cornelius Charlton at a ceremony on December 11, 1999, officiated by Maj. Gen. Mario F. Montero, Jr. and Charlton's sister, Fairy M. Papadopoulos, christened the ship. His hometown of the Bronx honored him in 1952 by creating a park eventually named Charlton Garden. It fell into disrepair and after a group of local veterans discovered that it had been named in honor of a Medal of Honor recipient, they took over its care and launched a campaign to revitalize it. Their efforts bore fruit and, in August 2011, the park was renamed Charlton—Thompson Garden, in honor of Sergeant Charlton and Private First Class William Thompson. These two heroes are the only Medal of Honor recipients to hail from the Bronx and the only African Americans to receive their Medals for action in the Korean War.

Jonathan D. Sutherland

Further Reading

Bowers, William T., William M. Hammond, and George L. MacGarrigle. *Black Soldier, White Army: The 24th Infantry Regiment in Korea*. Washington, DC: U.S. Army Center for Military History, 1996.

Reef, Catherine. *African Americans in the Military*. New York: Facts on File, 2010.

Williams, Albert E. *Black Warriors: The Korean War*. Haverford, PA: Infinity, 2004.

Cherry, Fred Vann

Born: March 24, 1928
Home State: Virginia
Service: U.S. Air Force
Conflict: Korean War, Vietnam War
Age at Time of Award: 39

Fred Vann Cherry, a fighter pilot in the 35th Tactical Fighter Squadron based in Thailand, was the first African American pilot to be captured by the North Vietnamese and incarcerated at the "Hanoi Hilton" (Hoa Lo Prison).

Born March 24, 1928, one of eight children in a poor Virginia family, Fred Vann Cherry graduated from Virginia Union College in 1951. He had already taken flight school tests at Langley Air Force Base, Virginia. Of the 20 men in his group, he was the only African American, and he achieved the highest scores. He originally wanted to join the navy as a pilot, but the recruiter's overt racism prompted him to join the U.S. Air Force. He flew 51 missions in F-84G fighter bombers over Korea.

In 1965, now a major and fighter pilot with the 35th Tactical Fighter Squadron, Cherry flew bombing missions from his base in Thailand into North Vietnam. On October 22, 1965, he was shot down flying a F-105D, while leading a bombing mission against surface-to-air missile sites north of Hanoi. For his actions on this day, he was awarded the Silver Star and was cited for "gallantry and devotion to duty." Captured by the North Vietnamese, he was sent to the prisoner-of-war camp known as the Hanoi Hilton. Cherry was the first African American pilot to become a prisoner of war and be held in this infamous jail. Here, he and other prisoners suffered appalling conditions and daily interrogations and torture at the hands of their captors.

After some time he was transferred to Cu Loc Prison (called "the zoo"), where he shared a cell with a white pilot, a navy lieutenant from Tennessee, Porter Halyburton. After an initial period of mistrust, they became friends and depended heavily on one another.

Cherry had been wounded when he had been shot down, and only in February 1966, did the North Vietnamese operate on him. They gave him no anesthetic or medication, and the wound became infected. It is unlikely that Colonel Cherry would have survived had it not been for the care provided by Halyburton. By March, Cherry was in a pitiful state and had lost nearly half of his weight. The North Vietnamese took off his torso cast, and washed him down with gasoline. He was given a blood transfusion and operated on twice more, in April and July 1966. He described the second operation: "They just took a scalpel and cut away the dead flesh, scraping at the infection on the bones. It was the worst straight pain I had yet known.

They had my face covered with a sheet. And they kept raising it to see if I'm going to beg for mercy, going to scream. And each time they looked down at me, I would look at them and smile."

Halyburton continued to care for him, but four days after the second operation the Vietnamese began intensive interrogation on Cherry. He was kept in solitary confinement, and they wanted him to make a statement denouncing the U.S. government. He was interrogated between four and five hours a day; still his wounds were not healing, and finally the North Vietnamese gave him antibiotics.

Cherry was finally released and returned to the United States in 1973. He was awarded the Air Force Cross for his outstanding conduct while a prisoner of war, two Bronze Stars, and two Purple Hearts to add to his Distinguished Flying Cross and Silver Star.

Cherry's experiences as a prisoner of war and his relationship with Porter Halyburton were central in his life story, as told in the book *Two Souls Indivisible: The Friendship That Saved Two POWs in Vietnam*. After Cherry's retirement in 1981, he worked in industry and eventually opened his own engineering consulting firm. He was asked by President Reagan to serve on the Korean War Veteran's Memorial Advisory Board. Among the many honors he has received are the Award for Outstanding Service to the Military Community from the Tuskegee Airmen and the naming of a college scholarship for him, the Colonel Fred V. Cherry Scholarship, awarded annually to a graduating senior from one of Suffolk, Virginia's high schools.

Jonathan D. Sutherland

Further Reading

Terry, Wallace. *Bloods: An Oral History of the Vietnam War by Black Veterans*. New York: Ballantine Books, 1984.

Westheider, James E. *The African American Experience in Vietnam: Brothers in Arms*. New York: Rowman & Littlefield, 2008.

Westheider, James E. *Fighting on Two Fronts: African Americans and the Vietnam War*. New York: New York University Press, 1997.

Corbin, Todd

Born: 1973
Home State: Ohio
Service: Marine Corps
Conflict: Iraq War
Age at Time of Award: 32

Lance Corporal Todd Corbin hails from Norwalk, Ohio, and served during Operation Iraqi Freedom as a member of 3rd Battalion, 25th Marine Regiment, 4th Marine Division, a reserve unit headquartered in Brook Park, Ohio.

Assigned to action in the dangerous Al Anbar Province, Corbin's unit was serving as part of the 2nd Marine Division conducting stability and security operations in the vicinity of Haditha Dam. Corbin was a transport driver who regularly served as a member of the battalion commander's personal security detachment. On May 7, 2005, shortly after returning from patrolling, the detachment received word that a marine platoon was pinned down and they rapidly prepared to move out as a Quick Reaction Force to rescue the trapped marines. While en route to the beleaguered marines' position, insurgents bent on preventing the rescue of the trapped platoon ambushed the Quick Reaction Force.

The enemy hit the rescue column with a suicide vehicle improvised explosive device, rocket-propelled grenades, and machine gun fire. Of the four vehicles in the column, three were hit in the initial engagement and severely damaged. Of the 16 marines in the rescue mission, 11 became casualties in this initial attack. Lance Corporal Corbin recognized the need to protect the wounded marines and positioned the remaining vehicle between them and the enemy fire. After radioing to higher headquarters for assistance, he moved forward into the combat and ran to his wounded patrol leader. Corbin threw the wounded marine over his shoulder under fire and used his free hand to engage the enemy with his weapon. Once the patrol leader was safe, Corbin ran across the kill zone again, this time reaching the wounded navy corpsman. After doing immediate first aid on the corpsman, Corbin began moving him to safety. Before he could complete this move, enemy fire forced him to cover the body of another wounded marine with his own until his unit could provide adequate suppressive fire. Reaching his unit's fighting position, he reorganized the marines still actively engaged and worked to repel the ambush. Lance Corporal Corbin reentered the kill zone five more times to recover dead or wounded marines. Once all of the patrol's members were behind his truck, Corbin got his damaged vehicle to start and got his unit out of the kill zone entirely. He was able to keep the vehicle running long enough to evacuate his wounded and dead to the battalion aid station nearly five miles away. Lance Corporal Corbin's actions reflect the sacrifice and valor that young marines long for from boot camp on. His actions as a member of the Quick Reaction Force near Haditha saved numerous lives. As a result of his actions on May 7, 2005, Lance Corporal Todd Corbin was awarded the Navy Cross for valor.

Corbin, a sheriff's deputy in civilian life, displayed an amazing level of courage that day and was honored with an award for valor that is second only to the Medal of Honor. When interviewed, Corbin refuses to acknowledge his courage or importance, instead constantly moving the conversation and credit to his relationship with God. Corbin returned from Iraq in late September 2005 with the 3/25 and returned to civilian life. On Independence Day 2006, at the 3/25th Headquarters in Brook Park, Ohio, Lance Corporal Corbin received his Navy Cross. The ceremony also included the presentation of the Silver Star to Corporal Jeff Schuller for his actions during the same fight near Haditha Dam. Beyond the recognition accorded to Corbin by the Department of the Navy, he also received the Richard K. Sorenson Award for being named the 4th Marine Division Association's Marine of the Year in 2006. He and his wife, Tonya, celebrated the birth of their first child, Tyra Olivia, in August 2006. Corbin continues to serve as a deputy sheriff and his wife as a policewoman in their home town in Ohio.

James B. Martin

Further Reading

"The Richard K. Sorenson Award." www.fightingfourth.com (accessed January 27, 2013).

Wilson, Kimberly. "Lance Cpl. Todd Corbin." www.beliefnet.com (accessed January 27, 2013).

Zimmerman, Beth. "Marines Brave 'Hell' in Haditha." *Marine Corps Times*, September 18, 2006.

Crecy, Warren G. H.

Born: January 4, 1923
Died: October 26, 1976
Home State: Texas
Service: Army
Conflict: World War II, Korean War
Age at Time of Award: 21

Warren G.H. Crecy, called Harding by his close friends, was born in Corpus Christi, Texas, on January 4, 1923. He was a mild-mannered child, but had a strong streak in him that showed in athletics and later in combat. Though only 150 pounds, reports show that he played offensive guard on the football team at Solomon M. Coles High School and apparently excelled, as his coach indicated that he was the toughest football player he had ever coached. After graduating from high school and only months after the attack at Pearl Harbor, Crecy enlisted in the army on April 12, 1942, at Ft. Sam Houston, Texas.

Crecy was among a small group of African American recruits selected to be trained as armored crewmen and went through basic training at Ft. Knox, Kentucky. He was then assigned to Company D, 761st Tank Battalion at Camp Hood, Texas, for unit training. Crecy was one of the original members of this famous African American unit that was formed in March 1942 with African American soldiers and mainly white officers. His platoon sergeant in Texas remarked that Crecy was the most gung-ho of any soldier in the unit and just wanted to do everything better than anyone else. This refrain of Crecy's drive and courage is a common theme from anyone who served with him in peacetime or combat. Though quiet and often stoic, when he entered the environment of athletic competition or combat, he became a different person and was driven to succeed with little fear of the consequences. An important factor in Crecy's life, and his future combat in Europe, was his friendship with Horatio Scott, another member of the 761st. Scott and Crecy became inseparable at Camp Hood, as interviews with Crecy's wife Margaret bear out. He and Scott swore an oath to stick together, even to the point of agreeing not to accept promotion until the other was ready for the same step in grade.

Crecy and his unit were alerted for deployment to the European Theater of Operations in August 1944, landing by ship at Dorset, England, on September 7, 1944. After drawing their new tanks and equipment, the unit crossed the English Channel and landed at Omaha Beach, following in the footsteps of the units that came ashore on D-Day. The 761st was assigned to General George Patton's Third Army and fought across France and Germany with this famous organization. Crecy was a tank commander and sergeant by the time the unit landed in Normandy and prepared to see combat for the first time.

The 761st Tank Battalion saw its first combat in the Lorraine Campaign near the town of Morville-lès-Vic from November 8 through 10. Crecy's unit went into action on November 9, 1944, at the northern end of Morville and encountered stiff resistance. An antitank emplacement immobilized Crecy's tank. Totally ignoring the danger he was in, Crecy dismounted the relative safety of his tank and moved to destroy the antitank emplacement. He commandeered a jeep with a .30 caliber machine gun and attacked the German position, routing its occupants and killing the majority of them. He and his crew dismounted and found a replacement tank, entering combat again as quickly as possible. His second tank became stuck in the thick mud in the fields around Morville and before it could free itself, it came under fire from German machine guns. Crecy again dismounted and tried to brace the tank tracks so that it could pull itself out of the quagmire, but as he was doing so he saw an infantry unit being raked by the machine gun positions firing on his vehicle. He mounted the back deck of the immobilized tank and began to provide covering fire with the .50 caliber machine gun on the turret. Though exposed to direct fire and artillery, Crecy continued to pour fire into the enemy positions and allowed the exposed infantry unit to withdraw to safety. All of the tank companies in the battalion were engaged and suffered significant casualties, but the hardest hit was Company C, Horatio Scott's unit. Scott himself was badly wounded and, though he sent word to Crecy that he would be fine, he succumbed to his wounds later that day. Scott's death hit Crecy hard and he requested a transfer to Company C to fight in Scott's place. This request was granted and he took command of a tank in Company C.

All reports indicate that Crecy's tenacity only grew after the death of his close friend. He continued to display courage and valor beyond any other member of the unit on a day-to-day basis. He became known by a number of nicknames, such as "Iron Man" or "The Baddest Man in the 761st," because of his constant disregard for enemy fire. He was recommended for the Silver Star for his actions on November 9 and 10 around Morville and later for saving the life of the 761st Battalion Commander, Lieutenant Colonel Paul Bates. Eventually, he would be awarded the Silver Star and a number of other awards for valor. After the war, members of the 761st nominated three of their comrades for consideration in the Shaw University study that resulted in Medals of Honor for African American soldiers in World War II. While Ruben Rivers from the 761st was selected for the final group considered as Medal of Honor recipients, Warren Crecy was not.

Crecy received a battlefield commission to lieutenant in May 1945 and stayed in the army after the war. He served in occupation duty in Germany, participating in the security surrounding the Nuremberg Trials and later returned to the United States to command an all-white unit at Ft. Benning, Georgia. He was deployed to Korea in 1952 and was severely wounded when a mortar shell exploded close by. He suffered significant wounds to his face and spent most of the rest of his life in and out of hospitals trying to repair the damage. He spent the last years of his life in San Francisco, California, around Letterman General Army Hospital and the Presidio of San Francisco. Reports indicate that though he was suffering from his own trauma, he spent considerable time trying to motivate injured soldiers and put them on a stronger path to recovery. He was medically retired from the army as a major in 1965, never having been able to return to a tank battalion as he had wished. In 1976, Crecy experienced a year with wonderful highs and devastating lows for his family. His son, Warren Jr., graduated from West Point and he attended his first and only reunion of the 761st. The man who was universally acknowledged as the most courageous soldier in the most storied African American tank unit in history finally died from complications of his Korean War wounds on October 26, 1976. He was buried with full military honors at Arlington National Cemetery.

James B. Martin

761ST TANK BATTALION (THE BLACK PANTHERS)

As with every segregated African American unit in American military history, the 761st Tank Battalion had to prove themselves worthy of combat to a degree not required of other units. This was particularly true as the U.S. Army moved into the mechanized age with the introduction of large numbers of armored units. White officers, many of whom had long scorned the ability of African Americans as soldiers, now claimed that armored combat required quickness of thought that African Americans were not capable of delivering. Regardless of the success of previous segregated units, such as the 369th Infantry Regiment during World War I, reasons were always found to exclude African American units from active combat. The 761st took another long stride to showing this stereotype to be false and once again showed the combat prowess of well-trained African American soldiers.

The 761st Tank Battalion, eventually known as the Black Panthers, was activated on April 1, 1942, at Camp Claiborne, Louisiana. As the law in 1942 forbid the integration of military units, but the manpower needs of the nation were expected to be great, the commander of Army Ground Forces in the United States, Lieutenant General Leslie J. McNair, pushed for the creation of segregated combat units to be used in Europe or Asia as necessary. The 761st was one of the original units created as part of the experiment he designed. The unit was initially trained in the use of the M5 Stuart light tank and by all accounts was well trained, as evidenced by their performance in a Third Army exercise in the Kisatchie National Forest in April 1943. They were observed during the exercise by none other than General McNair, who was reportedly pleased with their performance. Upon returning from this exercise, the unit was transitioned to the M4 Sherman medium tank, which was the mainstay of the armored units in the European Theater, and provided them a weapon system from which they could fight against the German panzers.

The 761st continued to train, now at Ft. Hood, Texas, and were finally shipped to the European Theater after the commander of the U.S. Second Army, General Benjamin Lear, certified them as combat ready. They embarked to England and, after a short stay there, eventually entered the continent across Omaha Beach on October 10, 1944. The unit arrived in Germany with 6 white officers, 30 African American officers, and 676 African American enlisted men. They were assigned to Lieutenant General George Patton's Third Army, though they did not stay with the unit throughout the war. It is reported that Patton had requested the best tank battalion left in the United States and the 761st was identified as the appropriate unit. Reports of Patton's welcome speech to the unit exist in many forms, but in typical Pattonesque form, he told them he wanted nothing but the best and that their task was to kill Germans, regardless of the color of their skin. What he did not say, but the historical record makes clear, is that he was one of the officers who did not believe African American soldiers were mentally equipped to fight in the armored corps.

The 761st entered combat for the first time on November 8, 1944, at Moyenvic, France, and in doing so became the first African American armored unit to ever see combat. From Moyenvic, the battalion participated in 183 days of continuous combat. In November 1944 alone, the battalion suffered 156 casualties, with 24 killed, 88 wounded, and 44 more nonbattle casualties. Transferred between Third Army, Seventh Army, and Ninth Army, the battalion saw combat in northern France, the Rhineland, Ardennes-Alsace, and Central European campaigns.

Probably most notable among their combat exploits was their participation in the Battle of the Bulge and the drive into Germany that followed. Moving to support the encircled 101st Airborne Division, the battalion engaged in two days of continuous combat against German panzer and infantry units, eventually splitting the German lines, thus preventing the resupply of those enemy forces which were encircling the 101st. After supporting the airborne division, the 761st served as the armored lead element for the 103rd Infantry Division and was part of the lead elements that breached the Siegfried Line—Germany's fortifications protecting the homeland. During this action, from March 20 through 23, 1945, the battalion operated beyond the range of U.S. artillery and racked up an impressive scorecard against German forces. During this three-day period, the 761st captured seven German towns, 400 vehicles, 80 heavy weapons, and significant numbers of small arms, and inflicted more than 4,000 German casualties. The historical record indicates that during this period the battalion fought against elements of 14 different German divisions. As the war ended, the battalion became one of the first U.S. units to link up with our Russian allies when they joined hands at the Enns River near Steyr, Austria.

During the course of the six months that the 761st saw combat in Europe, they fought in six different European countries under three different numbered U.S. Armies. The official tallies indicated that the battalion inflicted 130,000 casualties, liberated or destroyed 30 towns, destroyed 34 tanks, 461 wheeled vehicles, and 113 large guns. This was accomplished with a friendly casualty rate of nearly 50 percent and the loss of 70 American tanks. In a war that saw African Americans shut out of valorous recognition in large part, the members of the battalion were awarded 11 Silver Stars, 70 Bronze Stars, and 296 Purple Hearts. One member of the unit, Staff Sergeant Ruben Rivers, was among seven African American soldiers chosen to have their earlier awards upgraded to the Medal of Honor after the Shaw University study in the early 1990s. Two other members of the unit, Warren G. H. Crecy and First Sergeant Samuel Turley, were recommended by numerous individuals, but the Senior Awards Board that reviewed each case determined that their actions did not warrant upgrade. The 761st Tank Battalion was recommended during the war for the Presidential Unit Citation, but neither President Truman nor Eisenhower would sign the award. The battalion eventually received the citation in 1978, after it was signed by President Jimmy Carter. In 2005, a monument to the 761st Tank Battalion was unveiled at Ft. Hood, Texas, during a ceremony attended by many surviving veterans of the battalion. The monument, made out of marble and black granite, was designed by the same artist who created the Buffalo Soldier Monument at Ft. Leavenworth, Kansas.

An interesting note, though not concerning the 761st combat record, is the service of Lieutenant Jackie Robinson, who was assigned to the 761st before its departure for Europe. Robinson had a run-in with a white bus driver, who ordered him to move to the back of the bus. Robinson refused and, after an altercation with military police, was taken into custody. When the battalion commander of the 761st would not prefer charges, the post commander had Robinson transferred to a battalion with a more compliant commander and sought to court-martial him. After a trial, Robinson was found not guilty and eventually left the army. In just a couple of years, he was again pushing back against racism by breaking the color barrier in major league baseball.

James B. Martin

Further Reading

Booker, Bryan D. *African Americans in the United States Army in World War II.* Jefferson, NC: McFarland, 2008.

Pfeifer, Kathryn Browne. *The 761st Tank Battalion (African-American Soldiers).* New York: Twenty-First Century Books, 1994.

Wilson, Joe, Jr. *The 761st "Black Panther" Tank Battalion in World War II.* Jefferson, NC: McFarland, 1999.

Davis, Benjamin Oliver, Jr.

Born: December 18, 1912
Died: July 4, 2002
Home State: Washington, D.C.
Service: Army Air Corps, Air Force
Conflict: World War II, Korean War
Age at Time of Award: 31

Benjamin Oliver Davis Jr. was born on December 18, 1912, in Washington, D.C., the son of Elnora and Benjamin Davis. His father, in 1940, became the first African American to be promoted to the rank of brigadier general in the U.S. Army. Benjamin Davis Jr. lived on a number of military bases during his youth. After leaving Cleveland High School, Davis entered Cleveland Western Reserve University and was then transferred to the University of Chicago.

In 1932, Davis entered West Point. He was nominated for entry to the academy by the African American Chicago Congressman, Oscar DePriest, and passed the entrance examinations. During his time at West Point, Davis was subjected by his classmates to a shunning technique known as silencing. This meant that Davis roomed alone and ate alone and was spoken to by other cadets only when on official business. This silencing made Davis more determined to succeed, and he graduated 35th out of a class of 276 in 1936, becoming the first African American to graduate from the academy in 47 years. Davis also became one of only two African American line officers in the U.S. Army at the time, the other one being his father. With a commission as a second lieutenant, Davis applied to join the Air Corps but was refused because there were no black squadrons.

In June 1937, Davis entered infantry school in Georgia. After graduating a year later, he accepted the position of professor of military science at Tuskegee Institute, Alabama, where he remained for the next four years. During his time at the institute, President Franklin D. Roosevelt approved changes about the enlistment of African Americans into the armed services, and a training program for African American pilots at the Tuskegee Institute was established. In May 1941, Davis entered the Advanced Flying School at the Tuskegee Air Base and received his pilot wings in the spring of the following year. He was given command of the 99th Fighter Squadron at Tuskegee, the first African American air unit to be formed.

Davis, along with the 99th Pursuit Squadron, served in North Africa and Sicily during World War II. After four months of active service in the Mediterranean, he returned to America in October 1943 to take command of the 332nd Fighter Group, a larger African American unit, based at Selfridge Field, Michigan. The unit was deployed to Italy in January 1944 and proved to be a highly efficient and effective force. On June 9, the unit, flying P-47 Thunderbolts and escorting B-24 bombers, flew to Munich, Germany, led by Davis. During this mission, the unit successfully destroyed several Me–109s. For his leadership skills and bravery on this mission, Davis was awarded the Distinguished Flying Cross—the first of many such awards. The medal was presented to Davis at the Ramitelli Air Base in Italy and was pinned on his chest by his father, Brig. Gen. Benjamin O. Davis Sr.

Following the end of World War II, Davis returned to America in June 1945 to take command of the 447th Composite Group at Codman Field, Kentucky. He then commanded the base and the 332nd Fighter Wing at Lockbourne Army Air Base in Ohio. Between 1949 and 1953, Davis graduated from the Air War College in Alabama and was assigned to the deputy chief of staff for operations in Washington, D.C.

Davis again saw combat during the Korean War when he assumed command of the 51st Fighter-Interceptor Wing of the Far East Air Forces (FEAF). Commanding this racially integrated flying unit, Davis was promoted to brigadier general, becoming the first African American to attain the rank in the U.S. Air Force. From 1954 until 1955, Davis served as director of operations and training at the FEAF headquarters in Tokyo and then took up the post of vice commander of the 13th Air Force in Taipei, Formosa (Taiwan). After serving as chief of staff in Ramstein and Wiesbaden, Germany, Davis returned to the United States in July 1961.

In the positions of director of manpower and organization and deputy chief of staff, programs, and requirements, Davis remained at the headquarters of the U.S. Air Force until April 1965, when he was assigned as chief of staff for the United Nations Command and U.S. Forces in Korea.

During the Vietnam War, Davis commanded the 13th Air Force at Clark Air Force Base in the Republic of the Philippines. In 1968, he was assigned as deputy commander in chief of the U.S. Strike Command at MacDill Air Force Base in Florida, with additional duties as commander in chief, Middle East, Southern Asia, and Africa.

General Davis retired from military service in 1970, moving to Arlington, Virginia, and served as assistant secretary at the Department of Transportation for environment, safety, and consumer affairs under President Richard M. Nixon until 1975. In 1978, Davis served, as his father had before him, on the Battle Monuments Commission. In 1991, he published his autobiography, *Benjamin O. Davis, Jr., American.* Davis was a trailblazer who was the first African American to achieve the ranks of brigadier general, major general, and lieutenant general in the U.S. Air Force. In 1998, President Clinton promoted him to the rank of four-star general on the retired list.

Davis died on July 4, 2002, and was buried with full military honors at Arlington National Cemetery. A memorial service was also held at the Bolling Air Force Base chapel that attracted many former Tuskegee airmen. Alan Gropman, chairman, Grand Strategy Department, National Defense University, said:

> Gen. Benjamin O. Davis Jr. is an American hero. . . . General Davis risked his life for his nation, for his people and also for his country. He believed all his adult life in racial integration and thought he could bring this essential reform to America once World War II began. If he demonstrated blacks could fly and fight and lead with the same skill and courage as whites, a notion foreign to white America of 1941, he believed he could destroy the myth of racial inferiority. The Tuskegee Airmen shared his vision and courage, and he and they succeeded. (quoted in Lopez 2002)

At the Arlington ceremony, former members of the Tuskegee Airmen served as honorary pallbearers, and a heritage flyover, including two P-51s, an F-16, and an F-15, honored Davis with a missing-man formation.

Jonathan D. Sutherland

INTEGRATION OF THE U.S. ARMED FORCES

African American soldiers, sailors, airmen, and marines have served in the U.S. Armed Forces in a variety of capacities during the history of the republic. Some services accepted African Americans early in our history, while others finally agreed only after being issued orders by the president. The history of African Americans in the armed forces has, like the history of the society that it protects, been one of racial discrimination and segregation. African Americans fought during the American Revolution to help create this country. In the Civil War, African Americans enlisted in units like the 54th Massachusetts to fight against the racial oppression embodied by the southern slave system. On the western frontier, a significant amount of the fighting with Native Americans was done by Buffalo Soldier units, which earned respect of their enemy for their tenacity and bravery. At San Juan Hill and Kettle Hill, during the Spanish-American War, Buffalo Soldiers in the infantry and cavalry charged alongside Teddy Roosevelt's Rough Riders and acquitted themselves at a level equal to their white comrades.

The turn of the century saw an entrenchment in the military of the racism that was prevalent in society. Military leaders determined that the African American soldiers were not fit to be in combat units and attempted to relegate them to support units at the beginning of World War I and World War II. Throughout the first 173 years of American history, African Americans serving in the U.S. military were required to serve in segregated units, which were normally commanded by white officers. While some African American officers were commissioned and led the segregated units, the leadership of all the services hesitated to believe in the ability of African Americans to command or think at the rate necessary to lead men in combat. It should be remembered that in these shortcomings, the military leadership was consistent with the stereotypes heaped on

African Americans in our society at large. In fact, the ability to serve even in segregated units was often an opportunity for success that was much harder to find in civilian life.

As African American soldiers performed well in conflict after conflict, some more enlightened military leaders began to lobby for the integration of the U.S. Armed Forces. The last service to admit African Americans was the U.S. Marine Corps. They were finally forced into recruiting African American marines by Presidential Order in 1941. The marines they trained at Montford Point, North Carolina, broke through the last whites-only military service barrier and carried the pride of their community into service in the Pacific in World War II. The first African American army general, Benjamin O. Davis, was promoted to his first star in October 1940. Slowly, all of the official barriers to military service were removed except for segregation. That is not to say that discrimination disappeared, or even abated, but the official policies of the armed forces that denied opportunities to African American soldiers solely based on race were slowly being corrected.

The final official barrier, the regulations requiring segregated units for African Americans and whites were overturned by another Presidential Order in 1948. In the aftermath of World War II, the military services were required to take a fresh look at the use of African Americans in the military and identify how this important human resource would be used moving forward. The largest branch of service, the army, also had the largest proportion of African Americans in service. Shortly after the war's end, the Gillem Board, named after its chairman Lieutenant General Alvan C. Gillem Jr., proposed to change the way that African American soldiers were used in the army. While the document ignited more than a little controversy in the army and African American communities, its intentions were focused on how best to use the resource of African American soldiers rather than on solving problems of civil rights. Many senior officers in the army wanted to keep the status quo simply because they were products of the largely racist white culture of American society. While that pronouncement may seem harsh, there is no other honest way to express the fact. Making small changes around the edges of military personnel policy without dealing with the heart of the matter, segregation, was the simplest way to avoid major repercussions in the force.

In the end, the services proved unable to take the lead and solve the race problem that had haunted them for decades. On July 26, 1948, President Harry S. Truman signed Executive Order 9981 calling on the military to provide equal opportunity and treatment for all servicemen, regardless of race or color. Even though the president is the commander in chief, this change did not occur overnight or anywhere near quickly. The segregated 24th Infantry Regiment in Korea is a testament to segregation's continuing survival. Eventually, the military leadership bent to the order of the president and individual replacement of African American soldiers into formerly all-white units began to occur. Discrimination continued to occur, as it does today, but the opportunities for African American soldiers to work alongside white soldiers were created and African American officers began to be placed in command over white soldiers and white junior officers.

Although the racial story of the U.S. Armed Forces is not one of fairness and equality, it is probably better than the racial story of our country at large. The armed forces were integrated well ahead of American society, and not just in the south. It would be eight years after the executive order that integrated the armed forces before the story of a little girl in Topeka, Kansas, would finally end the official sanction of "separate, but equal" in America. In this way, the military may have been out in front a bit, but this would be a hard argument to make to the millions of African American soldiers who had to endure the segregation and discrimination of the military simply to try and serve their country.

James B. Martin

Further Reading

Astor, Gerald. *The Right to Fight.* Novato, CA: Presidio Press, 1998.

Buckley, Gail. *American Patriots: The Story of Blacks in the Military from the Revolution to Desert Storm.* New York: Random House, 2001.

Cohen, William S. Speech, December 9, 1998. http://www.defenselink.mil/speeches/1998/c19981209-secdef.html (accessed August 2, 2003).

Davis, Benjamin O., Jr. *Benjamin O. Davis, Jr., American: An Autobiography.* Washington, DC: Smithsonian Institution Press, 1991.

Lopez, Todd. "Pioneering Tuskegee Airman Laid to Rest in Arlington." http://www.defenselink.mil/news/Jul2002/n07172002_200207174.html, posted July 17, 2002 (accessed August 2, 2003).

Nalty, Bernard C. *Strength for the Fight.* New York: The Free Press, 1986.

Reef, Catherine. *Benjamin Davis, Jr.* New York: Scholastic, 1992.

Smithsonian National Air and Space Museum. http://www.nasm.si.edu/features/black wings/hstudent/bio_davis.cfm (accessed August 2, 2003).

Davis, Calvin Clark

Born: September 2, 1912
Died: November 30, 1944
Home State: Michigan
Service: Army Air Corps
Conflict: World War II
Age at Time of Award: 29

Calvin Clark Davis was born on September 2, 1912, in Bear Lake, Michigan, where he was orphaned as a young child and raised by his sister. His family could trace their ancestry back to an African American slave and a white plantation owner. Davis attended Malcolm School and later graduated from Bear Lake High School in 1932, where he excelled at track.

Davis was very light skinned and consequently when he enlisted with the 5th U.S. Army Air Force in May 1941, no one inquired as to his race and he subsequently joined the 90th Bomber Group of the 400th Squadron on May 15. The unit was known as the "Jolly Rogers" (not to be confused with a U.S. Navy fighter squadron of the same nickname, VF-17), and Davis became a member of the aircrew on board a B-24 Liberator. He took part in more than 50 combat missions in the Pacific. Davis and the rest of the bomber crew were awarded the Distinguished Flying Cross for their heroism when they attacked a Japanese airfield in on August 29, 1943. Davis's aircraft had already been damaged but they continued the attack out of formation to help protect the other bombers in their unit. Having completed the required 50 missions, Davis was eligible to seek a noncombat role because of the number of missions he had flown, but instead he volunteered for service in Europe, joining the 8th U.S. Army Air Force, 570th Squadron, 390th Bomber Group, known as the Jokers. He flew combat missions over Europe in a B-17.

On November 30, 1944, while the squadron was attacking German oil refineries at Merseburg, Germany, his bomber Asterisk collided with another American aircraft. Davis, then a radio operator, and five other members of the crew were killed, while three managed to bail out. Davis's story might well have remained undiscovered had one of his descendants, Calvin Murphy, not found a contemporary (2000) newspaper article about Davis and his exemplary service. Davis's records had been destroyed in a fire in 1973. Nevertheless, Murphy contacted Michigan Congressmen Peter Hoekstra and John Conyers Jr. to help him in his search for evidence.

This war hero, who was not relegated to noncombat roles because the army did not ask about his race, served his country during World War II and was belatedly honored in February 2002. Calvin Murphy received posthumous medals on Davis's behalf. For his heroism, Calvin Davis was awarded the Distinguished Flying Cross with two Oak Leaf Clusters, the Purple Heart, along with numerous service medals.

German civilians discovered Tsgt. Calvin Clark Davis's body intact, with his dog tags still attached. He was buried in Ardennes American Cemetery, Neupre (Neuville-En-Condroz), Belgium, where his grave was reportedly adopted and is regularly visited by a Belgian civilian.

Jonathan D. Sutherland

Further Reading

Motley, Mary Penick, ed. *The Invisible Soldier: The Experience of the Black Soldier, World War II*. Detroit: Wayne State University Press, 1975.

Osur, Alan M. *Blacks in the Army Air Forces during World War II: The Problem of Race Relations*. Washington, DC: Office of Air Force History, 1977.

Davis, Rodney Maxwell

Born: April 7, 1942
Died: September 6, 1967
Home State: Georgia
Service: Marine Corps
Conflict: Vietnam War
Age at Time of Award: 25

Rodney Maxwell Davis was born in Macon, Georgia, on April 7, 1942, to Gordon and Ruth Davis. He attended all of his schooling in Macon and shortly after his graduation from Peter G. Appling High School on May 29, 1961, he joined the U.S. Marine Corps on August 31 and was trained at the First Recruit Training Battalion, Marine Corps Recruit Depot Parris Island, South Carolina, until December. He then went on to the Marine Corps base at Camp Lejeune, North Carolina, for combat training with the 2nd Battalion, 1st Infantry Training Regiment, graduating in February 1962. Davis was assigned to Company K of the 3rd Battalion, 2nd Marine Regiment, 2nd Marine Division, Fleet Marine Forces, as a rifleman until May 1964. During this assignment, he was initially promoted to private first class and eventually lance corporal. Following his tour in North Carolina, Davis was assigned in London, England, to provide security for the naval headquarters there. During this three-year tour, Davis was again promoted, this time to sergeant, and volunteered for an assignment to Vietnam and arrived in the country in August 1967. Davis was assigned to 2nd Platoon, Company B, 1st Battalion, 5th Marines, 1st Marine Division and operated in the Quảng Nam Province during Operation Swift. On September 6, 1967, Sergeant Davis's unit came under attack from a much larger enemy force. Before the day was through, of the original 48 Marines in 2nd Platoon, all but 11 would be killed or wounded enough to need medication evacuation. Of the 11 still fit for duty, 7 of those would receive the Purple Heart for wounds suffered that day. 2nd Platoon was pinned down in the Que Son Valley by heavy enemy fire in a trench line. Sergeant Davis gallantly directed his men's fire and moved from marine to marine encouraging them, all the while maintaining his own firing rate and throwing grenades at the advancing enemy. Davis continued to lead his men until an enemy grenade fell into the trench among a group of five marines. Without hesitation, Sergeant Davis dove toward the grenade and used his hands to pull it under him and absorb the blast. His actions saved at least five marines, and one of those marines later indicated that there were at least seven other marines in the blast radius. Sergeant Rodney Davis's valor was recognized by the Marine Corps and the nation, with the presentation of a posthumous Medal of

Honor. Vice President Spiro Agnew officiated at the White House ceremony and presented the Medal to his parents on March 26, 1969. Sergeant Davis also was awarded the Purple Heart, the Good Conduct Medal, the National Defense Service Medal, the Armed Forces Expeditionary Medal, the Vietnam Service Medal, the Military Merit Medal, the Gallantry Cross with palm, and the Republic of Vietnam Campaign Medal.

To honor Sergeant Davis and the sacrifice he made for his country and fellow marines, the USS *Rodney M. Davis* (FFG-60), whose motto is "by valor and arms," was commissioned by the Department of the Navy on May 9, 1987. In Macon, Georgia, the town has done its best to honor its only Medal of Honor recipient. A bronze bust of Sergeant Davis stands in a park near the Macon Centreplex and another monument commemorating his courage stands just across the street from the Macon City Hall. Though his family was offered the honor of burying Sergeant Davis in Arlington National Cemetery, his mother believed it was more fitting for him to be buried in the neighborhood in which he grew up. He was buried in Linwood Cemetery near his Macon neighborhood. Over the years, the cemetery fell in disrepair and Davis's grave fared no better. One of the marines that Davis saved that day in Quảng Nam Province stopped to visit the grave and was appalled at the conditions he found. His work, along with that of other organizers, produced the Sgt. Rodney Davis Project. The project raised $80,000 to build a suitable monument and begin a scholarship fund in Sergeant Davis's name. At the dedication of the Sgt. Rodney M. Davis Memorial Monument on November 10, 2012, symbolically the 237th birthday of the Marine Corps, members of his platoon and family spoke of what Sergeant Davis had given them. An important point was made that, of the six men in the immediate area of the hand grenade that September day, five were white and one was an African American. That the lone African American chose to save five unknown white marines in a time of intense racial turmoil in the United States speaks to the unity of the Marine Corps and the overwhelming sacrifice of Sergeant Rodney Maxwell Davis. Sergeant Davis is honored on Panel 26E, Row 8 of the Vietnam Veterans Memorial.

James B. Martin and Jonathan D. Sutherland

Further Reading

Crenshaw, Wayne. "Marine Recalls Heroic Act of Medal of Honor Recipient Rodney Davis." Macon.com. http://www.macon.com/2012/11/10/2244622/new-memorial-unveiled-for-medal.html, posted November 10, 2012 (accessed August 18, 2013).

Greene, Robert Ewell. *Black Defenders of America, 1775–1973.* Chicago: Johnson, 1974.

Hollis, John. "Medal of Honor Recipient Sgt. Rodney M. Davis to Be Honored in Macon." *Atlanta Blackstar.* http://atlantablackstar.com/2012/11/09/medal-of-honor-recipient-sgt-rodney-m-davis-to-be-honored-in-macon/, posted November 9, 2012 (accessed August 18, 2013).

Shaw, Henry I., Jr., and Ralph W. Donnelly. *Blacks in the Marine Corps*. Washington DC: History and Museum Division, Headquarters United States Marine Corps, 1975.

Dillard, Oliver W.

Born: September 28, 1926
Home State: Alabama
Service: Army
Conflict: World War II, Korean War, Vietnam War
Age at Time of Award: 23

Oliver W. Dillard was born in Margaret, Alabama, on September 28, 1926, to Stonewall Jackson and Josiephine Dillard. His father was a graduate of Tuskegee Institute and a schoolteacher. Dillard excelled in school and earned a scholarship to Tuskegee Institute in 1942. He earned awards at Tuskegee before being drafted in 1945.

Dillard went to basic training at Ft. McClellan, Alabama, and then was deployed to Germany for service with the 349th Field Artillery group on January 1, 1946. His education and natural leadership qualities gained him rapid promotion to technical sergeant and he successfully applied to Officer's Candidate School. He completed OCS at Ft. Benning, Georgia, in July 1947, and was commissioned a second lieutenant. Dillard continued to earn accolades, as he was the honor graduate of his Infantry Officer's Basic Course before his initial assignment to a unit at Ft. Dix, New Jersey. In 1950, he was assigned to the 3rd Battalion, 24th Infantry Regiment, 25th Infantry Division in Japan.

With the outbreak of the Korean War, the 24th Infantry Regiment was deployed from Japan to the Pusan Perimeter. As a platoon leader in Company L, 3/24 Infantry, Dillard first saw combat on July 21, 1950, near the village of Yecheon. Just days later, during the period from July 26 through 31, 1950, Dillard saw significant combat as the new company commander of Company L. Assigned defensive positions in the vicinity of Sangju, the 3rd Battalion was partially overrun by North Korean units and Company L was cut off from the rest of the regiment. Dillard led his unit in the defense of their position and later withdrew them to safety, returning under the cover of darkness to rescue a seriously wounded soldier he had not been able to evacuate earlier. For his actions in the combat near Sangju, Dillard was awarded the Bronze Star with V device for his courageous leadership.

Dillard continued his wartime service in Korea and was assigned as the intelligence officer for the 3rd Battalion. On September 14, 1950, while aiding the battalion commander in establishing the battalion's defensive positions near Masan, Dillard and a small group of men responded to an enemy attack in the area of his old unit, Company L. For the next day-and-a-half Dillard fought heroically alongside his former soldiers and was awarded the Silver Star for his bravery on September 14 and 15. His Silver Star was presented to him by Brigadier General Joseph Bradley.

After completing the Infantry Officer's Advanced Course at Ft. Benning, Georgia, and serving in a Reserve Officers Training Corps assignment, Dillard was deployed to Germany and commanded Company C, 1st Battalion 12th Infantry Regiment. Upon finishing command, he was assigned as the regimental communications officer and later to a teaching position at the Seventh Army Noncommissioned Officers Academy.

After promotion to major, Dillard attended the Command and General Staff College at Ft. Leavenworth, Kansas, in 1958, as one of the few African American officers in the class. After CGSC, he was allowed to finish his bachelor's degree at the University of Omaha, as his induction into the army had interrupted his studies at Tuskegee before he could complete his degree.

Dillard continued to advance through assignments in New York and Liberia, where he developed an expertise in military intelligence. After promotion to lieutenant colonel, he was assigned to the army's Assistant Chief of Staff for Intelligence (Army G2) and then stayed in the Washington D.C. area to become the first African American graduate of the National War College in 1965. After senior staff assignments, Dillard commanded a battalion in the 5th Combat Support Training Brigade at Ft. Dix, New Jersey, and eventually spent a year in command of the brigade itself.

In 1969, now a colonel, Dillard was deployed to the Republic of Vietnam to serve in the U.S. Military Assistance Command—Vietnam as a province senior advisor. As with everything he had done in the army, he excelled at this assignment and was rewarded with a return assignment to the Army G2, but this time as the Deputy Assistant Chief of Staff for Intelligence, a position never before held by an African American officer. On February 1, 1972, Dillard was promoted to brigadier general and became only the fifth African American officer to be promoted to general officer in the U.S. Army.

After his promotion, Dillard returned to work in Military Assistance Command—Vietnam until it was disbanded in March 1973. He served in successive assignments in the United States as the senior intelligence officer at Forces Command

and then as the Assistant Division Commander—Maneuver for the 2nd Armored Division at Ft. Hood, Texas. Promoted to major general on August 1, 1975, he finished his army career with assignments in Germany and Ft. Dix, New Jersey.

After his retirement, Dillard continued to be active in the army, particularly when it came to the 24th Infantry Regiment's history in Korea. He was one of the loudest voices in the campaign to correct what the members of the regiment saw as unfair treatment in the original official history of the period published by the army's Center for Military History, *South to Naktong, North to the Yalu*, which was written by Roy Appleman. He believed that the treatment of the African American unit was tinged by racism and argued that it performed no worse or better than similar all-white units. He was extensively interviewed for the Center for Military History's official history of the regiment, *Black Soldier, White Army*, written by William Bowers, William Hammond, and George MacGarrigle. Beyond the combat decorations that Dillard earned, which included the Silver Star, Bronze Star with V Device, and Purple Heart, he was a highly decorated and honored officer. In June 2011, the Military Intelligence Corps Association honored him with the Lieutenant Colonel Thomas W. Knowlton Award for Excellence in Intelligence and in September 2012 he was inducted into the Army Military Intelligence Hall of Fame. Likewise, he was inducted into the Officer Candidate School Hall of Fame later in May 2012. Major General Dillard and his wife, Helen, raised four children during this very successful career in the army.

James B. Martin

Further Reading

Appleman, Roy. *South to Naktong, North to the Yalu*. Washington, DC: U.S. Army Center for Military History, 1961.

Bowers, William T., William M. Hammond, and George L. MacGarrigle. *Black Soldier, White Army: The 24th Infantry Regiment in Korea*. Washington, DC: U.S. Army Center for Military History, 1996.

Williams, Albert E. *Black Warriors: The Korean War*. Haverford, PA: Infinity, 2004.

Dorman, Isaiah

Born: 1820–1832
Died: June 25, 1876
Home State: Unknown
Service: Army
Conflict: Indian Wars
Age at Time of Award: 44–55

Isaiah Dorman was an African American born somewhere around 1832. Some authors believe he was born free in Philadelphia in 1832, while others believe him to be an escaped slave, born in Louisiana in 1820, due to his last name and its similarity to a plantation owner of French extraction. DNA testing by a woman who indicates that Dorman was her grandfather gives another possible explanation, as she indicates that genetic markers show him to have African American and Jewish backgrounds. This might account for the Dorman surname. It is hard to be certain of his background before the 1850s, but by then he was firmly identified living in the Dakota Territory near Ft. Rice. He was by all accounts a large man and capable of much hard work. He was hired in 1865, as a woodcutter by the trading firm of Durfee and Peck because of his ability to cut so much wood in a short period of time. Dorman had lived among the Sioux for a number of years and had married a woman of the Santee Sioux tribe. His knowledge of the Lakota language would serve him well when he worked for the army.

Because of his language capacity and his knowledge of the Sioux's tribal area, he was hired to carry mail on foot between Ft. Rice and Ft. Wadsworth, a nearly 360-mile round trip. He was well paid by the standards of the day, as he had unique skills that could not be easily found. In the early 1870s, he worked for the Northern Pacific Railroad as it surveyed the Dakota Territory in preparation for railroad construction. He may also have worked for Colonel George Armstrong Custer, commander of the 7th Cavalry, as early as 1873, but it has not been proven.

Owing to his language skills with Lakota and his knowledge of the territory, Custer issued Special Order No. 2 requesting Dorman as an interpreter for the operation that would culminate at the Little Bighorn River, at a contracted fee of $75 a month. Dorman would return to the land of the Sioux, but this time he would not ride into their lands as a friend or brother, but with the dreaded blue coats of the U.S. Cavalry.

Dorman was riding with Major Reno's column when the Battle of the Little Bighorn began on June 25, 1876. He apparently survived the initial encounter but was lost when the column began to retire across the river seeking the protection of the high bluffs nearby. All accounts are consistent in their picture of him having his horse shot out from under him and his legs becoming pinned under the fallen horse. He apparently continued to fight and killed a number of Sioux warriors with his nonregulation rifle, only to be wounded to the point that he could not resist. At least two accounts have him speaking to Pvt. Roman Rutten, infamous at the Little Bighorn for his horse taking him on an interminable ride among the fighting, out of fear of Indians. His reported comment to the private, "Good-bye, Rutten!" exudes a sense of foreboding and calmness in the face of certain death. As with almost anything having to do with the debacle at Little Bighorn that day, there are conflicting stories as to Dorman's death. Some say he was spared torture or mutilation because of his former relationship with Sitting Bull, but the most convincing evidence indicates that he was tortured by being repeatedly shot with either a small caliber handgun or very large buckshot in his legs below the knees. He was reportedly killed by Indian women who were following the warriors and then beaten severely with stone hammers. Whether he was mutilated further by having his body cut open or body parts removed remains an open question. Dorman died at one of the most infamous battlefields in American military history, the only African American combatant at this military disaster.

While there is ample evidence to prove that Isaiah Dorman was at Little Bighorn with Colonel Custer and the 7th Cavalry, he is predictably missing from the patriotic paintings and drawings that depict the scene. The one graphic that includes an African American among those on the battlefield that day is a pictograph done by an Indian artist. Isaiah Dorman did not win a medal for valor that day, but probably earned one from all accounts. An African American who died with such a large number of white soldiers, he had little chance for recognition from a society that would not even depict him in the scenes of the battlefield.

James B. Martin

Further Reading

Connell, Evan S. *Son of the Morning Star.* New York: Harper and Row, 1984.

Custer, Elizabeth B. *"Boots and Saddles": Or, Life in Dakota with General Custer.* Norman: University of Oklahoma Press, 1961.

Katz, William Loren. *The Black West.* Garden City, NY: Doubleday, 1973.

Mapp, Zoey. "Elaine Matlow: DNA Spectrum Hung the Moon." DNA Spectrum Web site. http://highlights.dnaspectrum.com/elaine-matlow-dna-spectrum-hung-the-moon/, posted April 3, 2013 (accessed August 24, 2013).

McConnell, Roland. "Isaiah Dorman and the Custer Expedition." *The Journal of Negro History* 33(3) (July 1948): 344–52.

Dorsey, Decatur

Born: 1836
Died: July 11, 1891
Home State: Maryland
Service: Army
Conflict: Civil War
Age at Time of Award: 28

Decatur Dorsey was born into slavery in Howard County, Maryland, probably in 1836. The birth records for slaves at this time were often inexact, and Dorsey's year of birth comes into question because of information on his army enlistment papers. Dorsey was freed by his master so that he could enlist in the U.S. Army, and he did so on March 22, 1864, at Baltimore, Maryland. His enlistment papers state his age to be 25, which would make 1839 his year of birth. Regardless of the exact date of birth, Dorsey became a private in Company B, 39th U.S. Colored Troops on that day. Dorsey apparently showed leadership qualities early on in Company B, as shortly after his enlistment, on May 17, 1864, he was promoted to corporal.

Dorsey, along with the remainder of 4th Division, had spent weeks preparing to lead the charge at what would come to be known as the Battle of the Crater. Brigadier General Edward Ferraro's division had prepared for this position of honor, in what would have been a marked change for United States Colored Troops units. At the last possible moment, the commanding general of the Army of the Potomac, Major General George Meade, changed his mind and moved the 1st Division, commanded by Brigadier General James Ledlie, into this role. Historians have debated this decision, apparently brought on by Meade's concern that he would be held accountable if the African American units were seen as having been used in a role that was seen as sacrificial. Regardless of the reason, the 4th Division was held in reserve.

The Battle of the Crater gets its name from the plan to use former coal miners to dig a substantial tunnel under Confederate earthworks near Petersburg and then fill the tunnel with explosives. The intent was to blow a hole in the enemies' lines and create such confusion that the Union troops would have a great advantage and roll up the Confederate position and break the stalemate at Petersburg. The initial plans had been to attack around the left and right shoulders of the blast area, thus avoiding the rubble and quickly moving to seize either side of the penetration. Unfortunately, as the 1st Division had not been trained for the mission, they did what many units did late in the Civil War; they attacked head on into the enemy and hope to gain the ground by sheer weight of numbers. Just before sunrise on July 30, 1864, the four tons of explosives that had been loaded into the tunnel were ignited and a huge crater blown in the Confederate lines. The 1st Division, attacking right through the sizeable hole, became slowed and trapped by the steep sides of the crater that was left after the blast. They began to take fire from the slowly recovering Confederates and wilted under it. Two more white divisions were sent into the crater, with the same results as seen with the 1st Division attack. By now, the crater was a bowl of panicked Union soldiers being shot at from three sides by small arms and cannon. Finally, the Division Commander Ambrose Burnside, dispatched the 4th Division into the battle in an attempt to carry the Confederate works. The unit rushed into the crater, as the left and right approaches were no longer available once the element of surprise was gone, and with difficulty moved through the retreating white divisions. Decatur Dorsey was acting as the colors sergeant for the 39th USCT and held the colors high as he made his way forward in the crater. He gained the top of the Confederate fortifications and planted the unit colors, only to have to retrieve them as the unit was thrown back by a counterattack. The accounts indicate that Dorsey once more called for his regiment to follow the colors and he made it to the top of the fortifications once again. This time the unit held the ground for some time and captured prisoners and unit colors, but they were eventually thrown back by the concerted counterattacks from a now fully recovered Confederate Army.

While the white divisions of the Army of the Potomac can be excused on some level for their performance, due to the lack of training for the mission, the leadership cannot. Poor decisions by general officers and poor leadership by junior officers resulted in a resounding defeat and loss on nearly 5,300 lives. The commitment of the 4th Division came too late and this unit alone totaled casualties in excess of 1,300 African American soldiers.

For his bravery in the crater, leading his regiment in charging the earthworks twice, Corporal Decatur Dorsey received the Medal of Honor on November 8, 1865. After the Battle of the Crater, Dorsey was promoted to sergeant on August 1, 1864. The records of Company B show him mustering out as first sergeant on December 4, 1865, at Wilmington, North Carolina. He initially returned to Maryland, but at some point moved to Hoboken, New Jersey. It was here, on July 11, 1891, that he succumbed to the effects of typhoid and rheumatism he had contracted prior to being mustered out at Wilmington. First Sergeant Decatur Dorsey was initially buried in an unmarked grave in the Flower Hill Cemetery in North Bergen, New Jersey. In 1984, concerned citizens discovered Dorsey's grave and sought to correct the error in his original internment. They reburied Dorsey with full military honors and a new headstone now indicates his valor with its reference to his Medal of Honor.

James B. Martin

Further Reading

Claxton, Melvin, and Mark Puls. *Uncommon Valor: A Story of Race, Patriotism, and Glory in the Final Battles of the Civil War*. Hoboken, NJ: John Wiley and Sons, 2006.

Hanna, Charles W. *African American Recipients of the Medal of Honor: A Biographical Dictionary, Civil War through Vietnam War*. Jefferson, NC: McFarland, 2002.

Wilmer, L. Allison, J. H. Jarrett, and George W. F. Vernon. *History and Roster of Maryland Volunteers, War of 1861–5*. Baltimore, MD: Guggenheimer, Weil & Co., 1899.

Fisher, Aaron R.

Born: May 14, 1895
Died: November 22, 1985
Home State: Indiana
Service: Army
Conflict: World War I
Age at Time of Award: 26

Aaron R. Fisher was born in Lyles, Indiana, on May 14, 1895. He was the son of a former member of the United States Colored Troops, Benjamin Fisher, who had served during the American Civil War. He enlisted in the army in 1911 and was assigned to the 366th Infantry Regiment prior to the American entry into World War I. Deployed to France as a sergeant, Fisher was commissioned a 2nd lieutenant in the Infantry in the 366th Infantry Regiment of the 92nd Division on June 1, 1918. He continued to lead in the 366th at his new rank and moved into the St. Die Sector with the regiment in September 1918. Operating near the village of Lesseux on September 3, 1918, Fisher's unit was attacked by a superior force of Germans. He responded to the penetration by standing his ground and leading his troops while under constant fire. He refused to leave the position though he was severely wounded, and continued to fight until the enemy was eventually forced to withdraw due to an Allied counterattack. For his actions at Lesseux, 2nd Lieutenant Fisher was awarded the Distinguished Service Cross and the Purple Heart. Later, because his actions occurred as part of a joint United States–French operation, the French commander awarded him the Criox de Guerre with Gold Star for his heroism and referred to him in the citation as an "officer of admirable courage." His actions at Lesseux marked 2nd Lieutenant Fisher as one of the heroes of the American actions in France, with him receiving the second highest award for valor the United States could bestow and the highest award for valor that France had to give. 2nd Lieutenant Fisher left the active army after World War I, but received a commission as a captain in the U.S. Army Reserve. It was customary for African American commissioned officers to be reduced to warrant officer after the war, but because of his record and his decision to move to the Reserves, it appears he was allowed to retain his commission. Fisher was discharged in 1919, but later chose to return to active duty as a noncommissioned officer. He worked his way back up to a chief warrant officer by the time he retired from the army in 1947. After the war, Fisher became a fixture at Wilberforce University as a member of the Reserve Officers Training Corps cadre. Wilberforce University's ROTC program was one of the top African American programs in the nation, with its cadre including luminaries like Colonel Charles

Young of the original 9th Cavalry Buffalo Soldiers and 1st Lieutenant Benjamin O. Davis. While on the staff at Wilberforce, "Cap" Fisher was an instructor to future Medal of Honor recipient John R. Fox, who would receive the Medal for valor in the same battalion and division in which Fisher fought in World War I. Fisher went on after his retirement, in 1947, to work for the Air Force at Wright Patterson Air Force Base in Dayton and eventually received recognition for 50 years of service to the U.S. military. Fisher and his wife continued to serve in the community in central Ohio. He lived in Xenia, Ohio, until his death on November 22, 1985. His place of burial is currently unknown.

James B. Martin

Further Reading

Fletcher, Marvin. *The Black Soldier and Officer in the United States Army, 1891–1917.* Columbia: University of Missouri Press, 1974.

Scott, Emmett J. "The American Negro in the World War." Washington, DC, 1919. http://net .lib.byu.edu/estu/wwi/comment/scott/ScottTC.htm (accessed January 26, 2013).

Williams, Chad L. *Torchbearers of Democracy: African American Soldiers in the World War I Era.* Chapel Hill: The University of North Carolina Press, 2010.

Fleetwood, Christian

Born: July 21, 1840
Died: September 28, 1914
Home State: Maryland
Service: Army
Conflict: Civil War
Age at Time of Award: 24

Christian Fleetwood was born in Baltimore, Baltimore County, Maryland, on July 21, 1840. His parents were free African Americans and, while he grew up in a slave state, he never felt the bonds of slavery directly. By 1860, he had traveled to Africa, visiting Liberia and Sierra Leone, and had graduated from Ashman Institute (which would become Lincoln University) in Pennsylvania. He had a good job as a clerk in the shipyards of his hometown and was not convinced that racial problems evident in Maryland were his problem. He planned to move to Liberia to live among free blacks to avoid the prejudice notably present in his homeland.

Though a small man, barely five foot four inches and weighing only 125 pounds during the war, Fleetwood had great inner strength. He was an active member of the Episcopal Church and at one point considered becoming a minister. He had not been beaten down by working in bondage and turned out to be a leader once he enlisted in the army. That day came on August 11, 1863, as he enlisted in Company G,

4th United States Colored Troops as a private. He enlisted in his hometown of Baltimore because by 1863 he had become convinced of his need to fight to help save his country and his people. He received a promotion to sergeant eight days later, as the white leadership of his unit recognized his education and natural leadership abilities.

By September 1864, Christian Fleetwood's unit had fought in the initial assaults on Petersburg, had been present but not committed at the Battle of the Crater, and was a hardened group of soldiers. Their most senior commander, Major General Benjamin Butler, had great faith in these African American soldiers and chose them to break the circle that protected the Confederate capitol of Richmond, Virginia. Butler proposed a plan to Lieutenant General Grant to penetrate the

Sergeant Christian Fleetwood received the Medal of Honor for his valorous actions during the Battle of New Market Heights. (Library of Congress)

enemy's thinly held lines at a point called New Market Heights, near Chaffin's Farm, and open a pathway to Richmond and the end of the war. To accomplish this breakthrough, Butler deployed the African American regiments under Colonels Draper and Duncan, which included now Sergeant Fleetwood's 4th United States Colored Troops. Because of the perceived need for stealth and speed, Butler ordered the initial attacks on the entrenched Confederates to come without artillery support or the firing of weapons by the soldiers. He wanted the fortifications taken at the point of the bayonet. The area was highly fortified, with downed trees and sharpened sticks as obstacles called abatis, all intended to slow down the Union troops and channelize them into kill zones. Duncan's unit led the initial charge and was badly mauled by intense Confederate fire at close range as they attempted to seize the high ground using only their bayonets. As directed, they did not fire back and had removed their percussion caps to prevent any accidental firing. As the initial charge surged forward, it faltered even though the African American troops fought with bravery and courage. Fleetwood was situated at the left of the regiment, owing to his position as the sergeant major. As the 4th charged from the abatis toward the Confederate fortifications, they were cut down in droves by the intense enemy fire. Fleetwood exhorted his men to move forward, while directly exposed to this fire, and looked to his right to the regimental colors. The color-bearers for the regimental and national colors were hit and the standards were close to being lost. Beyond the symbolic importance of these flags, they were critical in Civil War battles to allow the progress of units to be tracked and for members of the regiments to be able to guide on in the midst of the chaos of battle. Seeing the flags start to waiver, Fleetwood moved to grab the national standard just as Corporal Veal reached the regimental flag. Though caught in a crossfire from the Confederates concentrating fire on the regimental colors, with a bullet passing through his pants leg and tearing the strap of his right boot, Fleetwood held the flag high and rallied his men toward the fortifications. A second push forward saw them enter the enemy positions for a short period of time but were driven back to the abatis to seek cover. The colors were safe, but the 4th USCT and its sister units had failed to take New Market Heights. They had lost 365 of their original 683 members killed in action or as casualties during their bayonet charge against some of the Confederate Army's best known units. Although Duncan's units had been mauled and he had been severely wounded, Draper was able to follow up the attack of the first wave and carry the fortifications. The way to Richmond was opened at New Market Heights through the bravery and sacrifice of African American troops from numerous USCT regiments. For his bravery and leadership at the Battle of New Market Heights on September 29, 1864, Sergeant Major Christian Fleetwood received the Medal of Honor.

In addition to the recognition given him through the Medal of Honor, Fleetwood was recommended by his white officers for an officer's commission. This was against army regulations in the fall of 1864 and the request was denied. This denial soured Fleetwood on his army service and he chose to leave the military once the war was over on May 9, 1866. Regardless of his courage or capacity to lead, the U.S. Army was simply not ready to allow the advancement of African Americans into the ranks of officers.

After the war, Christian Fleetwood initially settled in Columbus, Ohio, and made his living as a bookkeeper. He eventually moved to Washington, D.C., and was employed by the Freedmen's Bank and the War Department. He was active with the District of Columbia National Guard, retiring from the organization as a major in 1892. He continued to be active in his church and after he died of heart failure on September 28, 1914, his services were held at St. Luke's Episcopal Church. He was initially buried in Columbian Harmony Cemetery, Washington, D.C., but his body, along with everyone else buried there, was moved in 1959 to National Harmony Memorial Park in Landover, Maryland.

James B. Martin

Further Reading

Claxton, Melvin, and Mark Puls. *Uncommon Valor: A Story of Race, Patriotism, and Glory in the Final Battles of the Civil War*. Hoboken, NJ: John Wiley and Sons, 2006.

Hanna, Charles W. *African American Recipients of the Medal of Honor: A Biographical Dictionary, Civil War through Vietnam War.* Jefferson, NC: McFarland, 2002.

Price, James S. *The Battle of New Market Heights: Freedom Will Be Theirs by the Sword.* Charleston, SC: The History Press, 2011.

Forrest, George G.

Born: April 13, 1938
Home State: Maryland
Service: Army
Conflict: Vietnam War
Age at Time of Award: 27

George G. Forrest was born in Leonardtown, Maryland, on April 13, 1938, to James and Harriet Forrest. He grew up in Leonardtown with his three brothers and a sister, experiencing the sting of a segregated Maryland town. His father was a telephone lineman and eventually became the first African American to serve on the St. Mary's County School Board. George left Leonardtown to attend college at Morgan State College, in Baltimore. While at Morgan State (today Morgan State University), he played intercollegiate football and was part of the Reserve Officer Training Corps. Upon graduating with a degree in political science, Forrest entered the U.S. Army and reported for schooling at Ft. Benning, Georgia. In the early 1960s, Forrest was assigned to the 3rd Infantry Division's Old Guard, the ceremonial unit that guards the Tomb of the Unknown Soldier and conducts military funerals at Arlington National Cemetery. While serving in this assignment, Forrest participated in a number of historical events, most notably standing guard over the casket of President John F. Kennedy in the Capitol Rotunda in 1963.

Forrest was assigned to the 1st Cavalry Division in 1965 and was deployed to the Republic of Vietnam with the division. His unit was assigned to operate in the central highlands of Vietnam in the area around Pleiku. His unit, Company A, 1st Battalion, 5th Cavalry, was attached to 2nd Battalion, 7th Cavalry for operations in the Ia Drang Valley, about 35 miles southwest of Pleiku. This operation has become probably the most famous of the entire Vietnam War, as it was immortalized by *We Were Soldiers Once . . . and Young*, a book and movie detailing the actions of Colonel Harold Moore and the 1st Battalion, 7th Cavalry. The Battle of the Ia Drang Valley took place from November 14 to 18, 1965, and Forrest's unit came into the famed landing zone (LZ) X-Ray on November 16 to reinforce Moore's command.

On November 17, Forrest's company was the trail company in a tactical move to LZ Albany for extraction from the Ia Drang. Just as the battalion's lead elements reached LZ Albany, the column was caught in an ambush along the entire 500–700 meter flank of the unit. Forrest, along with the other company commanders, was at the head of the column, having been called forward by the battalion commander. As soon as the firing began, Forrest recognized that his place was with his unit and set off at a full sprint to rejoin his command. The entire run, approximately 600 meters long, was across the kill zone of the Vietnamese ambush, but Forrest was able to make it into his unit's position and resume command. He lost both of the radio operators who tried to make the run with him, but returning to his unit, he was able to organize them and save many lives through his leadership. For his actions on November 17, 1965, George Forrest was awarded the Silver Star.

In 1993, a very nervous Forrest returned to Ia Drang. He described the men who had fallen there as "seventeen guys who could have been absolute national treasures. They were gallant, noble, afraid young men. . . . They did what they thought their country needed them to do." While he rightly focused on the men he lost, Forrest also tells the story of meeting the son of one of his surviving soldiers. This young man, relating discussions he had with his father about Vietnam, shared his father's belief that without Forrest's leadership, he too would have died. In the end, the young man thanked Forrest, indicating that without him making that run in November 1965, the young man would not be alive now.

Forrest stayed in the army after the Vietnam War ended and completed a 21-year military career. He served as the professor of military science at St. Norbet's College, was on the faculty of the U.S. Army Command and General Staff College at Ft. Leavenworth, Kansas, and was a staff planner at North Atlantic Treaty Organization headquarters. Along with the Silver Star he earned in the Ia Drang Valley, Forrest also was awarded the Legion of Merit, the Bronze Star with V device (with oak leaf cluster), and three Vietnamese Crosses of Gallantry.

After retirement from the army, Forrest coached football at his alma mater and worked in business, education, and government. In 2007, he retired from his position as the county administrator of St. Mary's County. He served on the boards of St. Mary's Hospital, Tomorrow's Child, Sotterley Historical Foundation, and the Governor's Southern Maryland Higher Education Center. He has received honors from multiple service organizations, was inducted into Morgan State University's ROTC Hall of Fame in 1992, and served as a torchbearer for the State of Maryland during the 1996 Olympic Games.

Jonathan D. Sutherland

Further Reading

Buckley, Gail. *American Patriots*. New York: Random House, 2001.

Cash, John A. *Seven Firefights in Vietnam*. Washington, DC: Office of the Chief of Military History, United States Army, 1985.

Moore, Harold G., and Joseph L. Galloway. *We Were Soldiers Once . . . and Young: Ia Drang—The Battle That Changed the War in Vietnam*. New York: Random House, 1992.

Nawrozki, Joe. "Honoring the Men of Ia Drang." *The Baltimore Sun*, November 11, 2003. http://articles.baltimoresun.com/.../0311110242_1_drang-valley-ia-drang-forrest (accessed November 24, 2013).

Fox, John Robert

Born: May 18, 1915
Died: December 26, 1944
Home State: Ohio
Service: Army
Conflict: World War II
Age at Time of Award: 29

Born in Cincinnati, Ohio, on May 18, 1915, John Robert Fox grew up in Ohio and graduated from Wyoming High School in 1934. Fox enlisted in Ohio's 372nd Infantry Regiment, where he served until graduating from Wilberforce University (located in Wilberforce, Ohio). Upon graduation, he received his Army ROTC commission in 1940.

Following his commissioning, Fox attended training at Ft. Devens, Massachusetts, and later at the Infantry School at Fort Benning, Georgia. Upon completion of his training, he was assigned to Cannon Company of the 366th Infantry Regiment. The 366th was deployed to North Africa and assigned to the 15th Air Force to secure airfields. In November of 1944, the 366th was attached to the 5th Army, 92nd Infantry Division (the historically all-black Buffalo Soldiers) and moved to Italy to participate in the liberation of Europe.

In November 1944, the 366th entered combat with the 92nd Infantry Division in the Serchio Valley. During the Battle of the Serchio Valley, in the vicinity of Sommocolonia, Italy, Lieutenant Fox was attached to the 598th Field Artillery Battalion to serve as a forward artillery observer. In this role, Lieutenant Fox was to call in adjustments to bring effective artillery fire on the enemy. On the evening of December 25, 1944, Lieutenant Fox set up his observation post on the second floor of a house in the village. The next morning, the village came under heavy fire from German and Italian forces that had infiltrated the area during the night. The Allied troops, who were greatly outnumbered, were forced to withdraw. Lieutenant Fox stayed in his position to adjust friendly artillery fire to cover the withdrawal of his comrades. As the Germans advanced to pursue the retreating Americans, Fox adjusted the artillery closer and closer to his position. Finally facing overwhelming odds, Fox called in an artillery barrage onto his own position. The fire direction center advised him that he would not survive the barrage; he insisted, saying, "Fire it!" During the ensuing barrage, Fox was killed, but his selfless act delayed the enemy advance. Later, when a counterattack retook the position, they found Lieutenant Fox's body along with the bodies of approximately 100 Axis soldiers.

Although Lieutenant Fox was recommended for the Distinguished Service Cross (DSC) at the time by the battalion commander, Lieutenant Colonel William Colbern, the recommendation was never processed through channels. Various historians have posited reasons for this oversight, but members of the 366th and 92nd continued to press for adequate recognition for Lieutenant Fox. Whether it was because of racial prejudice or because of the unique perspective of the division commander of the 92nd that awards were not submitted for missions that did not succeed, Fox's well-deserved award for heroism was denied to his family. It was only after a supporter supplied adequate information to the Army Awards Branch that an official investigation was opened and, on April 15, 1982, Fox was awarded the DSC posthumously. His family had previously received the Bronze Star and Purple Heart he had earned.

Throughout World War II, African American soldiers performed with the same courage and dedication that was the hallmark of all American soldiers. Unfortunately, due to racial prejudice at both an institutional and individual level, no African American soldiers received the Medal of Honor, although a number were recommended for our nation's highest honor. Following an investigation commissioned by the Department of Defense in 1993, it was determined that a number of African Americans had not received the Medal of Honor for actions during World War II due to their race. In 1996, Congress approved granting the Medal of Honor to seven African American soldiers from World War II. Lieutenant Fox was one of these men. On January 13, 1997, more than 50 years after Fox gave his life for his comrades, President Bill Clinton presented the Medal of Honor to Fox's widow, Arlene, in a White House ceremony honoring the seven African American World War II veterans whose earlier awards had been upgraded. The only one of the seven still living was Vernon Baker.

In 2005, the Hasbro Toy Company released an action figure commemorating Lt. John Fox in its GI Joe Medal of Honor series.

Christopher S. Trobridge

Further Reading

Astor, Gerald. *The Right to Fight: A History of African Americans in the Military*. Cambridge, MA: Da Capo Press, 1998.

Converse, Elliott V., III. *The Exclusion of Black Soldiers from the Medal of Honor in World War II*. Jefferson, NC: McFarland, 1997.

Gibran, Daniel K. *The 92nd Infantry Division and the Italian Campaign in World War II*. Jefferson, NC: McFarland, 2001.

Hargrove, Hondon B. *Buffalo Soldiers in Italy: Black Americans in World War II*. Jefferson, NC: McFarland, 1985.

Hall, Charles B. "Buster"

Born: August 25, 1920
Died: November 22, 1971
Home State: Indiana
Service: Army
Conflict: World War II
Age at Time of Award: 24

Charles Blakely Hall was born in Brazil, Indiana, on August 25, 1920. He grew up in Brazil and after high school attended college at Eastern Illinois State Teacher's College in Charleston, Illinois, in 1938. When the U.S. Army decided to recruit and activate an all-African American Air Corps squadron, Hall jumped at the chance. He left college early, in 1941, and reported to the Tuskegee Institute for flight training. He graduated with the fourth class of pilots to come out of Tuskegee and received his commission as a second lieutenant and his silver flight wings on July 3, 1942. While at Tuskegee, Hall picked up the nickname of Buster, which would follow him throughout his military career. Hall was assigned to the first African American fighter squadron, the 99th Pursuit Squadron, and deployed with it to North Africa on April 24, 1943. Lieutenant Hall was obviously one of the top pilots, because he was chosen to be among the first four pilots in the 99th to fly combat missions alongside the white 33rd Fighter Group. He took part in the 99th's first mission, a bombing attack on the Italian island of Pantelleria on June 2, 1943. Just one month later, on July 2, 1943, Lieutenant Hall became the first African American to shoot down a German Focke-Wulf 190 during a mission escorting bombers over Sicily. This single act of shooting down an airplane pushed Hall and the 99th Pursuit Squadron through an invisible barrier, as an African American pilot had been good enough to outfight a German pilot, silencing to some extent critics in Germany and the United States. The unit history provides a wonderful anecdote, as the 99th had been saving a single bottle of Coca Cola in the squadron safe to celebrate this first kill. With a little ice, Hall gladly took a sip from this honor bottle. The next day, General Dwight D. Eisenhower, Major General James "Jimmy" Doolittle, and General Carl Spatz arrived on base to personally congratulate him for "shooting down that Jerry."

While his kill on July 2, 1943, may have been his most famous, the most prolific combat day of his career came on January 28, 1944, over the beach at Anzio. Leading a flight of eight aircraft from the 99th, now Captain Hall spotted a flight of six German aircraft below his formation moving to strafe the soldiers on the beach. Diving into the enemy formation, he broke them up and eventually shot down two aircraft, a Focke-Wulf 190 and an ME-109. The remaining members of his flight shot down two additional German aircraft and chased off the final two. For his actions above Anzio on January 28, Captain Hall received the Distinguished Flying Cross.

After flying 108 combat missions, Captain Hall returned to the United States and took part in a 105-day bond drive, trying to raise money for the war and raise spirits at home. He remained in the Army Air Corps until 1946, spending his postwar service as an instructor pilot back home in Tuskegee. Hall got out of the army with a desire to fly commercial aircraft for the growing airline industry, but because of racial discrimination he could not find a flying job, even though he was one of the best pilots in the Army Air Corps. He took a position managing a restaurant in Chicago, until he moved to Nashville, Tennessee, to work for an insurance company. He married for the first time in Nashville and moved to Oklahoma City, Oklahoma, in 1948. Evidently tired of his position in a drug store, Hall got hired at Tinker Air Force Base in Oklahoma City and worked there until 1967. He remarried in 1961 and had two children by his second wife. In 1967, the Federal Aviation Administration opened a new center at the Oklahoma City Airport and Hall was hired to work there, the only employee of the new center to come from outside the FAA.

During these years, Hall remained a member of the reserves, eventually rising to the rank of major. He died in Oklahoma City on November 22, 1971, and was buried at Hillcrest Cemetery in Ardmore, Oklahoma. Since his death, Hall has been honored for his service and bravery by having the Tinker Air Force Base chapter of the Tuskegee Airmen named after him and having his portrait included with the heroes in the Military Hall of Fame in Washington, D.C., and the Ralph Ellison Library in Oklahoma City.

James B. Martin

TUSKEGEE AIRMEN

As World War II came into view, the nation had moved to include African Americans in the fight to save the world from domination and protect the American way of life. The Selective Service Act, passed on September 16, 1940, prohibited racial discrimination in military conscription and opened the door for African Americans to serve with distinction, though in segregated units. In the 1940s, as it is now, the most technologically advanced weapon systems in a nation's arsenal were its aircraft. If an African American could successfully operate them and perform at a high level as a fighter or bomber pilot, what was there in American society that they did not have the intellect to successfully accomplish? To many whites, this was the greatest fear of African Americans in the army and specifically in the Air Corps. While combat soldiers in the army were enlisted men who almost always reported to white officers, pilots were officers who held sway by virtue of rank over enlisted men, African American or white. Well beyond the Korean War, African American officers were unfairly criticized and labeled as poor leaders, largely because of entrenched feelings of racism from white senior commanders. There were relatively few African American officers in the army or navy in World War II and literally none in the Marine Corps. The largest grouping of African American officers in any service was created by the inclusion in the Air Corps of the Tuskegee Airmen. This potential problem of African American officers, and the possibility that they could outrank whites, was one of the major undertones in the military as those who maintained their racial prejudice sought to ensure the failure of the units that made up the Tuskegee Experiment.

The 99th Pursuit Squadron was activated at Chanute Field, Illinois, on March 22, 1941. The first class of pilots-in-training began their schooling at Tuskegee Institute in July of that year, with Captain Benjamin O. Davis Jr., the fourth African American graduate of West Point and the son of the first African American general officer in the U.S. Army, as a member of the 13-person class. Following this class would be many other African Americans from across the nation, who would endure the toughest screening process the army had and represent probably the most educated and highly qualified single group of African American young men in the country. It was truly an elite group that manned the aircraft of what would become known as the Red Tails, after the color of the tails on their airplanes. Soon to follow were the 100th Pursuit Squadron, 301st Fighter Squadron, 302nd Fighter Squadron, and the parent organization for these squadrons, the 332nd Fighter Group. Pilots continued to come out of the school at Tuskegee, with the second and third classes graduating in the spring of 1942. Until June 1942, the squadrons were all commanded by white officers, but in that month First Lieutenant George Roberts became the first African American to command an Air Corps squadron. In August 1942, the 477th Bombardment Group was activated as a parent unit for a series of bomber squadrons that were planned for combat duty in the Pacific Theater. While the fighter squadrons saw service in Europe and North Africa, for a variety of reasons, the bomber units never left the United States. One of the prominent issues that prevented them from attaining the readiness status needed early enough in the war was the racial unrest and resulting morale problems caused by racial policies on and off the bases where they trained and were stationed.

The 99th Pursuit Squadron was the first all-African American Air Corps unit to see combat when, after arriving in North Africa on May 31, 1943, it was dispatched on June 2 to attack the Italian island of Pantelleria. Finally seeing aerial combat about a week later, the unit continued to perform at a very high level and eventually earned two Distinguished Unit Citations during the war. In January 1944, the elements of the 332nd Fighter Group arrived in the European Theater and began to fly from the air base at Ramitelli, Italy. By July, the 99th Fighter Squadron (now renamed along with the 100th) joined the 332nd in Italy and flew with the group for the remainder of its combat tour. The Red Tails made their name in Europe escorting bombing raids against targets in Germany and other parts of Europe. These African American pilots flew over 15,000 combat sorties, destroying 94 aircraft in the air and over 150 on the ground. They shot everything on the ground that moved and some things that were stationary. They were credited with shooting down three of the newest German jet aircraft, the ME-262, while protecting bombers on a mission to bomb Berlin. Over 200 bomber escort missions have been documented and, while the original stories of the group never losing a bomber they were escorting have been debunked, the verified number of losses is 27 bombers over those 200 missions. That rate is far better than the average number lost for escort units that flew as many missions as the Red Tails. Their numbers put them in the upper echelon of quality when it came to escort units in World War II. When your life is on the line, you want the best and it was not a secret in the 15th Air Force that the Red Tails fit that moniker. The group eventually received three Distinguished Unit Citations (two to the 99th and one to the entire 332nd Group) for their actions. Sixty-six members of the group were killed in action and another 32 were captured. The pilots of the four squadrons were effective, efficient, and brave, eventually earning 96 Distinguished Flying Crosses, 14 Bronze Stars, and 8 Purple Hearts.

The Red Tails were certainly combat heroes, but they were much more. Their story, told in books and movies over the past 70 years, is one of inspiration and struggle against all odds. Historians have talked of the two Vs of World War II for African Americans—victory over the enemy and victory over racism at home. Author Barry Stentiford appropriately takes it a bit further, when he extends this for the Tuskegee Airmen to the three Vs: the enemy, racism at home, and victory over the official racism in the armed forces. They were mid-20th century pioneers who followed earlier African American pioneers and took the integration of the military as far as it could go, eventually playing a big role in the decision to officially integrate the armed forces by President Truman in 1949. The members of the organization were all heroes and some of them are individually identified in this volume. In the end, they attained the highest levels of military expertise available to their generation and, for their courage and sacrifice, were recognized by Congress and President George W. Bush as heroes when they were awarded the Congressional Gold Medal. This award, the highest award the nation has to offer civilians, was presented to the group at the U.S. Capitol on March 29, 2007.

James B. Martin

Further Reading

Francis, Charles E., and Adolph Caso. *The Tuskegee Airmen: The Men Who Changed a Nation.* Boston: Branden Publishing, 1997.

Gubert, Betty Kaplan, Miriam Sawyer, and Caroline M. Fannin. *Distinguished African Americans in Aviation and Space Science.* Westport, CT: Oryx Press, 2002.

Homan, Lynn M., and Thomas Reilly. *Black Knights: The Story of the Tuskegee Airmen.* Gretna, LA: Pelican Publishing, 2001.

Moye, J. Todd. *Freedom Flyers: The Tuskegee Airmen of World War II.* New York: Oxford University Press, 2010.

Stentiford, Barry M. *Tuskegee Airmen.* Santa Barbara, CA: Greenwood, 2012.

James, Daniel "Chappie," Jr.

Born: February 11, 1920
Died: February 25, 1978
Home State: Florida
Service: Army Air Corps, U.S. Air Force
Conflict: World War II, Korean War, Vietnam War
Age at Time of Award: 30

James was born on February 11, 1920, in Pensacola, Florida. He graduated from Washington High School in June 1937 and for the next five years attended Tuskegee Institute in Alabama, where he earned a bachelor of science degree in physical education and took civilian pilot training under a government-sponsored program. On November 3, 1942, he married Dorothy Watkins of Tuskegee, with whom he would have a daughter, Danice, and two sons, Daniel III and Claude.

After graduating from Tuskegee, James worked at the institute as a civilian instructor pilot in the Army Air Corps Aviation Cadet Program. In January 1943, he entered the program as a cadet and, in July 1943, he received a commission as a second lieutenant and was transferred to Selfridge Field, Michigan. There he completed fighter-pilot combat training, after which he was assigned to a variety of different units throughout the country.

In September 1949, James served in the Philippines as flight leader for the 12th Fighter-Bomber Squadron, 18th Fighter Wing, at Clark Field. The following year, he served in Korea, where he flew F-51 and F-80 aircraft and was involved in more than 100 combat missions. In 1950, while leading a flight of F-51s in close air support of U.N. troops, James and his unit saved the

Daniel "Chappie" James received the Distinguished Flying Cross for his valor with the Tuskegee Airmen in World War II. Becoming an Air Force officer when the service was created, he went on to become the first African American to achieve four star rank in the Air Force. (Defense Visual Information Center)

ground troops from annihilation. For his heroism in this action, he was awarded the Distinguished Flying Cross.

In 1951, James joined the 58th Fighter-Interceptor Squadron (FIS) at Otis Air Force Base in Massachusetts, becoming first its operations officer and then, in 1953, commander of the 437th FIS. In August 1955, James was given command of the 60th FIS and received the 1954 Young Man of the Year award for his community relations efforts. Two years later, in June 1957, he graduated from the Air Command and Staff College at Otis Air Force Base.

James spent the next three years as a staff officer at the headquarters of the U.S. Air Force and, in 1960, was transferred to the Royal Air Force Station, Bentwaters, England, serving as assistant director of operations. He was promoted to director of operations and, in 1962, was promoted to deputy commander for operations for the 81st Wing. He then returned to the United States, serving first as director of operations, training, and then deputy commander for operations for the 4453rd Combat Crew Training Wing at Davis-Monthan Air Force Base in Arizona.

During the Vietnam War, James, now in his mid-40s, took part in 78 combat missions into North Vietnam, particularly in the Hanoi and Haiphong areas. He led a flight into the Bolo MiG sweep, which destroyed seven North Vietnamese MiG-21s, the highest number in any Vietnam War mission. He was deputy commander for operations, then wing vice commander of the 8th Fighter Tactical Wing, operating out of Ubon Royal Thai Air Force Base in Thailand. Increased administrative responsibilities came to restrict the number of combat missions he flew. But on one occasion he accompanied an air raid on Hanoi, where he had to shut down one of the engines on his Phantom, which had been punctured with 56 holes from antiaircraft fire. Desperate for fuel, James radioed an airborne tanker and ordered his flight to refuel while his stricken craft headed for the rendezvous. The pilots in his group refused to leave him, stating that their radios were defective and that they could not hear his orders. James and the others made their rendezvous with the tanker and flew safely back to Thailand.

In December 1967, James was named wing vice commander of the 33rd Tactical Fighter Wing at Elgin Air Force Base in Florida. He was also awarded the George Washington Freedom Foundation Medal in both 1967 and 1968 and received Florida's Outstanding American of the Year in 1969 as well as the Distinguished Service Award. By August 1969, he was commander of the 7272nd Fighter Training Wing based at Wheelus Air Force Base in the Libyan Arab Republic. In 1970, he received the Arnold Air Society Eugene M. Zuckert Award for outstanding contributions to air force professionalism. His citation called him "[a] fighter pilot with a magnificent record, public speaker, and eloquent spokesman for the American Dream we so rarely achieve." In 1970, he also became the deputy assistant secretary of defense (public affairs). He remained in this post until April 1973, when he was designated principal deputy assistant secretary of defense and then, in September 1974, he was named vice commander of the Military Airlift Command headquartered at Scott Air Force Base in Illinois.

On September 1, 1975, James became the first African American to be promoted to four-star general in the U.S. Air Force, and he was appointed commander in chief of NORAD/ADCOM (Aerospace Defense Command), based in Colorado. This joint role gave James the responsibility for operational command of all United States and Canadian air defense and for providing warning and assessment of hostile attacks from bombers or missiles.

General James retired at the end of January 1978. He had the reputation of being extremely tough on African American officers, taking the attitude that they had to work harder than their white counterparts in order to gain rewards. Barely one month after his retirement, he suffered a heart attack and died. He was buried with full military honors at Arlington National Cemetery.

Jonathan D. Sutherland

Further Reading

Astor, Gerald. *The Right to Fight*. Novato, CA: Presidio Press, 1998.

Buckley, Gail. *American Patriots*. New York: Random House, 2001.

Nalty, Bernard C. *Strength for the Fight*. New York: Free Press, 1986.

James, Miles

Born: 1829
Died: August 28, 1871
Home State: Virginia
Service: Army
Conflict: Civil War
Age at Time of Award: 34–35

Miles James was born in Princess Anne County, Virginia, sometime in 1829. Some authors list his occupation prior to army service as laborer and others as a farmer, but he was working in Virginia in some capacity when, on November 16, 1863, he enlisted in what was then Company B, 2nd North Carolina Volunteers at Portsmouth, Virginia. The unit was raised by Major General Edward Wild, a former physician, who had lost an arm at the Battle of Antietam and was now raising an African American regiment to fight in Virginia. Wild's unit was later renamed the 36th United States Colored Troops and carried that designation throughout the remainder of the war.

James's first action during the Civil War came in December 1863, during an expedition to capture or kill guerrillas operating in North Carolina and Virginia against Union forces and sympathizers. Along with 1,600 other African American soldiers, comprised also of 700 members of the 1st USCT and 530 soldiers from the 5th USCT, James marched south from the encampments around Norfolk and Portsmouth, Virginia. His unit, under the command of Colonel Alonzo Draper, bloodied themselves against guerrilla forces in North Carolina before heading back into Virginia on December 21. An incident during this expedition, where an African American soldier was hanged by Confederate guerrillas with a promise to do the same to the remaining African American soldiers, drove home to the new troops that they would get no quarter and needed to give none.

By September 1864, Miles James's unit had fought at Petersburg and was a hardened group of soldiers. Their most senior commander, Major General Benjamin Butler, had great faith in these African American soldiers and chose them to break the circle that protected the Confederate capitol of Richmond, Virginia. Butler proposed a plan to Lieutenant General Grant to penetrate the enemy's thinly held lines at a point called New Market Heights, near Chaffin's Farm, and open a pathway to Richmond and the end of the war. To accomplish this breakthrough, Butler deployed the African American regiments under Colonels Draper and Duncan, which included now Corporal James's 36th United States Colored Troops. Because of the perceived need for stealth and speed, Butler ordered the initial attacks on the entrenched Confederates to come without artillery support or the firing of weapons by the soldiers. He wanted the fortifications taken at the point of the bayonet. The area was highly fortified, with downed trees and sharpened sticks as obstacles called abatis, all intended to slow the Union troops and channelize them into kill zones. Duncan's unit led the initial charge and was badly mauled by intense Confederate fire at close range. As directed, they did not fire back and had removed their percussion caps to prevent any accidental firing. As the initial charge surged forward, it faltered even though the African American troops fought with bravery and courage. Seeing the attack lose momentum, Corporal James's regiment was ordered forward but now allowed to fire on the enemy as necessary. Their attack was also met with a withering fire, but the momentum and the burning desire for victory that had built up in the African American soldiers would not let them fail. With soldiers like Miles James performing heroic acts, even though their white officers went down dead and wounded, the African American soldiers of Draper's regiment eventually surged over the top of the earthworks and opened the way to Richmond. James was badly wounded during this final surge, taking a bullet in his arm that made it almost useless. Rather than falling back to seek medical attention, Corporal James continued to load and fire his weapon with one arm while less than 30 yards from the enemy and rallied the members of his company forward to take the works. For his bravery during the Battle of New Market Heights on September 29, 1864, Corporal Miles James received the Medal of Honor.

While many white leaders during the war did not want to lead African American troops or did so under duress, a story exists about Miles James that shows the high regard in which he was held by his commander. After New Market Heights, although James's arm had to be amputated, he wanted to remain in the army. His service records include a letter from then Brigadier General Alonzo Draper to the surgeons at the hospital supporting Corporal James's desire to serve and offering to have him serve as the sergeant of his own provost guard. James was such a recognized hero that his former commander sought to support him when he did not have to do so.

Miles James was promoted to sergeant and allowed to stay with his regiment for over a year longer, eventually being mustered out on October 13, 1865. He and his wife, Sarah, had a son named James. First Sergeant Miles James died near Norfolk on August 28, 1871, and was buried somewhere in Norfolk County, Virginia.

James B. Martin

Further Reading

Claxton, Melvin, and Mark Puls. *Uncommon Valor: A Story of Race, Patriotism, and Glory in the Final Battles of the Civil War.* Hoboken, NJ: John Wiley and Sons, 2006.

Hanna, Charles W. *African American Recipients of the Medal of Honor: A Biographical Dictionary, Civil War through Vietnam War.* Jefferson, NC: McFarland, 2002.

National Archives, Washington DC. Miles James's service records. http://www.rootsweb.com/~ncusct/medals.htm.

Price, James S. *The Battle of New Market Heights: Freedom Will Be Theirs by the Sword.* Charleston, SC: The History Press, 2011.

James, Willy F., Jr.

Born: March 18, 1920
Died: April 8, 1945
Home State: Missouri
Service: Army
Conflict: World War II
Age at Time of Award: 25

Willy F. James Jr. was born in Kansas City, Missouri, on March 18, 1920. Very little is known about his early life, but he enlisted in the U.S. Army on September 11, 1942, in his hometown. He was not part of one of the more famous all-black units, but arrived in France in 1945 as an individual replacement. Willy had evidently volunteered for combat duty and, after infantry training in France, he was assigned to Company G, 413th Infantry Regiment, 104th Infantry Division as a combat infantryman in an all-black platoon.

James's regiment established a bridgehead over the Weser River in Germany as part of the drive toward Berlin in the latter stages of the war. As with any bridge-head operations, the heady task was to push the Germans out from the river that was just crossed, in order to secure room for the reinforcements necessary to hold the crossing and exploit it. As part of these operations, Company G was assigned the mission of taking the town of Lippoldsberg. On April 7, 1945, PFC James was the lead scout for his platoon nearing the town when he took fire from German posi-tions in Lippoldsberg. He took cover and was soon joined in this forward position by his platoon leader. James was given the mission of moving farther forward and providing reconnaissance of the enemy positions in order to plan the platoon's at-tack. He advanced approximately 200 yards farther across relatively open terrain, taking fire constantly, and observed from his covered position for nearly an hour.

James returned to his platoon, again having to cross over 200 yards of open ter-rain under fire and provided his platoon leader with the positions of the enemy in and around the outlying buildings of Lippoldsberg. James volunteered to lead a squad in the assault, as he knew the terrain and situation, and was in the lead elements moving out to assault the town. The fire from the town was again intense and as the assault got underway James's platoon leader was hit by enemy fire and went down. James immediately began to cross open ground to aid his wounded leader, only to be killed by machine gun fire from Lippoldsberg. Despite his death, the reconnais-sance mission he had earlier performed and his demonstration of heroism provided the impetus for his platoon's successful assault and the accomplishment of the unit mission of seizing Lippoldsberg and protecting the bridgehead on the Weser River.

PFC James's platoon leader survived his wounds and six weeks later, on May 26, 1945, recommended Willy F. James Jr. for the Distinguished Service Cross for his actions at Lippoldsberg. The recommendation for the DSC moved quickly, gaining endorsements from his division and corps commanders and eventually the deco-rations board at Seventh Army Headquarters. He was awarded the Distinguished Service Cross (posthumously) on September 14, 1945.

Throughout World War II, African American soldiers performed with the same courage and dedication that was the hallmark of all American soldiers. Unfortu-nately, due to racial prejudice at both an institutional and individual level, no Af-rican American soldiers received the Medal of Honor, although a number were recommended for our nation's highest honor. In 1993, the Department of Defense commissioned an investigation into the question of whether such prejudice was the reason for this oversight and which African American soldiers who had been awarded lesser decorations had deserved the Medal of Honor. The study, conducted by Shaw University, examined the records of multiple African American soldiers and, in 1995, recommended that 10 soldiers receive America's highest award for heroism. Congress eventually decided to award the Medal of Honor to 7 of the 10 soldiers who had been recommended and on January 31, 1997, President Bill

Clinton presented the medals during a ceremony at the White House. Only one of the seven, Vernon Baker, was alive to receive his Medal in person, but Willy F. James Jr. officially had his Distinguished Service Cross upgraded to the Medal of Honor for his actions in April 1945.

PFC James was buried in Europe, eventually interred in the Netherlands American Cemetery and Memorial in Margraten, Holland. In an effort to recognize James's actions and memorialize his name in the army's history, the 7th U.S. Army Reserve Command (ARCOM) Reserve Center in Bamberg, Germany, was dedicated in his memory during a ceremony in November 2001.

James B. Martin

Further Reading

Booker, Bryan D. *African Americans in the United States Army in World War II*. Jefferson, NC: McFarland, 2008.

Converse, Elliott V., III. *The Exclusion of Black Soldiers from the Medal of Honor in World War II*. Jefferson, NC: McFarland, 1997.

Moore, Christopher Paul. *Fighting for America: Black Soldiers—The Unsung Heroes of World War II*. New York: Ballantine Books, 2005.

Jenkins, Robert H., Jr.

Born: June 1, 1948
Died: March 5, 1969
Home State: Florida
Service: Marine Corps
Conflict: Vietnam War
Age at Time of Award: 20

Robert H. Jenkins Jr. was born in Florida, in Putnam County's small town of Interlachen. His mother and father were Robert and Willie Mae Jenkins. He attended Palatka Central Academy and after graduation made the decision to join the U.S. Marine Corps on February 2, 1968. After graduating from recruit basic training at Parris Island, South Carolina, he went on to more advanced training at Camp Lejeune, North Carolina.

In July 1968, Jenkins was deployed to Vietnam with the 3rd Recon Battalion, 3rd Marine Division, Fleet Marine Force and was assigned as a machine gunner with Company C. The unit was stationed at Fire Support Base Argonne, Quảng Trị Province, Republic of Vietnam. Argonne was situated on Hill 1308 and was a critical location due to its close proximity to the Laotian border and the ability to observe the Ho Chi Minh Trail from that position. On the morning of March 5,

1969, Private First Class Jenkins and 11 other members of his reconnaissance team were occupying defensive positions at Fire Support Base Argonne. During an early morning attack by a North Vietnamese Army unit in platoon-sized strength, they responded to incoming fire. Jenkins and his assistant gunner moved into a two-man fighting position and began to use their machine gun to great effect on the North Vietnamese force. In the midst of the fighting, a North Vietnamese soldier was able to throw a grenade that came to rest inside the fighting position occupied by Private First Class Jenkins and his comrade. Fully understanding the gravity of the situation, Jenkins pushed the assistant gunner to the bottom of the fighting position and shielded the marine with his own body. The blast of the grenade was absorbed by Private First Class Jenkins's body, and the assistant gunner's life was spared. Jenkins was badly wounded by the grenade blast and he eventually died of the wounds suffered during the attack. For his bravery and self-sacrifice, Private First Class Robert H. Jenkins Jr. received the Medal of Honor. Because of his actions at Fire Support Base Argonne that spring day in 1969, Private First Class Jenkins became the last of five African American marines to receive the Medal of Honor during the Vietnam War and the most recent African American marine to receive America's most prestigious award for valor.

Jenkins's family received his Medal of Honor from Vice President Spiro Agnew in a White House ceremony on April 20, 1970. Private First Class Jenkins was buried with honors at Sister Spring Baptist Cemetery in Interlachen, Florida. Palatka Central Academy, his alma mater, has now been renamed the Robert Jenkins Middle School in his honor. In addition, the Veteran's Administration has preserved his memory by naming the Robert H. Jenkins Jr. Veterans Domiciliary Home of Florida, located in Lake City, Florida, in his honor. Private First Class Jenkins is memorialized on the Vietnam Memorial at Panel 30W, Row 046.

James B. Martin

Further Reading

Greene, Robert Ewell. *Black Defenders of America, 1775–1973*. Chicago: Johnson, 1974.

Hanna, Charles W. *African American Recipients of the Medal of Honor: A Biographical Dictionary, Civil War through Vietnam War*. Jefferson, NC: McFarland, 2002.

Jones, Maxine D., and Kevin M. McCarthy. *African Americans in Florida*. Sarasota, FL: Pineapple Press, 1993.

Smith, Charles R. *U.S. Marines in Vietnam: High Mobility and Standdown, 1969*. Washington, DC: Headquarters United States Marine Corps, Marine Corps in Vietnam Series, 2002.

Westheider, James E. *Fighting on Two Fronts: African Americans and the Vietnam War*. New York: New York University Press, 1997.

Joel, Lawrence

Born: February 22, 1928
Died: February 4, 1984
Home State: North Carolina
Service: Army
Conflict: Vietnam War
Age at Time of Award: 37

Born on February 22, 1928, Lawrence Joel spent his youth in Winston-Salem, North Carolina, growing up on the east side of the city, a predominantly African American section of the city at the time. Although only 17 years old when World War II ended, he, nevertheless, joined the Merchant Marines during the war and served for one year. In 1946, after completing his stint in the Merchant Marines, Joel joined the U.S. Army. As a result of the army's still-segregationist policies, he did not have many career opportunities during the early part of his service, though he did see combat during the Korean War.

In November 1965, Specialist Five Joel was a medic in the Headquarters and Headquarters Company (HHC), 1st Battalion, 503rd Infantry Regiment, 173rd Airborne Brigade in South Vietnam. On November 8, he took part in Operation Hump, a large search-and-destroy mission involving his battalion and the 1st Battalion, Royal Australian Regiment. After a 20-minute helicopter ride from Bien Hoa, Joel's unit was prepared for a full day of searching for the Viet Cong (VC) insurgents. Joel thought that the day began "fairly routine . . . just like back at Ft. Bragg—going to play war games." Unfortunately, the day would prove to be anything but routine.

Shortly before 8:00 AM, Company C, 1st Battalion, 503rd Infantry

Specialist Five Lawrence Joel was both the first medic to receive the Medal of Honor for service in Vietnam and the first living African American to receive the Medal of Honor since the Spanish-American War in 1898. (U.S. Army Medical Department Regiment)

Regiment encountered a dug-in VC regiment on Hill 65. Rather than easily overwhelming these enemy troops, the American forces quickly realized that they were facing a much larger and determined foe. The 1st Battalion's Company B was ordered to assist Company C and, without realizing it, managed to strike the VC regiment on their right flank. While many of the VC soldiers retreated in the face of this unexpected assault, the VC commander realized retreat would result in annihilation by superior American air and artillery fire. Instead, he ordered his men to close with the enemy in order to negate the American air and artillery advantage. If the VC moved in close enough, the Americans would be unable to use air and artillery fire without hitting their own troops. During the hand-to-hand fighting that followed, the VC used their superior numbers—they outnumbered the Americans by approximately six to one—to isolate and almost overrun the American units.

Throughout the battle, Joel repeatedly risked his life to provide medical aid to wounded American soldiers. When hit in the right calf by an enemy rifle round, he simply bandaged himself, administered a dose of morphine, and continued to help the casualties around him. After administering aid to all the nearby wounded, Joel fashioned a makeshift crutch and, under heavy fire, hobbled to a nearby unit to assist with more injured soldiers. Completely ignoring the warnings of other Americans, the bullets striking the ground around him, and his own pain, he knelt while holding up plasma bottles, completely engrossed in his mission. After receiving a second wound—this time in the right thigh—Joel continued to drag himself from casualty to casualty. Displaying resourcefulness when his medical supplies ran out, he saved the life of one soldier by placing a plastic bag over a severe chest wound to congeal the blood. When the 24-hour battle finally ended, more than 400 VC were dead, but at least 13 Americans had been saved by Joel's efforts.

Joel spent three months recuperating from his injuries in American hospitals in Saigon and Tokyo. Initially, he only received the Silver Star, the third highest U.S. decoration for valor, for his actions. It took more than a year for the paperwork for his Medal of Honor to be processed and approved. On March 9, 1967, President Lyndon B. Johnson presented the Medal to him in a White House ceremony. In his speech, President Johnson referred to Joel's bravery as a "very special kind of courage—the unarmed heroism of compassion and service to others." Joel was both the first medic to receive the Medal of Honor for service in Vietnam and the first living African American to receive the Medal of Honor since the Spanish-American War in 1898. He returned to Vietnam in 1969, having volunteered for a second tour as a combat medic.

President Johnson invited Joel as a special guest for the State of the Union Address in 1966. Later, on April 8, 1967, his hometown of Winston-Salem held a parade in Lawrence Joel's honor that the *New York Times* called the biggest tribute the city had ever staged to honor an individual. Joel retired from the U.S. Army in 1973 after 27 years of active service. He died of complications from diabetes on February 4, 1984, and was buried at Arlington National Cemetery. Five years after his death, in 1989, his hometown once again honored Joel by naming the new home of the Wake Forest Demon Deacons, opening the Lawrence Joel Veterans Memorial Coliseum on August 28.

Alexander M. Bielakowski

Further Reading

"Laggard Draft Boards." *Baltimore Afro-American*, January 20, 1966, p. 2.

Murphy, Edward F. *Vietnam Medal of Honor Heroes*. New York: Ballantine Books, 1987.

Tillman, Barrett. *Heroes: U.S. Army Medal of Honor Recipients*. New York: Berkley, 2006.

Johnson, Dwight H.

Born: May 7, 1947
Died: April 30, 1971
Home State: Michigan
Service: Army
Conflict: Vietnam War
Age at Time of Award: 20

Dwight H. Johnson was born in Detroit, Michigan, to Joyce Johnson Alves. His father did not choose to stay with the family and he grew up with his mother; though for a period of time, he had a stepfather of Jamaican descent. The family lived in the E. J. Jeffries Homes, a public housing project in Detroit. Johnson attended public schools in Detroit until he entered the army on July 28, 1966, in his hometown. Prior to deploying to Vietnam, Johnson served in stateside assignments at Ft. Knox, Kentucky, and Ft. Carson, Colorado. He was deployed to the Republic of Vietnam in February 1967, joining Company B, 1st Battalion, 69th Armored Brigade, 4th Infantry Division near Đắk Tô in Kontum Province.

Johnson was nearing the end of his year in Vietnam when his commanding officer asked him to begin driving a different M-48 tank because of the illness of another soldier. Johnson moved to the new tank crew and was serving there when his tank was included in a reaction force dispatched to the aid of another portion of the unit. As the column of four M-48 tanks rolled to rescue their comrades, they were hit with an ambush fueled by antitank rockets. The North Vietnamese Army unit initially damaged two of the tanks, including Johnson's, and began to press the attack against the surprised American unit. Seeing the members of his former crew in trouble in their badly damaged tank, Johnson exited the relative safety of his armored vehicle and moved to try and save the crew. He was able to rescue one fellow soldier before the vehicle's ammunition exploded and killed the remainder of the crew. Johnson turned his anger and frustration on the North Vietnamese soldiers and moved among them firing his .45 caliber pistol until he ran out of ammunition.

Grabbing a submachine gun from another tank he again engaged the enemy, doing significant damage to the unit and blunting the force of the attack. Once again running out of ammunition with the submachine gun, he killed an enemy soldier in close combat with a blow from the weapon's stock and mounted a nearby tank to continue the fight. He joined the crew of that tank in firing the main gun until it malfunctioned and then he exposed himself again, firing at the enemy with another .45 caliber pistol as he made his way to his original tank. Here, he mounted the tank and continued the fight by providing devastating fire from the .50 caliber machine gun mounted above the turret until the action subsided. It is reported that Johnson's anger at seeing his former crew killed fueled his actions and he had to nearly be restrained in his anger once the fighting was over. For his bravery in this fight and his personal role in breaking up a potentially disastrous enemy ambush, Specialist Fifth Class Dwight H. Johnson received the Medal of Honor.

After his discharge from the army in July 1968, Johnson returned to Detroit, but like so many returning Vietnam veterans of the day, he found it difficult to get a job or adjust to civilian life. In the days following the November 19, 1968 White House ceremony where President Lyndon B. Johnson presented Specialist Fifth Class Johnson the Medal of Honor things should have improved greatly.

Unfortunately, either because of the inability to deal with newfound celebrity status or a severe case of posttraumatic stress, Johnson simply struggled to get a firm grip on life. He was hired by the army as a recruiter and spent some time doing public relations for the service. As the stress again wore thin, he was apparently admitted to a military hospital in Valley Forge, Pennsylvania, for the emotional and mental effects of his Vietnam service. He continued to receive treatment for his emotional challenges and was on a pass to visit his family when his life was cut short. In the morning hours of April 30, 1971, in his hometown of Detroit, Johnson was shot and killed by the clerk of the Open Pantry Market convenient store near his home as he allegedly tried to rob the store. Though his life ended tragically, Dwight H. Johnson was one of America's heroes of the Vietnam War. He had proven himself when tested in the crucible of combat, but could not find himself in civilian life. In honor of his actions in Vietnam and befitting his status as a recipient of the Medal of Honor, Johnson was buried in Arlington National Cemetery, Arlington, Virginia on May 6, 1971. His grave can be found in Section 31, Lot 471.

James B. Martin

Further Reading

Hanna, Charles W. *African American Recipients of the Medal of Honor: A Biographical Dictionary, Civil War through Vietnam War.* Jefferson, NC: McFarland, 2002.

Westheider, James E. *The African American Experience in Vietnam: Brothers in Arms.* New York: Rowman & Littlefield, 2008.

Westheider, James E. *Fighting on Two Fronts: African Americans and the Vietnam War.* New York: New York University Press, 1997.

Johnson, Henry

Born: June 11, 1850
Died: January 31, 1904
Home State: Virginia
Service: Army
Conflict: Indian Wars
Age at Time of Award: 29

Johnson was born in Boydton, Mecklenburg County, Virginia on June 11, 1850. He enlisted in Detroit, Michigan, and joined F Troop of the 10th Cavalry. After fighting in several engagements against the Cheyenne on the Republican River, he was promoted to corporal in January 1868. He became a sergeant in November 1869 but was reduced to a private in March 1871, possibly because of brawling.

In June 1877, he joined D Troop of the 9th Cavalry, based at Ft. Wallace, Kansas, eventually regaining his stripes. D Troop was posted to Ft. Union, New Mexico; in 1878, D Troop was sent to Colorado as part of the Ute expedition, and by the end of the year it was based for the winter at Pagosa Springs.

As a member of a small group of Buffalo Soldiers under the command of Captain Francis S. Dodge, Johnson left D Troop's encampment on the Grand River and traveled the 70 miles to the Milk River to reinforce Captain J. Scott Payne's small unit from the Fifth Cavalry. The black soldiers and their officers joined the white troopers in makeshift fortifications surrounded by a larger force of Utes. Descriptions of the situation indicate that conditions were poor, with almost all horses killed or wounded within the fortifications and the Utes having clear fields of fire at the cavalry troopers. While the fortifications were near the Milk River, the position of the Indians on the high ground made resupply of water very dangerous and it was accomplished only during the night at great risk.

Serving as sergeant of the guard, Johnson organized the forward screen to protect the entrenchments and regularly made the rounds to issue instructions to the troopers. In doing so, he was constantly exposed to fire from the Indians who were on the high ground and well within effective rifle range. In addition to these heroic actions, Johnson also led a group of troopers who made a dangerous trip to the Milk River to secure water resupply and provide adequate water for the wounded within the fortifications. In 1890, he applied for a Medal of Honor for his gallantry at Milk River in 1879. Captain Dodge and Lieutenant Martin B. Hughes, the two officers with D Troop during the action at Milk River, supported his application for the award. For his actions during the four-day siege at the Milk River from October 2 to 5, 1879, Johnson eventually received the Medal of Honor on September 22, 1890. His citation simply read: "Voluntarily left fortified shelter and under heavy fire at close range made the rounds of the pits to instruct the guards, fought his way to the creek and back to bring water to the wounded."

Johnson lost his stripes again and spent six months in prison in 1881 because of a court martial conviction. He accepted a discharge from the army in January 1883 at Ft. Riley, Kansas, after his enlistment expired.

After just two months, Johnson rejoined the 10th Cavalry at Ft. Grant, Arizona, and after another five-year enlistment he joined the 9th Cavalry and had been promoted to sergeant by 1889, but he lost his stripes again following a fight with a bartender at Ft. Robinson, Nebraska.

As a member of K Troop (9th Cavalry), Johnson saw action on the Pine Ridge Sioux Reservation in the winter of 1890, and in the spring of 1891, he and K Troop were transferred to Ft. Myer, Virginia. K Troop was one of the most decorated of the Buffalo Soldier units, with three different members of the unit having received the Medal of Honor. In the summer of 1893, at the beginning of his sixth enlistment, Johnson and K Troop were sent back to Ft. Robinson, where he applied for a Certificate of Merit to complement his Medal of Honor. The Certificate of Merit came with a two-dollar-per-month bonus and was normally reserved for actions such as saving lives or preventing the destruction of government property. As Johnson's heroic efforts at Milk River had already been recognized through the Medal of Honor, the War Department determined that the Certificate of Merit was not warranted. While Johnson had shown an ability to get himself in trouble and face occasional disciplinary action, his quality as a trooper apparently still carried weight with his superiors. At the time of the application for the Certificate of Merit, he was serving under now Captain Hughes who supported Johnson's request to the War Department.

In the spring of 1898, as the 9th Cavalry was preparing to depart for Cuba, Johnson, now 49, requested furlough. When he returned from furlough on July 26, he requested retirement and returned to the Washington, D.C., area.

Johnson died in January 1904. He had been promoted to sergeant three times and had been reduced to private each time, not an unusual set of circumstances for long-serving troopers in the American West, regardless of the soldier's race. As a long-serving and respected soldier, who had received his country's highest honor, he was buried with full military honors in Arlington National Cemetery.

James B. Martin and Jonathan D. Sutherland

Further Reading

Amos, Preston E. *Above and beyond in the West: Black Medal of Honor Winners, 1870–1890.* Washington, DC: Potomac Corral, Westerners, 1974.

Leckie, William H. *The Buffalo Soldiers: A Narrative of the Negro Cavalry in the West.* Norman: University of Oklahoma Press, 1967.

Schubert, Frank N. *Black Valor: Buffalo Soldiers and the Medal of Honor, 1870–1898.* Wilmington, DE: Scholarly Resources, 1997.

Johnson, Henry L.

Born: 1897
Died: July 5, 1929
Home State: New York
Service: Army
Conflict: World War I
Age at Time of Award: 21 or 22

Henry Lincoln Johnson was born in Alexandria, Virginia, in 1897. As a teenager his family moved to Albany, New York, where he worked as a railway porter before joining the 15th Infantry Regiment of the New York National Guard shortly before the United States entered World War I in 1917. Once the U.S. government had officially declared war against Germany, the 15th New York was incorporated into the U.S. Army as the 369th, an all-black infantry regiment.

Shipping out to France with the rest of the American Expeditionary Force (AEF) in late 1917, the 369th was almost immediately assigned to support the 161st Division of the French Army, which had suffered tremendous losses, along with the rest of the French Army, over the course of four years of grueling warfare.

Henry Johnson is honored during a victory parade in New York City. (National Archives)

Delegating African American units to the command of the French was a common practice in World War I, as U.S. military authorities were unenthusiastic about having black troops and labored under the impression that the French were better suited to command black soldiers, given their long tradition of enlisting units from French colonies in Africa. To some extent, they were right. The French harbored less prejudice than the Americans and treated the African American soldiers with a greater degree of equality than they could have expected from their own countrymen.

Stationed on the frontlines of the fighting, the 369th quickly gained a great deal of combat experience and earned for themselves the reputation of being tough fighters. Their French colleagues hailed them as being perfectly suited for dangerous night patrols, not only because of their bravery but also because their skin color provided them with natural camouflage. The Germans had also learned a grudging respect for the black troops, erroneously calling them the "French Moroccans" because they did not realize American troops had supplemented the French force at this point of the lines.

On the night of May 14, 1918, Johnson was a member of a five-man patrol ordered to advance to the very foremost of the French positions to listen for a possible German attack. Taking turns standing guard, Johnson and his compatriot Needham Roberts stood watch, while the other three members of the team rested in a nearby dugout. Suddenly, the Germans launched a fierce grenade attack against the patrol's position that seriously wounded both Johnson and Roberts. The concussion of the blast temporarily knocked the other three men unconscious. When the Germans followed the grenade barrage by launching 24 men in a frontal assault on the position, both Johnson and Roberts fought back despite their wounds. Roberts was nearly overcome, but Johnson managed to drive off the Germans by shooting some, injuring others by beating them over their heads with the butt of his rifle, stabbing others with his small "bolo" knife, and hurling grenades at the rest. Daunted by such a show of ferocity, the Germans retreated, leaving behind their dead and wounded and a considerable amount of weapons, ammunition, and supplies. Johnson and Roberts both remained conscious, although each man had sustained several severe wounds. Johnson was later reported to have received more than 20 wounds in the incident.

Johnson was hospitalized and then returned to his unit, although they were both given the option of receiving an honorable discharge and going home, an offer that Roberts accepted. Johnson, though, remained with the regiment, which the Allied forces dubbed the "Harlem Hellfighters," for the rest of the war, gaining promotion to sergeant. The unit became famous for never having a single man captured or losing a foot of ground, despite high casualty rates.

The U.S. Army paid scant attention to Johnson's and Roberts's heroics, filing a routine report on the matter that did little to highlight the soldiers' bravery. The French handled the matter differently, however, conducting their own investigation into the event. Their report stressed the men's gallantry. In fact, the French commander in charge of the investigation later wrote to the U.S. commander of the AEF, Gen. John J. Pershing, that "the American report is too modest. As a result of oral information furnished me, it appears the blacks were extremely brave. This little combat does honor to all Americans." As a result of the French report, both Johnson and Roberts received the Croix de Guerre with Gold Palm Leaf, one of the highest French military honors. They were the first Americans, black or white, to receive such an honor in the war.

Johnson and Needham became instant heroes in the African American community in New York when their story was told by a journalist in *The Saturday Evening Post*. They provided their community the heroes it had yearned for and were a visible demonstration of the quality and valor of African American soldiers when given the opportunity to serve in combat. African American publications lauded their exploits, while white publications downplayed their actions or liberally sprinkled treatments of their story with racial stereotypes.

After the war, Johnson was shipped home with his regiment, which marched in a victory parade in New York City on February 17, 1919. Because of his fame and because he never fully recovered from his injuries, Johnson was accorded a special car to ride in for the parade. Many hailed him as the nation's most popular African American hero, praise that former President Theodore Roosevelt topped by declaring him "one of the five bravest Americans."

Despite this glory, Johnson struggled during the 1920s. He left the army and returned to Albany, but permanently disabled by his injuries, he was unable to return to his job as a railway porter. Suffering from what would now be termed posttraumatic stress disorder, he began to abuse alcohol as an escape from the feelings of frustration, anger, and sadness that plagued him. At that time, few recognized the effect warfare could have on the combatants, and so his depression went untreated. He died at the young age of 31 or 32 in 1929.

Roughly 60 years later, Johnson returned to the spotlight when the city of Albany named a street after him and placed a monument to his feats nearby. State and local officials took a second look at the war record of this man who had been passed over during his lifetime for honors from the U.S. government. With the support of Johnson's son Herman (who was also a war hero, flying with the Tuskegee Airmen during World War II), politicians such as Governor George Pataki and several state assemblymen began to push for national recognition for Johnson. Their first effort was to locate Johnson's grave, which some believed was in a pauper's cemetery on the outskirts of Albany. Research proved that it was instead in Arlington National Cemetery, where a funeral with military honors had been held for the war hero on July 5, 1929. Second, Pataki initiated a campaign to convince the army and the government to give Johnson his due, albeit posthumously. In March 2002, the U.S. Army complied, awarding Johnson the Distinguished Service Cross. Efforts to secure the Medal of Honor for Johnson, a feat that requires presidential approval, continue.

Jonathan D. Sutherland

369TH INFANTRY REGIMENT (THE HARLEM HELLFIGHTERS)

As with many conflicts in U.S. military history, World War I provided an opportunity for African American soldiers to prove their worth, but also displayed the problems of racial prejudice that have been endemic to America. With the American entry into World War I, units were raised in various parts of the United States for eventual service in Europe. In New York, the raising of an African American regiment was sponsored by the Union League Club of New York and was initially identified as the 15th New York Infantry Regiment. The club had previously sponsored the creation of the 20th U.S. Colored Infantry during the Civil War and their action in 1916 simply followed in that tradition. The regiment was initially commanded by Colonel William Hayward and recruited largely from the Harlem area of New York City.

The regiment initially trained in Spartanburg, South Carolina, and suffered significant racism during their time in the south. They embarked from New York City on December 27, 1917, en route to France as part of the 185th Infantry Brigade. The 369th was the first African American unit to ship out for France from the United States and would be the first such unit to see combat in Europe. Upon its arrival in France, the 369th was assigned to the 93rd Division (Provisional) which was made up of the African American units arriving on the continent. The leadership of the American Expeditionary Forces took some time in deciding how to utilize the segregated African American units and because of this the 369th spent some time engaged in labor service duties while waiting their chance for combat. The AEF decided in April 1918 to assign an African American unit to the French Army for the remainder of the war and the 369th was the initial unit chosen for this assignment. While the French were not particularly more racially liberal, they were in dire straits for manpower and put survival over race relations in their decisions on how to use the loaned American unit. The 369th was given French equipment, though they kept their American uniforms, and was made an active part of the French 16th Division. They immediately began training for their coming part in the division's combat operations and became combat ready well ahead of the other segregated units which had arrived in Europe from the United States. On April 29, 1918, the regiment was given responsibility for a five-mile portion of the French front, a responsibility and honor that had not been given to an African American unit to this point in the war. Seeing combat much earlier than their counterparts, the 369th quickly became a veteran combat force and provided the African American community back home the war heroes they were eager to recognize.

On May 13, 1918, Needham Roberts and Henry Johnson were the first to react to a German patrol's incursion into the 369th's area of responsibility and were recognized by the French Army with awards for gallantry. The newspapers in New York picked the story up after an officer from the unit relayed the story to a journalist from the *Saturday Evening Post*. The story created figures of legendary proportions in the African American publications and prompted stories that were more racially tinged in the mainstream publications. Nevertheless, the 369th had become a famous unit in America and France because of the actions of Roberts and Johnson. They began to be referred to as the Harlem Hellfighters and fought in combat through the remainder of World War I with the French Army. Their battlefield exploits included such important engagements as the Champagne-Marne, Meuse-Argonne,

Champagne 1918, and Alsace 1918. Over the course of the war, the unit was credited with having spent 191 days under fire and suffered approximately 1,500 casualties. A battalion commander in the 369th, who later wrote a book about the unit's time in France, maintained that the unit never lost a foot of ground nor had a single soldier captured. Members of the regiment received the Distinguished Service Cross from the U.S. Army and the Croix de Guerre and Legion of Honor from the French Army. Private Johnson became the first American ever awarded the Croix de Guerre from the French. In all, 171 members of the 369th received the Legion of Honor from the French and the unit received a Croix de Guerre with Silver Star for its actions at Sechault. On November 28, 1918, the 369th reached the banks of the Rhine River and became the first allied unit to advance that far into Germany.

The 369th proved what a segregated African American unit could do because they were given the opportunity by the French Army. Out of the French desperation came success for the Harlem Hellfighters and recognition of the positive role of African American soldiers during World War I. The unit returned to a heroes' welcome in New York City and was among the first units to march up Fifth Avenue to their armory in Harlem. Some historians have used this parade in Harlem as the event marking the beginning of the Harlem Renaissance.

James B. Martin

Further Reading

"American Hero: William Henry Johnson, New York National Guard." *StrategyWorld.com*: http://www.strategypage.com/respect/articles/20020321.asp.

Press Releases from Gov. George Pataki's Office. "Governor Pataki Honors WWI Hero Sgt. Henry Johnson." http://www.state.ny.us/governor/press/year02/jan10_1_02.htm, posted January 10, 2002; and "Governor Urges Awarding Medal of Honor to Henry Johnson." http://www.state.ny.us/governor/press/year01/feb12_2_01.htm, posted February 12, 2001.

Williams, Chad L. *Torchbearers of Democracy: African American Soldiers in the World War I Era*. Chapel Hill, NC: The University of North Carolina Press, 2010.

"WWI 'Harlem Hellfighter' Posthumously Nominated for Medal." National Guard Web site. http://www.ngb.army.mil/news/2001/02/12/johnson.shtml, posted February 12, 2001.

Johnson, Ralph H.

Born: January 11, 1949
Died: March 5, 1968
Home State: South Carolina
Service: Marine Corps
Conflict: Vietnam War
Age at Time of Award: 19

Ralph Henry Johnson was born in Charleston, South Carolina, on January 11, 1949, to Rebecca Johnson. He grew up in Charleston, attending both Courtenay Elementary School and Simonton Jr. High School in the city. By March 23, 1967, Johnson had found his way to the west coast and enlisted in the Marine Corps Reserve. Within four months, he was released from his commitment to the reserves so that he could enlist in the active portion of the U.S. Marine Corps on July 2, 1967. He was stationed at Marine Corps Recruit Depot San Diego and, after completing his training in September 1967, he was transferred to Camp Pendleton for further combat preparation. He completed basic infantry training at Camp Pendleton in November 1967, and was promoted to private first class.

Shortly after this promotion Johnson received orders to deploy to the Republic of Vietnam, and on January 1, 1968, he arrived in the country. He joined Company A, 1st Reconnaissance Battalion, 1st Marine Division as a reconnaissance scout and settled into the unit. On March 5, 1968, Private First Class Johnson's unit was operating in Quảng Nam Province in the vicinity of the Quan Duc Valley. Company A was engaged with North Vietnamese regulars and Viet Cong as part of Operation Rock. The small unit with which Johnson was operating had been inserted at Landing Zone Finch on March 2 and had occupied Hill 146 overlooking the valley. From this position, they had good observation into enemy-controlled territory and were providing intelligence to their parent unit. Each time they were able to identify enemy units, they called in artillery fire and were making themselves a problem for the North Vietnamese in the valley. Shortly after dawn, the 15-man patrol was manning positions on this scrub-covered hill. Suddenly they were attacked by a larger force of North Vietnamese, who attempted to penetrate their position with automatic weapons, grenades, and other explosives. Private First Class Johnson was in a three-man fighting position with two other marines when a grenade was thrown into the hole. Immediately recognizing the danger the hand grenade posed, he jumped forward on top of it and curled his body around it to shield the other marines from the blast. His actions saved the life of Marine Lieutenant Clebe McClary, the patrol's leader, and prevented the North Vietnamese from penetrating the perimeter, as the loss of all three members of the patrol in that fighting position would have opened an avenue for the enemy to pour into the marine position. Johnson's actions were those of a hero, sacrificing himself for his comrades and the good of the mission. For his courage and sacrifice, Private First Class Ralph Henry Johnson received the Medal of Honor.

On April 20, 1970, Vice President Spiro Agnew presented the posthumous Medal of Honor to Mrs. Johnson in her son's honor. Private First Class Johnson was buried at Beaufort National Cemetery in Beaufort, South Carolina, and his headstone can be found at Section 3, Grave 21. He is memorialized on the Vietnam Memorial on Panel 43E, Row 8.

In an effort to honor the memory of Private First Class Ralph Henry Johnson, in 1991, the Veteran's Administration renamed the VA medical center in Charleston,

South Carolina, as the Ralph H. Johnson VA Medical Center. The Department of the Navy also sought to honor the memory of this hero on February 15, 2012, by announcing the decision to name the newest Arleigh Burke-class guided missile destroyer the USS *Ralph Johnson* (DDG-114).

James B. Martin

Further Reading

Greene, Robert Ewell. *Black Defenders of America, 1775–1973.* Chicago: Johnson, 1974.

Hanna, Charles W. *African American Recipients of the Medal of Honor: A Biographical Dictionary, Civil War through Vietnam War.* Jefferson, NC: McFarland, 2002.

Westheider, James E. *The African American Experience in Vietnam: Brothers in Arms.* New York: Rowman & Littlefield, 2008.

Westheider, James E. *Fighting on Two Fronts: African Americans and the Vietnam War.* New York: New York University Press, 1997.

Jordan, George

Born: 1847
Died: October 24, 1904
Home State: Tennessee
Service: Army
Conflict: Indian Wars
Age at Time of Award: 33–34

George Jordan was born in Williamson County, Tennessee, sometime in 1847. He left rural Tennessee and enlisted in the army at Nashville, Tennessee, joining the 38th Infantry Regiment there. He became a career soldier in the army and spent the greatest part of his life serving as a Buffalo Soldier in the 9th Cavalry Regiment. He joined K Troop of the 9th Cavalry in 1870 and spent most of his remaining service there, eventually rising to first sergeant of the unit. In May 1880, the Apache leader, Victorio, was active in the American Southwest and elements of all four African-American regiments, the 9th and 10th Cavalry and the 24th and 25th Infantry, were all involved in actions against his forces. Sergeant Jordan was in command of 25 men in K Company on a mission to escort supply wagons when he was alerted by a courier to Victorio's nearby presence and potential plan to attack settlers at Old Fort Tularosa in the New Mexico Territory. The fact that Jordan was commanding a group of soldiers this large speaks volumes concerning the faith his officers had in him and his actions over the next 24 hours supported this faith. Though the courier made contact just at sundown on May 13, his information indicated that there was no time for the detachment to rest. Jordan informed his men of the situation and they began the forced march to Old Fort Tularosa, which was nearly a day's march distant. Jordan's unit reached their objective in advance of Victorio's forces and began to create defensive positions to resist the larger enemy force. The settlers were very happy to see the soldiers and provided what assistance they could. The Apache's attacked on the evening of May 14, with about 100 warriors challenging the 25 Buffalo Soldiers under Jordan. The Indians could not penetrate the defensive position around the settlement and turned their attention to the livestock enclosure. Jordan responded by dispatching troopers to reinforce the herders and eventually drove the Apache force away. Such a strong defensive position may have fooled the enemy into believing the larger portion of the regiment was nearby and caused an early end to the fight. Sergeant Jordan was recommended for the Medal of Honor for his actions at Old Fort Tularosa, but he would not officially be recognized for a full decade. As he continued to serve with K Troop, nearly a year later he was once again thrust into dangerous combat in which he distinguished himself. Victorio had been killed in combat and was replaced by a new war chief, Nana. On August 12, 1881, Sergeant Jordan was serving with Captain Parker, the commander of K Troop, and engaged the Apaches under Nana in a fierce firefight. Parker and his 19 Buffalo Soldiers, accompanied by First Sergeant Thomas Shaw, attacked Nana's forces near Carrizo Canyon, New Mexico. The troopers of K Troop chased the Indians into the canyon, with Jordan commanding the right flank of the unit. With First Sergeant Shaw spearheading the fight in the center and Sergeant Jordan anchoring the right flank, K Troop was able to hold their own against the larger force until the Indians broke contact. Nana and his 40–60 Apaches tried repeatedly to turn the cavalry unit's flank but were unable to defeat Jordan's flank position. Once again, Sergeant Jordan had commanded a small force of Buffalo Soldiers and defeated a much larger force of Apache's. His personal courage and leadership in this action was matched by First Sergeant Shaw's, who received the Medal of Honor for his actions. In December 1890, George Jordan received the Medal of Honor for his actions in New Mexico in 1880 and 1881. His Medal of Honor citation mentions both the actions at Old Fort Tularosa and Carrizo Canyon. His performance in either fight merited the award of the Medal of Honor and if the army had moved more quickly, he might well have been a double recipient of the Medal. Instead, his actions at Carrizo Canyon were also rewarded through a Certificate of Merit, the other high award that could be given to Buffalo Soldiers. Though he deserved separate Medals of Honor for his actions at Old Fort Tularosa and Carrizo Canyon, the Certificate of Merit brought with it a two-dollar-a-month increase in pay and probably meant more to Jordan at that time. Jordan would go on to become First Sergeant of K Troop and serve in that capacity during the Ghost Dance winter on the Pine Ridge Agency in the winter of 1890–1891. Jordan retired in 1897 in Crawford, Nebraska, near Ft. Robinson. He made a meager living among a group of former Buffalo Soldiers in Crawford, until illness in the fall of 1904 became a major problem. Jordan's plight, unable to get care at the Ft. Robinson Hospital because the senior doctor refused to allow a retired Buffalo Soldier admission, illuminated the fact that African American soldiers, even those that were heroes, were not well treated by the army once they were no longer needed. The doctor's advice that Jordan travel to the U.S. Soldiers' Home in Washington for care was ridiculous on so many levels. Without adequate medical care, Jordan died in Crawford, Nebraska, on October 24, 1904. He was buried in Ft. McPherson National Cemetery just south of Maxwell, Nebraska.

James B. Martin

Further Reading

Hanna, Charles W. *African American Recipients of the Medal of Honor: A Biographical Dictionary, Civil War through Vietnam War.* Jefferson, NC: McFarland, 2002.

Leckie, William H. *The Buffalo Soldiers: A Narrative of the Negro Cavalry in the West.* Norman: University of Oklahoma Press, 1967.

Schubert, Frank N. *Black Valor: Buffalo Soldiers and the Medal of Honor, 1870–1898.* Wilmington, DE: Scholarly Resources, 1997.

Utley, Robert M. *Frontier Regulars: The United States Army and the Indian, 1866–1890.* New York: Macmillan, 1973.

Lafayette, James

Born: 1748
Died: August 9, 1830
Home State: Virginia
Service: Continental Army
Conflict: Revolutionary War
Age at Time of Award: NA

James Lafayette worked as a double agent during the American Revolution. Originally named James Armistead, he adopted "Lafayette" as his surname.

Lafayette was born into slavery on William Armistead's farm in New Kent County, Virginia, in 1748. William Armistead gave him permission to join the Marquis de Lafayette's army in 1781. The Marquis de Lafayette was particularly impressed with James Armistead's memory and intelligence and sent him into British camps to collect intelligence. He posed as a camp worker, first with Benedict Arnold's troops and later with the men of Lord Cornwallis. He became a trusted servant and was privy to confidential conversations between the officers. He then passed on the information to other African Americans who passed the details on to the Marquis de Lafayette.

Cornwallis sent Armistead to spy on the Marquis de Lafayette, and so his work as a double agent began, but he remained loyal to the American cause. It is widely believed that without the information he provided, George Washington would not have won at Yorktown. In 1784, the Marquis de Lafayette wrote a certificate detailing Armistead's work and imploring that Virginia grant him his freedom. He was finally freed in 1787, by which time he had taken Lafayette's name as his own surname. Twenty-three years later, Virginia awarded James Lafayette a pension for his war contribution.

It is also widely believed that James Lafayette was instrumental in convincing the Marquis to press George Washington to free slaves. The Marquis de Lafayette did sponsor the Society of the Friends of the Blacks in Paris. The Marquis returned to America for the last time in 1824, when he had his final meeting with the 76-year-old James Lafayette. At this time James Lafayette, dressed in an American uniform, sat for a portrait, the only known image of a man who had played such a vital role during the American Revolution.

James Lafayette died at the age of 82 on August 9, 1830.

Jonathan D. Sutherland

Further Reading

Davis, Burke. *Black Heroes of the American Revolution.* San Diego: Harcourt Brace Jovanovich, 1991.

Kaplan, Sydney, and Emma Nogrady Kaplan. *The Black Presence in the Era of the American Revolution.* Amherst: University of Massachusetts Press, 1989.

Ploski, Harry A., and James Williams. *The Negro Almanac: A Reference Work on the African American.* New York: Bellwether, 1983.

Langhorn, Garfield M.

Born: September 10, 1948
Died: January 15, 1969
Home State: New York
Service: Army
Conflict: Vietnam War
Age at Time of Award: 20

Garfield M. Langhorn was born in Cumberland, Virginia, on September 10, 1948. At some point, his family moved to New York, as Langhorn attended high school at Riverhead High School, in Riverhead, New York, on Long Island. Langhorn graduated from Riverhead High School in 1967 and enlisted in the U.S. Army at Brooklyn, New York. Langhorn was deployed to Vietnam with the 7th Squadron (Airmobile), 17th Cavalry of the 1st Aviation Brigade in 1968. He was assigned to Troop C as a radio operator and performed downed aircraft recovery missions with a special unit nicknamed the "Blues." On January 15, 1969, a Cobra attack helicopter operating near Plei Djereng in Plieku Province was hit by enemy fire and crashed on a forested hillside. The Blues, with PFC Langhorn as the radio operator, were dispatched to rescue the crew or recover their bodies if they were deceased. The platoon landed near the crash site and moved to recover the bodies of the two pilots who were both killed in the crash. PFC Langhorn was orchestrating the communication with the command and control helicopter when the platoon came under attack from North Vietnam Army soldiers on the nearby hillsides. He called for fire support from the Cobra gunships overhead and directed their minigun fire against the enemy positions. With night closing in, the supporting fire became impossible because of low visibility and the platoon settled into a small, dangerous perimeter under fire from enemy bunker positions to their left and right. As the enemy began to probe the platoon's position, a grenade landed in front of PFC Langhorn very close to wounded members of the platoon. Seeing the danger, PFC Langhorn surged forward from his position between the platoon leader and another soldier and pulled the grenade under his body before it could explode and kill his fellow soldiers. PFC Garfield M. Langhorn died that day in Vietnam but saved the lives of numerous other troopers of his platoon. All the other members of Troop C on the landing zone that day survived, largely based on Langhorn's actions. In recognition of his valor and sacrifice, on April 7, 1970, President Richard M. Nixon presented the Medal of Honor to his mother, Mary Langhorn, as a posthumous representation of the country's gratitude. PFC Langhorn is honored on the wall of the Vietnam Veterans Memorial on Panel 34W, Row 009. He has also been honored by induction into the Army Aviation Hall of Fame in 1998. In the years after PFC Langhorn's death, the community of Riverhead has sought multiple ways to honor him. After working with local politicians for some time, the city was successful in getting the U.S. Congress to name the post office in Riverhead in Langhorn's honor. On September 27, 2010, the building was officially named the Private First Class Garfield M. Langhorn Post Office Building. As part of that honor, a bronze bust of PFC Langhorn is in a grassy area next to the post office. After a number of years during which the students at Pulaski Street School competed for prizes in a writing contest about his heroism, the library at the school was named the Garfield M. Langhorn Memorial Library on January 25, 2011. More recently, the street where Langhorn grew up in Riverhead, Maple Street, has been rededicated in his honor. Private First Class Garfield M. Langhorn is buried in Riverhead Cemetery in the town that continues to find ways to honor his courage.

James B. Martin

Further Reading

Hanna, Charles W. *African American Recipients of the Medal of Honor: A Biographical Dictionary, Civil War through Vietnam War.* Jefferson, NC: McFarland, 2002.

Westheider, James E. *The African American Experience in Vietnam: Brothers in Arms*. New York: Rowman & Littlefield, 2008.

Westheider, James E. *Fighting on Two Fronts: African Americans and the Vietnam War*. New York: New York University Press, 1997.

Lee, Fitz

Born: June 1866
Died: September 14, 1899
Home State: Virginia
Service: Army
Conflict: Spanish-American War
Age at Time of Award: 32

Fitz Lee was born in Dinwiddie County, Virginia, in June 1866. In the late 1860s, he moved to Philadelphia and worked until he enlisted in the army in 1889. He was a veteran at the time of the Spanish-American War, serving his third enlistment with Troop M of the 10th Cavalry. He and a number of other Buffalo Soldiers were assigned to a mission led by Lieutenant Carter P. Johnson, a former enlisted man with over two decades of experience in the army. The unit was given the task of resupplying and reinforcing Cuban rebels operating behind Spanish lines. After an abortive attempt to land the nearly 400 Cuban insurgents at an initial location, Johnson settled on landing near the small settlement of Tayabacoa. On June 30, 1898, a landing party of 300 insurgents and 28 American troopers attempted to land in the face of a blockhouse at the mouth of the Tayabacoa River. They were met with intense fire, despite supporting fires from a gunboat accompanying the naval landing vessels. The attacking force never seized a beachhead and they were forced to withdraw at night, but lacked the necessary boats to transport everyone, having lost at least two boats to Spanish cannon fire. Two wounded Americans and a number of wounded Cuban insurgents were stranded in the water at the shoreline.

The Cuban insurgent forces attempted to rescue the trapped men, only to have four successive rescue missions fail in the face of Spanish defensive fire. At the urging of his 10th Cavalry Troopers, Johnson eventually agreed to allow one additional attempt to rescue the stranded men. Five Americans, including Lee, were selected to carry out the rescue. Moving their landing boat through the water as quietly as possible, because the Spanish garrison was still on high alert for such a rescue mission, the five men made it to the wounded men and pulled them into the boat. As the Spanish positions poured fire into the ocean, the party successfully rescued the stranded men and returned to the *Florida* safely. Lieutenant Johnson is quoted as saying that the "rescue was pronounced by all who witnessed it, as a brave and gallant deed, and deserving of reward."

In early 1899, Lieutenant Johnson would petition the War Department for proper acknowledgment of the heroic actions of the five troopers at Tayabacoa.

The War Department made the decision quickly and determined that the four Buffalo Soldiers deserved the Medal of Honor. This is very interesting in hindsight, as these would be the last Medals of Honor awarded to black soldiers until well after World War II. No black soldiers were awarded the Medal of Honor during World War I or World War II, apparently due to the pervasive racism in the military during the intervening years. A number of black soldiers were belatedly honored in the 1990s for their actions during the two world wars.

Fitz Lee had returned to Texas with a portion of the 10th Cavalry and received his award on June 23, 1899, while recovering in the hospital at Ft. Bliss, Texas. He had suffered a decline in health since the deployment to Cuba and had begun to complain about problems with his eyesight shortly after the rescue mission. By June 1899, his health had deteriorated to the point where he could no longer serve, as he was suffering from a variety of ailments, including swollen limbs and abdominal pains. He was discharged from the army at Ft. Bliss in July 1899. He traveled to Ft. Leavenworth, Kansas, to visit a former Buffalo Soldier, Charles Taylor. Taylor and his wife, Cora, looked after Fitz Lee during his final days in the summer of 1899. He passed away on September 14, 1899, and was buried at the Ft. Leavenworth National Cemetery with full military honors. His grave is found at Section G, Site 3183. The post theater at Ft. Leavenworth is named Fitz Lee Hall in his honor.

James B. Martin

Further Reading

Hanna, Charles W. *African American Recipients of the Medal of Honor: A Biographical Dictionary, Civil War through Vietnam War.* Jefferson, NC: McFarland, 2002.

Johnson, Edward A. *History of Negro Soldiers in the Spanish-American War and Other Items of Interest.* Raleigh, NC: Capital Printing Company, 1899.

Schubert, Frank N. *Black Valor: Buffalo Soldiers and the Medal of Honor, 1870–1898.* Wilmington, DE: Scholarly Resources, 1997.

Schubert, Frank N. "Buffalo Soldiers at San Juan Hill." 1998 Conference of Army Historians. http://www.history.army.mil/documents/spanam/BSSJH/Shbrt-BSSJH.htm (accessed September 1, 2013).

Leonard, Matthew

Born: November 26, 1929
Died: February 28, 1967
Home State: Alabama
Service: Army
Conflict: Vietnam War
Age at Time of Award: 37

Leonard was born in Eutaw, Alabama, on November 26, 1929, and entered service in Birmingham, Alabama. He served in Vietnam as a platoon sergeant with Company B, 1st Battalion, 16th Infantry Regiment, 3rd Brigade, 1st Infantry Division.

On February 23, 1967, the 1st Battalion was airlifted from its base camp at Lai Khe to Suoi Da, where it was assigned to act as the reserve for the 3rd Brigade and to hold defensive lines at Suoi Da, Republic of Vietnam. Early the next day, the battalion received 120 rounds of mortar fire. Two men were killed and five were wounded. Six hours later, the battalion was airlifted to Route 4, north of Suoi Da, where the men took up night positions six kilometers south of Prek Klok. The battalion's mission was to secure the road and carry out search-and-destroy operations.

At 8:00 AM on February 28, Company B left the battalion's position and proceeded east. Only 2.5 kilometers ahead of the company was a stream called Prek Klok; the men never reached it. Company B advanced a little more than one kilometer, and at 10:30 AM, the 3rd Platoon engaged the enemy, who was supported by three concealed machine guns. Captain Donald S. Ulm of Company B marked the position of his men with colored smoke to enable the supporting artillery to fire. About 20 minutes after the 3rd Platoon made initial contact with the enemy, communication with it was lost. Ulm directed the 1st Platoon to move to the left to prevent the 3rd from being flanked, and the 2nd Platoon moved to the right. At 12:30 PM contact was reestablished, and the company now formed an arc with the 3rd in the center. Air strikes were now hitting the enemy positions. At 1:00 PM, the 2nd Platoon detected an enemy attempt to encircle the company, and elements of the 1st and 2nd Platoons were moved northwest and southwest. By 2:00 PM the battle had begun to die down, and the U.S. Air Force had flown 54 sorties in the engagement. At 2:30 PM, two other companies reinforced the northeast. These men now moved to assist Ulm. At approximately 3:00 PM, they lost contact with the enemy. At 4:45 PM, a third company landed and secured a landing zone. Ulm's men did not reach the landing zone until 9:30 PM that evening; they brought with them 25 dead and 28 wounded soldiers. A sweep of the area revealed that 167 enemy troops had been killed.

Among those killed was Platoon Sergeant Matthew Leonard, who would receive the Medal of Honor for organizing the platoon's defensive position, redistributing ammunition, and leading his comrades after the platoon leader was wounded in the initial stages of the Battle of Prek Klok.

The story that was told when Ulm's unit reached the landing zone chronicled the heroism displayed by Leonard and the role he played in keeping the casualties from being even worse. As was often the case in Vietnam, among the first soldiers hit when the enemy suddenly unleashed the withering fire was the platoon leader. Other key leaders were wounded in close succession and Platoon Sergeant Leonard assumed command of the unit. The unit was able to withstand the initial onslaught and bought precious time to create a makeshift defensive position. Moving swiftly among his men, Leonard saw to the critical elements of organizing the hasty position, redistributing what ammunition they had, and motivating the soldiers to prepare them for what was certainly to come next. Seeing a wounded soldier who had not been secured inside the perimeter, Leonard left the position and dragged the wounded man to safety. This effort cost him the use of his left hand, as it was rendered useless by a sniper's bullet. The expected second assault again came suddenly and Leonard moved around the position, directing fire and leading his platoon by example. During this attack, the enemy used the distraction of their main attack on one side of the defensive position to move a heavy machine gun to an elevated position that could easily engage the entire perimeter. As Platoon Sergeant Leonard moved to deal with this threat, the platoon machine gun assigned in this sector of the perimeter malfunctioned. The crew was working to clear the weapon jam when he was able to crawl to their assistance, but as he arrived, the gunner and his crew were hit by fire from the North Vietnamese machine gun and rendered helpless. Knowing that the unit could not survive with an automatic weapon raking the perimeter, Platoon Sergeant Leonard charged the North Vietnamese position and quieted the gun and its crew. Unfortunately, while he was quick enough to kill the entire crew, he was hit repeatedly during his attack and lost the ability to continue to move. Propping himself up the best he could against a tree, Leonard continued to engage the North Vietnamese until his wounds finally proved fatal. His heroic actions in destroying the machine gun position saved the platoon and motivated the unit to hold its defensive position until the reinforcements arrived.

President Lyndon B. Johnson presented Platoon Sergeant Leonard's Medal of Honor to his widow Lois on December 19, 1968. He is buried in the Ft. Mitchell National Cemetery in Ft. Mitchell, Alabama. Platoon Sergeant Leonard is memorialized on Panel 15E, Row 119 of the Vietnam Veterans Memorial.

James B. Martin and Jonathan D. Sutherland

Further Reading

Rogers, Bernard William. *Vietnam Studies Cedar Falls—Junction City: A Turning Point.* Washington, DC: Department of the Army, 1989.

Westheider, James E. *The African American Experience in Vietnam: Brothers in Arms.* New York: Rowman & Littlefield, 2008.

Westheider, James E. *Fighting on Two Fronts: African Americans and the Vietnam War.* New York: New York University Press, 1997.

Long, Donald Russell

Born: August 27, 1939
Died: June 30, 1966
Home State: Ohio
Service: Army
Conflict: Vietnam War
Age at Time of Award: 26

Donald Russell Long was born in Blackfork, Ohio, a small community in the southern Ohio county of Lawrence. His parents were Mr. and Mrs. Herman Long. He entered service on April 16, 1963, after being drafted while living in Ashland, Kentucky, and after basic training and advanced individual training, joined Troop C, 4th Cavalry, 1st Infantry Division at Ft. Riley, Kansas. Long's entire unit was deployed to the Republic of Vietnam together in the fall of 1965.

On June 30, 1966, Sergeant Long's unit was conducting a reconnaissance mission in Bình Long Province when a Viet Cong regiment attacked them. The enemy unit was heavily armed, with machine guns, recoilless rifles, and mortars, firing from covered and concealed positions along the road that Troops B and C were following. During the ensuing combat, Sergeant Long disregarded his own safety in order to save the lives of his fellow troopers who were wounded in the ambush. He repeatedly abandoned his armored personnel carrier and carried wounded cavalrymen to a landing zone so that they could be evacuated. The entire time he was in the ambush area recovering wounded soldiers, he was exposed to deadly enemy fire. Fighting forward to provide much-needed ammunition and supplies to the advanced elements of the troop, Sergeant Long again exposed himself to mortal danger by leaving the relative safety of his armored vehicle and providing resupply to the troopers, though he was constantly in danger from what his citation for valor referred to as "enemy fire at point blank range." During an assault on the Viet Cong positions, Long continued his valorous conduct and served as an inspiration to keep the rest of the troop fighting. He stood up without protection to gain a better line of fire at enemy soldiers attempting to board his armored vehicle, denying them access to the personnel carrier. Though he had fought the Viet Cong off of his own vehicle, another personnel carrier nearby was not as successful and Long moved to rescue the wounded men from this disabled carrier. While trying to reorganize some of the wounded that could still fight, Sergeant Long saw a grenade fall on the deck of armored personnel carrier where they were and leaped into action. Though he shouted an alarm to warn everyone, the clamor of the battle kept at least one man from hearing him, so Long pushed him to safety. Still knowing that the explosion would kill several of his men, Sergeant Long threw his body on the grenade and pulled it to him as it went off. His actions absorbed the blast and saved the lives of the men on the carrier deck and the man he pushed off, a total of eight troopers. Sergeant Donald Long's actions are those of a true hero. He fought his enemy to a standstill through cunning and courage and in the end made the ultimate sacrifice to save the lives of his comrades. For his courage and self-sacrifice, he received the Medal of Honor.

Sergeant Donald Russell Long's Medal of Honor was presented posthumously to his family on February 8, 1968. The Secretary of the Army presided at the Pentagon ceremony and praised the courage of this fine American. Sergeant Long was buried in the tiny Union Baptist Church Cemetery in his hometown of Blackfork, Ohio. He is memorialized on the Vietnam Veterans Memorial on Panel 8E, Row 112.

James B. Martin

Further Reading

Hanna, Charles W. *African American Recipients of the Medal of Honor: A Biographical Dictionary, Civil War through Vietnam War*. Jefferson, NC: McFarland, 2002.

Westheider, James E. *The African American Experience in Vietnam: Brothers in Arms*. New York: Rowman & Littlefield, 2008.

Westheider, James E. *Fighting on Two Fronts: African Americans and the Vietnam War*. New York: New York University Press, 1997.

McBryar, William

Born: February 14, 1861
Died: March 8, 1941
Home State: North Carolina
Service: Army
Conflict: Indian Wars, Spanish-American War, Philippine Insurrection
Age at Time of Award: 29

William McBryar was born on February 14, 1861, in Elizabethtown, North Carolina. After growing up in North Carolina, he attended college in Tennessee for three years and spoke Spanish and a bit of Latin. He was, for his time period, a well-educated African American in a country that had little opportunity for such men.

McBryan opted to join the 10th Cavalry Regiment of the famed Buffalo Soldiers in early 1887, choosing a career as a soldier in the African American regular army unit over the prejudice he found in the civilian world. His education and a strong character proved to be excellent qualities in the 10th Cavalry, and McBryar was successful in his chosen pursuit. By his second enlistment in Troop K, he was the troop first sergeant and highly regarded by his officers and men. He saw service with the 10th Cavalry around the San Carlos, Arizona, reservation that housed the Chiricahua Apaches after the surrender of Geronimo. This was very hard duty, with inhospitable conditions and long stretches of tedious boredom interspersed with tough rides to capture renegade Apache groups. On one such tough ride, First Sergeant McBryar distinguished himself and become one of the 10th Cavalry's greatest heroes.

In early March 1890, William McBryar's unit was stationed at Ft. Thomas, near the San Carlos Reservation, when word was received that a small raiding party of Apaches had ambushed a freight wagon and killed the man driving it. The commander of the Department of Arizona, General Benjamin Grierson, directed the 10th Cavalry to hunt down the perpetrators and bring them to justice. A small group of troopers, numbering only about 10 men, departed Ft. Thomas with one officer and First Sergeant McBryar in charge. They found the dead wagon driver and, meeting up with Indian scouts and a group of white cavalrymen, set off in pursuit of the small group of Apaches.

This small task force chased the band of Apaches, now estimated as only about five warriors, for five days and over 200 miles. This chase was over extremely rough country and wore down the troopers and their horses, but they pressed on. On March 7, 1890, they finally trapped the Apache raiding party in a canyon on the Salt River. The raiding party had discarded their horses to move into terrain unsuited for horses and the cavalrymen were forced to do the same. The Apaches took cover in a cave and chose to fight it out with the army from there. It was a tough fight and no progress was being made until First Sergeant McBryar maneuvered himself, under fire, to a spot where he could ricochet bullets into the cave off a flat rock at its front. He killed two of the five Apaches and the other three chose to surrender rather than die also.

McBryar's ingenuity and courage under fire were recognized by the 10th Cavalry and the army when he received the Medal of Honor for his actions at Salt River. His award was unique in the period of the Indian Wars, as it was awarded to him in May 1890, for an action that occurred in March of that same year. It was not unusual for such awards to take 10 to 15 years from the date of action until the Buffalo Soldier was recognized, but McBryar's actions were apparently so distinguished that the recommendation was approved in almost record time.

McBryar left the 10th Cavalry in 1893, transferring to the 25th Infantry Regiment as a new private. By 1898, he had risen again to the rank of quartermaster sergeant and was set to deploy to Cuba with the 25th to fight in the Spanish-American War. McBryar wanted to become a commissioned officer and every officer he had ever worked for supported him in this endeavor. He secured such a commission in the new 3rd North Carolina Volunteer Infantry Regiment, but the unit had not mustered into service yet when he was forced to deploy with the 25th to Cuba. He once again fought with distinction in Cuba and was with Company H, 25th Infantry, when it took the summit of El Caney, a hill situated close by San Juan Hill. With only one officer in Company H, McBryar was made the platoon leader of 2nd Platoon and performed the duties of a lieutenant during the fight at El Caney and the remainder of his time in Cuba. He was once again recommended for a commission and, in August 1898, he was made a lieutenant in the 8th Volunteer Infantry.

Volunteer infantry units were not part of the regular army, and once they were mustered out of service, the officers and men were simply out of the army. This is exactly what happened to the 8th Volunteers in March 1899, and McBryar reenlisted in the 25th Infantry Regiment to stay in service, beginning again as a private as the regiment headed to the Philippines to fight against the insurrection. He was quickly promoted to the sergeant major of his battalion but did not enjoy his four years in the Philippines. He continued to seek appointment as a commissioned officer in the regular army but was rebuffed at every turn. Before finishing his tour in the Philippines, he was again commissioned as a lieutenant in the 49th Volunteer Infantry Regiment, only to see the regiment mustered out in June 1900.

William McBryar wanted to stay in the army, but his options were extremely limited. The only possibilities presented to him by the War Department involved service in the Philippines again, which he sought to avoid. He lived for over three years in North Carolina, trying to make a living in the civilian world, but the lure of army life continued. His only option for service, by 1905, was to rejoin the Buffalo Soldiers as a private in the 9th Cavalry Regiment. He served with the unit at Ft. Leavenworth, Kansas, for less than a year until the wear and tear that his body had sustained during his military tenure made it impossible for him to serve as a regular soldier in a cavalry unit. He again left the army, never again to put on the uniform.

McBryar married in 1906 and worked at a long list of jobs in the civilian world, including a stint as a watchman at Arlington National Cemetery in Washington, D.C. Predictably, he offered himself to the government for service during World War I, but was informed that he was too old. In the end, his long years of service and the valor that he showed at the Salt River led to no long-term benefits for William McBryar, and by 1933, he was unable to work or care for himself. He lived his final years with his sister in Philadelphia, passing away on March 8, 1941. He was buried in the sacred place that he once watched over, occupying a grave in the hallowed ground of Arlington National Cemetery at Section 4, Lot 2738-B. He is identified on the grave marker as 1st Lieutenant William McBryar, a small touch that he might well find satisfying.

William McBryar's short stint at Ft. Leavenworth, Kansas, provided the opening for the modern army to honor him one last time. Home to the Buffalo Soldiers for many years, and the site of the beautiful Buffalo Soldiers' Monument, Ft. Leavenworth is the home of the army's Command and General Staff College. On March 21,

2009, William McBryar was inducted into the Ft. Leavenworth Hall of Fame, one of three noncommissioned officers ever inducted into the elite group. McBryar's photo is seen by hundreds of army officers every day as they pass it in the halls, situated alongside such well-known names as Douglas MacArthur, Dwight Eisenhower, George Patton, Colin Powell, and fellow Medal of Honor recipient Roger Donlon. His story lives on at Ft. Leavenworth, his final military home.

James B. Martin

Further Reading

Johnson, Tisha. "NCOs Inducted into Fort Leavenworth Hall of Fame." Fort Leavenworth Lamp. http://www.army.mil/article/21394/ (accessed September 1, 2013).

Leckie, William H. *The Buffalo Soldiers: A Narrative of the Negro Cavalry in the West.* Norman: University of Oklahoma Press, 1967.

Rickey, Don, Jr. *Forty Miles a Day on Beans and Hay: The Enlisted Soldier Fighting the Indian Wars.* Norman: University of Oklahoma Press, 1963.

Schubert, Frank N. *Black Valor: Buffalo Soldiers and the Medal of Honor, 1870–1898.* Wilmington, DE: Scholarly Resources, 1997.

Utley, Robert M. *Frontier Regulars: The United States Army and the Indian, 1866–1890.* New York: Macmillan, 1973.

McDade, Aubrey L., Jr.

Born: 1981
Home State: Texas
Service: Marine Corps
Conflict: Operation Iraqi Freedom
Age at Time of Award: 23

Aubrey McDade was born in Houston, Texas, and grew up in the rough parts of Ft. Worth and Dallas. His mother raised him by herself after his father was shot and killed in Ft. Worth when Aubrey was 11 years old. Pushing forward when others of his community did not, he became the first member of his family to graduate from high school and then tried to find a way to attend college and prepare himself for a better life. After graduating from Western Hills High School and finding every path to college blocked, McDade eventually met a Marine Corps recruiter and decided to join the Corps for a few years to prepare himself for life and then return to Ft. Worth and his family. He enlisted in November 1999, and was shipped to basic entry training at Marine Corps Recruit Depot, San Diego, where he got his first taste of Marine Corps life. While McDade had initially intended to just do his four-year enlistment and then leave the marines, his intentions were complicated by the terrorist attacks on September 11, 2001. The American reaction to Afghanistan and the follow-on involvement in Iraq left McDade in a position of wanting to help his family back in Ft. Worth, but not wanting to leave his young marines as they were going to the Middle East and combat. He reenlisted in the Corps and did his first tour of duty in Iraq from March to November 2003, near the northern city of Mosul. Returning to the United States, he did a tour of duty as a drill instructor and returned to Iraq in June 2004, as a machine gun squad leader with 1st Battalion, 8th Regiment, 1st Marine Division. Participating in the Second Battle of Fallujah, McDade and his unit were patrolling on the night of November 11, 2004, when they came under heavy fire in a narrow alley. Three marines were instantly struck and fell in the alley, exposed to heavy enemy fire. McDade's first reaction was to turn his machine guns toward the sound of the guns and return fire to suppress the enemy positions. As he looked out into the alley in front of his guns, he could not leave the three marines lying there and exposed to further fire. He turned to his platoon sergeant and indicated that he was going after the marines, only to be told that if he was hit trying it the platoon would not be able to come to his rescue. Understanding the risk, but unable to leave the marines there, McDade ran exposed into the alley and knelt to grab the first marine. He called for him to loosen his gear and hoisted him up to his shoulder, running back across the alley to the cover of the up-armored Humvees protecting the remainder of the unit. Though bullets had hit all around him on his first foray into the alley, McDade returned a second and third time to retrieve the other two marines who were hit in the initial contact. He then supervised the provision of first aid to the men and aided in removing the entire unit from danger. His actions saved the lives of the two marines who were not killed in the initial burst of fire and retrieved the body of the one who had been instantly killed. Sgt. Aubrey McDade was originally recommended for the Silver Star for his actions, but through the work of supporters, the commendation was eventually upgraded to the Navy Cross. After leaving Iraq, McDade was again assigned as a drill instructor, this time at Parris Island, South Carolina. He received the Navy Cross at a recruit graduation ceremony at Marine Corps Recruit Depot, Parris Island, on January 19, 2007. Members of his platoon from Camp Lejeune were present and honored to see him receive the Navy Cross they were convinced he deserved. McDade was later honored by being invited to join First Lady Laura Bush at the State of the Union Address on January 23, 2007. When McDade was asked if he told his recruits about his Navy Cross, he remarked that he did not until well into basic training. He indicated that he wanted them to respect him as a drill instructor before they found out about his medal. Always humble, Sgt. McDade continues to reflect that he would give up his Navy Cross to bring back the one marine he could not save. As of this writing, Sgt. McDade continues to serve in the U.S. Marine Corps.

James B. Martin

Further Reading

Dye, Julia. *Backbone: History, Traditions, and Leadership Lessons of Marine Corps NCOs.* New York: Open Road Media, 2013.

Lowry, Richard S. *New Dawn: The Battles for Fallujah.* Havertown, PA: Casemate Publishing, 2010.

Miller, Doris (Dorie)

Born: October 12, 1919
Died: November 24, 1943
Home State: Texas
Service: Navy
Conflict: World War II
Age at Time of Award: 22

Doris Miller was born in Waco, Texas, on October 12, 1919. He was the third of four sons born to Connery and Henrietta Miller, who lived on a small family farm.

Dorie Miller receives the Navy Cross. (Library of Congress)

He is today more commonly known as Dorie, a name which he gained either through a nickname in the navy or a misspelling in a newspaper article after he displayed an unending courage at Pearl Harbor. He attended A. J. Moore Academy in Waco, but even though he excelled at athletics, academics did not turn out to be a good fit for Miller and he eventually dropped out of school. He enlisted in the U.S. Navy on September 16, 1939, after unsuccessfully trying to join the Civilian Conservation Corps and tiring of working on the family farm. At that time, the only jobs open to African Americans in the navy were mess attendants and cooks, and Miller was sent to Norfolk, Virginia, for basic training and advanced training as a mess attendant. He was initially assigned to an ammunition ship, but on January 2, 1940, he was transferred to the battleship USS *West Virginia* (BB48). Doris Miller was still assigned to the *West Virginia* on December 7, 1941. By then, this large African American sailor had become the ship's heavyweight boxing champion and had been promoted to Ship's Cook, Third Class.

Miller awoke on that fateful day at 6:00 AM and was going about his duties when the call to general quarters sounded. The ship almost instantly took torpedo hits from aircraft off the Japanese carrier *Akagi*. Miller moved quickly to his general quarters battle station at the antiaircraft magazine amidships but found that it had been destroyed by one of the initial torpedoes. Needing a task to do amid the chaos, Miller moved to the main deck and was immediately put to work moving wounded seamen due to his size and strength. At one point, an officer grabbed him and took him to the bridge, where the ship's captain had been badly wounded. Unwilling to be removed from the bridge of his ship, Miller carried his captain to a less-exposed position and turned to get further orders. Two officers ordered him to accompany them, in order for Miller to serve as a loader on the .50 caliber antiaircraft machine guns on the conning tower. Miller had never fired a machine gun like these before, but when one of the officers hesitated over something else, he began to open fire on the Japanese aircraft attacking his ship. Miller would later indicate that he believed he had shot down one of the Japanese aircraft. When the guns ran out of ammunition, Miller again was ordered to move the captain to a safer location, though his commander was destined to die on the *West Virginia* that day. Eventually, the Japanese were able to hit the *West Virginia* with enough armor-piercing bombs and 18-inch torpedoes to cause her to list and begin to sink. The crew saved the ship by flooding specific compartments to restore balance and the *West Virginia* settled to the harbor bottom upright. Miller, along with the remaining crew, abandoned ship, but not until after he had moved more injured sailors to the quarterdeck where they could be rescued. Doris Miller's actions, on one of America's most infamous days, saved the lives of many navy personnel and were an image of courage and tenacity.

When the navy report on Pearl Harbor was released on January 1, 1943, there was a single commendation for an unnamed Negro sailor. That sailor was Doris Miller and the African American community at home had their first World War II hero. The NAACP and other organizations lobbied President Roosevelt to reward Miller with the Distinguished Service Cross and some in Congress pushed for the Medal of Honor. The African American press pushed forward to support honors for Miller, as they saw the opportunities that the war would provide to move the situation of African Americans in the United States forward in a positive way. The African American community in the United States needed its own heroes and the navy would not stand in the way. The Secretary of the Navy commended Miller in a letter on April 1, 1942, and referred to him as one of the "first heroes of World

War II." On May 27, 1942, Admiral Chester W. Nimitz, the commander in chief of the Pacific Fleet, gathered the crew of the USS *Enterprise* and presented Doris Miller the Navy Cross for gallantry in combat. This award was the third highest the navy could award in 1942 and Miller became the first African American to ever receive the award.

Some still pushed for Miller to receive the Medal of Honor, but that campaign was doomed to failure, as no African American received the award during World War II. The Shaw University study that was conducted decades later only examined the records of army personnel, so Miller was not considered. Miller returned to the United States for a period of time, as many white and African American war heroes would do, to participate in a war bond drive and to speak to audiences around the country. After one such trip on May 15, 1943, now a petty officer, Ship's Cook Third Class, Miller reported to Puget Sound Navy Yard, in Bremerton, Washington, to join his new ship, the escort carrier USS *Liscome Bay* (CVE-56). The *Liscome Bay* joined the fleet that was bound to attack the Makin and Tarawa Atolls in the Gilbert Islands. From November 20 to 23, 1943, aircraft from the *Liscome Bay* participated in onshore operations providing supporting fires. The next day, on November 24, the ship was cruising near a small island in the chain, when it was hit from a single torpedo fired by a Japanese submarine. The torpedo was well placed and tore directly into the ship's aircraft bomb magazine, causing a catastrophic explosion and the *Liscome Bay* sank to the bottom of the sea in moments. Of the 900 sailors on board, only 272 were rescued and Doris Miller was not among them. He was presumed dead and listed as missing in action.

Doris Miller was one of the first heroes in America's biggest war and was the only African American hero in the initial years. He has been honored in so many ways since his actions on December 7, 1941, that a list here is impractical. He was immortalized for current generations through Cuba Gooding Jr.'s portrayal of him in the 2001 film *Pearl Harbor* and was portrayed by other actors in similar movies over the years. The Doris Miller Foundation was founded in 1947 to reward outstanding actions in the field of race relations. The navy used Miller's likeness on a World War II recruiting poster and then named a Knox-class frigate, the USS *Miller* (FF-1091), after him on June 30, 1973. They have since dedicated the Bachelor Enlisted Quarters after him at Great Lakes Naval Base, named a housing community for officers after him in Maui, and even named the galley at Camp Lemonnier, Djibouti, in his honor. Between the Veteran's Administration and the American Legion, he has been honored at least five times and he has at least five schools and three streets named in his honor. One of his most recent honors came when the U.S. Postal Service chose him as one of four Distinguished Sailors of the 20th century and placed his likeness on a commemorative stamp.

Doris (Dorie) Miller was a well-known hero during World War II and because of the movies, books, and various honors listed previously, he has continued to be a constant reminder of the bravery and courage of African American warriors of all services.

James B. Martin

Further Reading

"Cook Third Class Doris Miller USN." Washington, D.C.: Naval History and Heritage Command. http://www.history.navy.mil/faq57–4.htm (accessed August 25, 2013).

Goodwin, Doris Kearns. *No Ordinary Time.* New York: Simon and Schuster, 1994.

O'Neal, Bill. *Doris Miller: Hero of Pearl Harbor.* Waco, TX: Eakin Press, 2007.

Washburn, Patrick S. *A Question of Sedition.* New York: Oxford University Press, 1986.

Olive, Milton Lee, III

Born: November 7, 1946
Died: October 22, 1965
Home State: Illinois
Service: Army
Conflict: Vietnam War
Age at Time of Award: 18

Milton Lee Olive III was born on November 7, 1946, an only child whose mother died very soon after his birth. Before Olive joined the army in 1964 in Chicago, Illinois, he had assisted civil rights workers in Mississippi, encouraging other African Americans to register to vote. Only a few years before, Emmett Till (also from Chicago) had been lynched in the area. When Olive's family heard of his activities, his father took him back to Chicago.

Olive began his tour of duty on Saturday, June 5, 1965. From Vietnam, where he served as a private first class, in Company B, 2nd Battalion (Airborne), 503rd Infantry, 173rd Airborne Brigade, he wrote to his father, not mentioning that he had already been slightly wounded

Private First Class Milton Olive III was the first African American to receive the Medal of Honor for valor during the Vietnam War. (AP Photo)

shortly after he had joined the unit: "Just a line to say hello. . . . I'm over here in Never Never Land fighting this hellish war. You said I was crazy for joining up, well, I've gone you one better. I'm now an official U.S. Army Paratrooper. How does that grab you? I've made six jumps already."

Early in the morning of October 22, 1965, the paratroopers were inserted by helicopter into the vicinity of Phu Cuong. Soon after, the Vietnamese claimed their first kill, Private First Class George Luis, hit by a sniper's bullet. According to Olive's citation for the Medal of Honor, the unit was ambushed and "subjected to a heavy volume of enemy gunfire and pinned down temporarily, it retaliated by assaulting the Viet Cong positions, causing the enemy to flee."

Olive's comrades included Vince Yrineo, a Mexican American former sailor and career soldier, aged 36 at the time. The officer in charge, 1st Lieutenant Jimmy Stanford, had rotated in only three days before. A career soldier who had joined the army in 1954, Stanford had been an enlisted man and had taken 11 years to earn his promotion to lieutenant. His great-grandfather had been a Confederate soldier, and his father had served in France during World War I. Stanford was a white Texan whose knowledge and experience of working with African Americans was scant.

Olive and four other soldiers were moving through the jungle when an enemy soldier threw a grenade into their midst. Walking alongside Olive were two African American privates, "Hop" Foster, 19, and Lionel Hubbard, 20, who both took cover as the enemy sprang the ambush. With bullets thudding into the tree stumps around them and grenades being thrown at them, the paratroopers began to return fire.

A grenade landed a foot or so from Stanford; without a second thought, Olive grabbed the explosive and pushed it under his body, which absorbed the bulk of the impact. Olive died just 16 days before his 19th birthday. Both Yrineo and Hubbard were hit by shrapnel, and Stanford was bleeding heavily. In all, some 12 paratroopers were wounded. These casualties would surely have been significantly higher except for the courageous actions of Private Milton Olive. His Medal of Honor citation lauds his bravery and recognizes the selfless sacrifice that he showed in thinking only of the safety of his comrades.

President Lyndon B. Johnson presented Private Olive's Medal of Honor to his family in a ceremony at the White House on April 21, 1966. Olive was the first African American serviceman to receive the Medal of Honor during the Vietnam War, a fact not lost on the president or the media. The Vietnam War was the first in American history to have been waged with a totally integrated military and it occurred at a time in the nation's history when questions about racism continued to boil. President Johnson's remarks that day included his opinion that "by his heroic death, Milton Lee Olive III taught those of us who remain how we ought to live" and pointed out that "Pvt. Olive's military records have never carried the color of his skin or his racial origin—only the testimony that he was a good and loyal citizen of the United States." Many in the United States would come to disagree with the president on this issue and Olive's father, Milton Olive Sr., indicated his belief that his son's death and heroism did speak to his race. While accepting the Medal of Merit from the City of Chicago on his son's behalf, Mr. Olive pointed out to all in attendance "that the service the colored soldier has given in Vietnam has erased for all time the disparaging statements made about him."

Private Milton Olive was buried in West Grove Missionary Baptist Cemetery near Lexington, Mississippi. He was memorialized by a new park, Olive Park, at the foot of East Ohio Street and the lakefront in Chicago. The Olive monument at the park is a large concrete slab faced with a bronze plaque bearing Olive's likeness and his Medal of Honor citation. Private First Class Olive is memorialized on Panel 2E, Row 131 of the Vietnam Veterans Memorial.

Jonathan D. Sutherland

Further Reading

Westheider, James E. *The African American Experience in Vietnam: Brothers in Arms*. New York: Rowman & Littlefield, 2008.

Westheider, James E. *Fighting on Two Fronts: African Americans and the Vietnam War*. New York: New York University Press, 1997.

Williams, Michael W. *The African-American Encyclopedia*. New York: Marshall Cavendish, 1993.

Petersen, Frank E.

Born: March 2, 1932
Home State: Kansas
Service: Marine Corps
Conflict: Korean War, Vietnam War
Age at Time of Award: N/A

Petersen was born on March 2, 1932, in Topeka, Kansas. In 1951, Petersen entered the Naval Aviation Cadet Program, having joined the U.S. Navy as a seaman apprentice in June 1950. In October 1952, he was made a second lieutenant in the Marine Corps upon completion of his flight training. During the Korean War, he was assigned to Marine Fighter Squadron 212 and flew 64 combat missions, for which he received six air medals as well as the prestigious Distinguished Flying Cross. He also gained the respect and admiration of those under his command, earning the nickname "the godfather."

During his career, Petersen was inspired by two African American military pioneers. Upon joining the service, he greatly admired the achievements of Jesse Brown, the first African American navy aviator who had died courageously in North Korea. During his flight training days, Daniel "Chappie" James, who would later become the first African American four-star general, was a mentor for the young and determined aviator.

Petersen pursued higher education later in his career, funded by the military, and received a Bachelor of Science (1967) and Masters in International Affairs (1973), both from George Washington University. In 1987, Virginia Union University presented him with an Honorary Doctor of Laws degree. Other institutions he attended were the Amphibious Warfare School in Quantico, Virginia, the Aviation Safety Officers Course at the University of Southern California, and the National War College in Washington, D.C.

Petersen spent 38 years in the Marine Corps, from 1950 through July 1988. He had more than 4,000 hours in fighter and attack aircraft and had served in Korea in 1953 and Vietnam in 1968. Altogether, he took part in more than 300 combat missions. Petersen achieved a Senior Aviator designation of Silver Hawk in the marines and Gray Eagle in the navy. His tour commanding Marine Fighter Squadron 314 in Vietnam resulted in other honors for Petersen. He was presented the Legion of Merit with V device for his combat leadership and the squadron received the inaugural Robert M. Hanson Award as the best fighter attack squadron in the Marine Corps in 1968. He also received the Purple Heart for his actions in North Vietnam in 1968 when he was forced to eject from a plane engulfed in flames from enemy fire.

Frank E. Petersen achieved many firsts during his illustrious career. At just 20 years of age, he became the first African American naval aviator in the U.S. Marine Corps. Later he would become the first African American marine to command a fighter squadron, a fighter air group, an air wing, and a major U.S. Marine base. He was also the first to attain flag rank in the Marine Corps.

Frank E. Petersen retired from the Marine Corps on August 1, 1988, relinquishing his position as the commanding general of the Marine Development Education Command at Quantico, Virginia. Throughout his career, he was affiliated with various educational and research-based organizations. He has worked with the Tuskegee Airmen headquarters, served on the board of directors for the National Aviation Research and Education Foundation from 1990 to 1992, and held the position of vice president for Dupont Aviation.

Petersen continues to be an active participant in corporate and military affairs, having been named by President Obama in 2010 to serve on the Board of Visitors of the U.S. Naval Academy. His autobiography, *Into the Tiger's Jaw: America's First Black Marine Aviator*, was published in 1998 and chronicled the story of this pioneer who faced the most racist service in the Department of Defense and broke down racial barriers for other generations to follow.

Jonathan D. Sutherland

Further Reading

African American Publications. 2001. "Frank Petersen, Jr." http://www.africanpubs.com/Apps/bios/1075PetersenFrank.asp?pic=none.

Petersen, Frank E. *Into the Tiger's Jaw: America's First Black Marine Aviator—The Autobiography of Lieutenant General Frank E. Petersen*. Novato, CA: Presidio Press, 1998.

MONTFORD POINT MARINES

The story of African Americans in the military service in the United States is one of segregation, prejudice, and courage. In no branch of the military was the hill for African Americans harder to climb than in the U.S. Marine Corps. From the Revolutionary War until the early part of World War II, the Marine Corps vehemently opposed the enlistment or service of African Americans in their small, tight-knit organization. The official historians of the Marine Corps posit a variety of reasons for this fact—whether it was the smaller size of the Corps, the predominance of white southerners among the officer corps, or just an overall prejudice that allowed them to stand firmer than the other branches of service. The issue was certainly not a sea service issue, as the navy had enlisted African Americans as able-bodied seaman in the early days of the Republic. While the marines continued to exclude African Americans, the army and the navy both used them in every conflict since the Revolution. African Americans had proven time and time again that they were excellent combat warriors and capable of whatever discipline required. In the end, the Marine Corps could not stand up to the political pressure applied by President Franklin D. Roosevelt and an executive order required the Marine Corps to open enlistment to African Americans. In August 1942, the marines opened up Montford Point as a segregated training facility for African American marines on the sprawling Camp Lejeune Marine base. The site was isolated and had originally been chosen to be the base headquarters area. The first African American marines to enlist signed up on June 1, 1942. These initial enlistees, Alfred Masters and George O. Thompson, were quickly followed by more and more African Americans wanting to make their way in the U.S. Marine Corps. Though Masters and Thompson were the first to enlist, the official history indicates that Obie Hall was the first marine in the first squad of the first regular recruit platoon; unofficially making him officially the first Montford Point Marine. The Montford Point Marines trained under white officers and initially under white drill instructors. The transition to African American drill instructors progressed steadily until by mid-1943 all of the drill instructors at Montford were African Americans. The last white drill instructor left the unit in late May of that year and Sergeant "Hashmark" Johnson took his place as the field sergeant major. While this was undoubtedly good for racial harmony within the organization, it also marked the advent of even tougher training for the young recruits at Montford, as the drill instructors were determined to turn out an African American recruit as good as any white marine. As in the other services, most of the marines trained at Montford were put into support units such as ammunition companies and depot companies. Two combat units were created, the 51st and 52nd Defense Battalions, and equipped with 155m howitzers, 20mm and 40mm guns, and heavy machine guns. Units from Montford began to deploy to the Pacific Theater in early 1944, with the 51st Defense Battalion embarking from San Diego on February 11, 1944. In an oddity of the Marine Corps organization, the two combat battalions trained at Montford Point saw little or no combat, as officers concerned about their performance isolated them as separate organizations and used them to backfill white defense battalions that were sent into combat. On the other hand, the ammunition and depot companies were created to supply ammunition and other essentials to all marine units, African American or white. Montford Point Marines saw combat with these units on the Mariana Islands, Saipan, Tinian, Peleliu, Iwo Jima, and Okinawa. The first African American marine death due to enemy fire occurred in the initial landings on Saipan, as Private Kenneth J. Tibbs of the 20th Marine Depot Company was killed. While the most highly trained of the Montford Point Marines were sitting in rear areas in the 51st and 52nd, the ammunition haulers and laborers of the depot companies were exposed daily to direct combat and deadly fire. Because of the late enlistment of African Americans in the Marine Corps, and the Corps policy of not putting African American combat units into direct combat, this volume sparsely represents African American war heroes in the Marine Corps in World War II and before. Awards for valor were earned, but they were lower than they would have been for white troops performing the same feat. Two marines specifically identified in the official history, Privates James M. Whitlock and James Davis of the 36th Depot Company, earned Bronze Stars for their actions in combat on Iwo Jima on March 26, 1945. The highest decoration awarded to an African American Marine in World War II came on Saipan to a member of the 4th Ammunition Company. Private First Class Luther Woodward grew up in Mississippi. One night in December 1944, he came upon fresh tracks and followed them, surprising six Japanese soldiers. He killed one and wounded another before the others fled. Woodward returned to the marine lines and recruited other members of the company and tracked the remaining four Japanese soldiers down, killing two. For his courage and initiative, Private First Class Woodward was awarded the Bronze Star, which was later upgraded to the Silver Star. In approximately two years from the opening of Montford Point, African American marines distinguished themselves in combat, to include winning the third highest award for valor the nation has to offer. In the approximately six years that the segregated training center was in operation, nearly 20,000 African American marines were trained for combat and support duties. While they were poorly treated by the Marine Corps and the white population in North Carolina near Camp Lejeune, they never wavered. Tried in combat, the men of the support units that got their opportunities proved their metal and made "Hashmark" Johnson proud of them. Montford Point did not go down in military lore like the Tuskegee Airmen and the Buffalo Soldiers. It was largely forgotten for many years, until a group of veterans from Montford got together and created a memorial association. Today, the group is vibrant and the Montford Point Marine Association is open to all veterans. The heroes who first populated Montford Point are slowly passing, as are all of our heroes from World War II. Many stayed in the Corps; others went home to find a new life in the civilian world. Some may have driven cabs in New York City and one of them was elected Mayor of the Big Apple. Through it all, this group of patriots faced far greater challenges than other marines but braved it all to serve their country and be called marines. In recognition of this courage and sacrifice, on November 23, 2011, the president and the Congress awarded the Congressional Gold Medal to all of the African American marines who trained in the segregated camp at Montford Point. This award is the highest award for distinguished service that the nation has for civilians and honors the memory of what these men did and who they were.

James B. Martin

Pinckney, William

Born: April 27, 1915
Died: July 21, 1976
Home State: South Carolina
Service: Navy
Conflict: World War II
Age at Time of Award: 27

William Pinckney was born in Beaufort, South Carolina, on April 27, 1915. He was the son of Renty and Jenny Pinckney, though his mother passed away when he was very young and his sister, Ethel, largely raised him from the age of eight on. William attended Robert Falls Elementary School but did not find school to his liking and eventually dropped out after completing the seventh grade. His one positive result from attending to school was meeting his future wife, Henrietta. William turned to the same craft as his father, carpentry, and worked on the waterfront in Beaufort until he decided to join the navy.

William Pinckney enlisted in the navy on August 3, 1938, and was sent to Great Lakes Naval Station for initial training as a seaman. As the only jobs open to African Americans at this time were as mess attendants or cooks, William went to cook school, was promoted to Cook, Third Class, and eventually assigned to the USS *Enterprise* (CV 6). He spent a total of three years on the *Enterprise*, only leaving the famous World War II fighting ship because of injuries sustained in combat. The *Enterprise*, along with the carrier USS *Hornet*, was taking part in the Guadalcanal Campaign in the Pacific Theater when it engaged with the Japanese Navy in the Battle of Santa Cruz. The *Hornet* was sunk and the *Enterprise* came under very heavy attack by Japanese aircraft, sustaining two direct hits from aerial bombs.

The second bomb struck very close to the ammunition magazine that was William Pinckney's battle station. It caused a five-inch gun shell to explode, instantly killing four of the six sailors manning the magazine. The explosion mangled the magazine, which was situated below the hangar deck of the *Enterprise*, and left it dark and dangerous. Sharp metal edges were everywhere; exposed electrical cables dangled from what remained of the ceiling, the smell of gas filled the air, and the decks above and below the magazine were hot enough to sear human flesh. William regained consciousness and began to move to the only light he could see, which was a hatch above him leading to the hangar deck. When he arrived at the ladder, he found Gunner's Mate James Bagwell, equally stunned and now badly burned from an attempt to climb the ladder to the hangar deck above. Pinckney threw the much larger Bagwell over his shoulder and started up the ladder, only to be shocked in the dark by an exposed electrical line that caused him to lose consciousness and both men to fall back to the deck of the magazine. Once Pinckney regained consciousness for a second time, he again hoisted Bagwell on his shoulder while ignoring his own badly burned right leg, hands, and back, and got him to the hanger deck and safety. Once he had gotten his comrade to medical care, Pinckney returned to the dangerous magazine from which he had just escaped to see if any of the other members of his work crew were still alive. Finding all four sailors dead, Pinckney finally returned to the hangar deck and sought medical attention for his own wounds and burns. For his valor and willingness to place himself in danger to save the lives of fellow sailors, William Pinckney was awarded the Navy Cross, the navy's third highest award in 1942. He became one of only four African American sailors to receive the award during World War II.

Pinckney was evacuated to Hawaii for medical care and recovered from his wounds and burns there. He was reassigned to the Boat Basin in San Diego, California, travelling back to Beaufort in November 1943, to marry Henrietta and bring her back to Oceanside, California, to live. William Pinckney stayed in the navy throughout World War II, finally leaving the navy from San Diego as a Cook, First Class on June 30, 1946.

He and Henrietta moved to Brooklyn, New York, and William worked for many years as a cook with the Merchant Marine. He served on such ships as the *African Moon* and the *Sir John Franklin*, finally retiring from the Merchant Marine after 26 years. He and Henrietta moved back to Beaufort after this and he stayed there for the remainder of his life. In July 1974, Pinckney was diagnosed with spinal cancer, an illness that would eventually take his life on July 21, 1976. He was buried in the Beaufort National Cemetery, where he can be found in plot number 3381.

In February 2000, the navy decided to honor Cook, First Class, William Pinckney by naming the 41st Arleigh Burke-class destroyer built after him. The USS *Pinckney* (DDG91) was the third iteration of this name on a U.S. Navy ship and this one was specifically named to honor William Pinckney. It was built in Pascagoula, Mississippi, commissioned on May 29, 2004, and is permanently stationed at Port Hueneme, California. People who knew William Pinckney said that he was humble and never thought of himself as a hero. They have indicated that he would often say that he was just "proud to serve" and that saying is now carried on as the motto of the USS *Pinckney*. One other specific is apparently carried over to the *Pinckney* from its namesake, according to the official navy history. Evidently, Pinckney loved almost all foods except beets. To this day in his honor, beets are never served on the USS *Pinckney*.

James B. Martin

Further Reading

Navy Office of Information. "Navy Secretary Names Destroyer to Honor World War II African American Hero." Press release, February 2000. http://www.pinckney.navy.mil/PR.htm (accessed August 29, 2013).

United States Navy. *USS Pinckney*. http://www.public.navy.mil/surfor/ddg91/Pages/ourship.aspx#.Uh-MAxbJAlI (accessed August 29, 2013).

Pitts, Riley Leroy

Born: October 15, 1937
Died: October 31, 1967
Home State: Oklahoma
Service: Army
Conflict: Vietnam War
Age at Time of Award: 30

Riley Leroy Pitts was born in Fallis, Oklahoma, on October 15, 1937. He grew up in Oklahoma, but chose to attend college in Wichita, Kansas, at the Municipal University of Wichita. He graduated from this institution, now called Wichita State University, and was involved in journalism activities and the Reserve Officer Training Corps during his tenure at the school. The 1960 edition of the school yearbook indicated that he was the news editor of the student newspaper, the *Sunflower*, and was active in the military fraternity of Scabbard and Blade. Riley graduated in 1960, with a degree in journalism and was commissioned an infantry officer in the Army Reserves. He worked at Boeing Aircraft Company in Wichita while serving in the reserves until 1966. He was called to active duty as a captain that year and deployed to Vietnam, where he initially worked

President Johnson presents the Medal of Honor to the widow of Captain Riley Pitts, the first African American officer to receive the Medal during the Vietnam War. (Bettmann/Corbis)

in public information until he was given command of Company C, 2nd Battalion, 27th Infantry (Wolfhounds) assigned to the 25th Infantry Division.

On October 31, 1967, Captain Pitts was commanding his company during an airmobile assault in the Mekong Delta, near Ap Dong. As was common in Vietnam, his unit was lifted into a landing zone by helicopters and he began to move them toward their objective. A very short way from the landing zone, Captain Pitts's company began to take fire from hidden enemy positions very close at hand. He did not hesitate, but led an assault on the enemy positions and routed the Viet Cong that had attacked them. Receiving orders to move out to relieve another company that was under heavy attack, his unit came under very heavy fire from bunkers situated in the dense jungle foliage. As he turned to engage the enemy in these four bunkers, two of which were reported to be within 15 meters of his position, he found that rifle fire was ineffective because of the very heavy jungle in which he was operating. Instead, he began to use a 40 mm grenade launcher that had a much heavier projectile and engaged the enemy to pinpoint the targets for the rest of his unit. He attempted to destroy a bunker with a grenade, only to have it bounce off the heavy foliage and come to rest among his men. Captain Pitts immediately jumped on the grenade and shielded his men with his body, but the grenade did not detonate and he returned to dealing with the Viet Cong bunkers. He maneuvered his unit under fire to a point where he could safely call in an artillery fire mission and followed that barrage with an assault on the enemy positions. He personally led the assault on the position, killing at least one additional Viet Cong in the process. Again, the heavy jungle foliage restricted their fields of fire and he rapidly maneuvered himself to a location where he could place direct fire on the enemy positions. Though this location exposed him to enemy fire, he continued to pour fire into the enemy positions and directed his men in the assault that finally captured the positions and saved the men in his company. During this final assault, Captain Pitts was hit by enemy fire and fell mortally wounded. While he and three other soldiers died that day, his quick thinking and gallantry under fire saved the lives of many more by silencing the enemy guns. For his bravery and self-sacrifice, Captain Riley Leroy Pitts received the Medal of Honor.

President Lyndon Baines Johnson presented his Medal of Honor to his wife, Eula, and his family in a White House ceremony on December 10, 1968. President Johnson, in speaking to the family about Captain Pitts, said, "He was a brave man and a leader of men. No greater thing could be said of any man." Leroy Pitts was survived by his wife Eula, a son Mark, and a daughter Stacie. He was buried in Hillcrest Memory Gardens in Spencer, Oklahoma. Captain Pitts is memorialized on the Vietnam Memorial at Panel 28E, Row 105.

Riley Leroy Pitts was a remarkable soldier and a true hero. He had already earned a Silver Star during his tour in Vietnam and became the first African American commissioned officer to ever receive the Medal of Honor, though another future commissioned recipient's actions had occurred earlier. He has been honored in a variety of ways in his home state since his death, including through a scholarship created at the University of Oklahoma that bears his name and being inducted with the class of 2000 into the Oklahoma Military Hall of Fame. The 5th Signal Brigade Headquarters building in Mannheim, Germany, was named Pitts Hall in his honor. In addition, the main road inside the gate of Funari Barracks in Mannheim was named after him in May 2007.

James B. Martin

Further Reading

Hanna, Charles W. *African American Recipients of the Medal of Honor: A Biographical Dictionary, Civil War through Vietnam War.* Jefferson, NC: McFarland, 2002.

Murphy, Edward F. *Vietnam Medal of Honor Heroes.* New York: Ballantine Books, 2005.

Reef, Catherine. *African Americans in the Military.* New York: Facts on File, 2010.

Poor, Salem

Born: circa 1747
Died: 1834
Home State: Massachusetts
Service: Army
Conflict: American Revolution
Age at Time of Award: N/A

Born a slave in roughly 1747, Poor later purchased his freedom and married another free black named Nancy; they subsequently had one son. Settling in Andover, Massachusetts, in May 1775, Poor joined the Continental Army, answering the call to arms for all able-bodied men in New England to besiege the British force holed up in Boston following the Battles of Lexington and Concord in April of that year.

On the night of June 16, 1775, the Continental Army secretly moved from their base in Cambridge to a hill in neighboring Charlestown that gave the Americans an important strategic position from which to bombard the British in Boston. When the British awoke on the morning of June 17, and saw the newly built fortifications, they immediately recognized the threat such an American position posed to their defenses and organized an assault against the hill. British overconfidence and the speed with which they launched an attack worked against them, and the British suffered tremendous casualties in their three attempts to assail the position. The last advance proved successful, however, and the Americans were forced to retreat and abandon the hill, but only after enormous loss of life on both sides. One British officer declared that another victory at such a price would cost them the war. The conflict became known as the Battle of Bunker Hill, and despite the American defeat, it served as an inspiration to patriots throughout the colonies.

Historians estimate that roughly three dozen African Americans fought in the Battle of Bunker Hill, but Poor's conduct elicited particular attention from his white compatriots. Six months after the fight, 14 American officers presented a petition to the Massachusetts legislature requesting that Poor be singled out with a monetary reward for his heroic deeds. Unfortunately, the petition does not list these deeds, stating that "to set forth particulars of his conduct would be tedious." No other account of Poor's actions survives, but it is noteworthy that of the more than 3,000 Americans who fought at Bunker Hill, Poor is the only one to receive such recognition. Tradition credits Poor with having fired the shot that killed British Lt. Col. James Abercrombie.

Such praise must have been welcome to Poor, especially as his position within the Continental Army was becoming increasingly untenable. Less than a month after Bunker Hill, the newly installed commander of the Continental Army, George Washington, announced that African Americans would not be recruited to serve, but those already enlisted in the army could remain, as long as they were free and not slaves. A few months later, Washington extended the policy to prevent African Americans from reenlisting after their initial terms of service had expired. By November 1775, the Continental Congress had enacted legislation banning all African Americans from the Continental Army, a policy that was once again changed within a few months to allow free blacks to serve in light of Lord Dunmore's Proclamation inviting slaves to join the British Army in exchange for their freedom.

Despite his changing status within the army, Poor stayed with it and served under Washington for several more years, accompanying the general's forces at Valley Forge and the Battle of White Plains among other smaller engagements. Surviving records fail to indicate whether or not he ever received his reward from the Massachusetts government, but in 1975, the U.S. Postal Service commemorated him on a stamp in its "Contributors to the Cause" series.

Jonathan D. Sutherland

Further Reading

Kaplan, Sidney, and Emma Nogrady Kaplan. *The Black Presence in the Era of the American Revolution.* Amherst: University of Massachusetts Press, 1989.

Nalty, Bernard C. *Strength for the Fight.* New York: Free Press, 1986.

Quarles, Benjamin. *The Negro in the American Revolution.* Chapel Hill: University of North Carolina Press, 1961.

Radcliffe, Ronald A.

Born: February 13, 1944
Home State: Illinois
Service: Army
Conflict: Vietnam War
Age at Time of Award: 28

Ronald A. Radcliffe was born on February 13, 1944, in Lincoln, Nebraska, to David and Elizabeth Radcliffe. He lived in Lincoln until his parent's divorce prompted a move to Chicago, Illinois, where he attended school until midway through his high school years. On the day he turned 17, Ronald dropped out of high school and enlisted in the U.S. Army, departing for basic training as an infantryman. After nearly six years in the army, Radcliffe was selected for Officer Candidate School and was sent to Ft. Benning, Georgia, to complete the training and obtain his commission. Graduating as an infantry officer on May 2, 1968, he chose to fly helicopters and was sent to flight school at Ft. Rucker, Alabama.

Radcliffe was deployed to Vietnam and by February 1972, was serving with Troop F, 4th Cavalry Regiment stationed at Long Binh. Troop F was a composite organization that had been created out of Troop D, 3rd Battalion, 4th Cavalry Regiment upon the departure of its parent unit, the 25th Infantry Division, from Vietnam. It was one of four such units created in Vietnam during the drawdown of troops and would be one of the last army units to leave the Republic of Vietnam.

On February 20, 1972, just days after his 28th birthday, Radcliffe and his unit were operating in the vicinity of the Cambodian border. They were operating in three teams of three aircraft each, with each team consisting of a Light Observation Helicopter (Loach), a Cobra gunship, and a Huey Utility Helicopter (Slick). Radcliffe was in charge of Team 3 and the day was coming to a close in the late afternoon after running multiple missions. Team 1 had completed their missions for the day and had departed for Long Binh, leaving Teams 2 and 3 to follow behind once they were released. The pilot of the Loach on Team 1 was flying near an area the aviators referred to as the Mushroom, because of its shape from the air, along the Saigon River near Củ Chi. He spotted enemy soldiers on top of a bunker complex and requested permission to engage from the battalion operations center. Though denied the authorization, he made a single pass to ascertain what the possible target was and report. During this single pass, the Loach pilot was hit in the head with a round from a Vietnamese heavy machine gun and the Loach flipped over and crashed. Its escorting Cobra was heavily damaged and had to pull out of the area and land at Fire Base Tennessee, which was in close proximity to the Mushroom.

Teams 2 and 3 were en route back to Long Binh by this time and were flying to the east of the Mushroom. Upon receiving the call indicating the Team 1 was in trouble, Radcliffe banked his aircraft to make a pass over the crash site. The standard belief was that the best time to rescue a downed crew was immediately after the crash, not leaving time for the enemy to move in around the site and lay an ambush for aircraft coming to the aid of the downed crew. Radcliffe and his crew made a pass through the area and immediately began taking intense ground fire. He turned and made a second pass, with his crew suppressing the ground fire as best they could while they searched for any sign of life. On that pass, Radcliffe's observer saw an American soldier scramble into a bomb crater and they knew they had to rescue at least one crew member before the enemy could get to him. On a third pass, Radcliffe got so low and fast to avoid incoming fire that he almost collided with a stand of bamboo, ultimately causing a severe vibration in his aircraft.

Needing to check to see if the aircraft was safe to fly, Radcliffe departed the crash area and flew to Fire Base Tennessee. While the aircraft from Team 2 covered the crash site, he determined his aircraft was safe to fly and left his crew at the Fire Base so as to endanger fewer people. Returning to the Mushroom alone, Radcliffe marked the northeast corner of a landing zone for the South Vietnamese rangers (Browns) who were inbound to aid in the rescue and recovery operations. Once the Browns were on the ground, Radcliffe vectored them to the crash site, where the pilot and a crew member were dead in the burned-out frame of the Loach. On the way to the downed aircraft, the rangers found the living member of the crew and Radcliffe maneuvered his aircraft under constant enemy fire to the bomb crater where the crew member had sought cover and picked him up. Once the rangers had recovered the bodies and loaded them on the Team 3 Slick, Radcliffe vectored in other aircraft to pick up the rangers and departed to return the crew member to safety. During this sequence of events, Captain Radcliffe flew into the crash area between 40 and 50 times, almost always under heavy fire. He and his crew killed an estimated 12 enemy, while sustaining 29 hits to the helicopter. For his courage and sacrifice in the Mushroom near Củ Chi, Radcliffe was awarded the Silver Star.

Just over two months later, Troop F was scheduled to operate in the vicinity of Quảng Trị, which had been largely cut off by North Vietnamese forces attempting to encircle the position. Now operating in three aircraft teams of a Loach and two Cobras, Radcliffe and his team flew into Quảng Trị and landed at Tiger Pad. On the first mission of the day, Radcliffe was only a kilometer off the pad when his observer indicated he had just seen an American armored personnel carrier. With this report not sounding right, Radcliffe banked hard and turned to find the vehicle. Ascertaining that it was not an American vehicle, but a North Vietnamese PT-76 amphibious tank, Radcliffe began to fire at the vehicle and flew to a location above it where his crew could mark it with white phosphorous for the Cobras. After the Cobras destroyed this tank, Radcliffe spotted another tank nearby that was hidden under a tight grove of palm trees. Concerned as to whether the Cobras could see this vehicle, Radcliffe put his aircraft right above it and had his crew chief drop another white phosphorous grenade, but this time through the open hatch of the turret. The tank exploded as the ammunition began to catch fire and one of the Cobras, which were now operating at very low altitudes because of the presence of surface-to-air missiles, began to climb away from the exploding rounds. Almost instantly, the Cobra took a 30 mm round in the transmission and began to lose altitude. The aircraft flipped onto its top as it came to the ground, hitting on the rotor blades and exploding with its full load of fuel and ammunition.

Radcliffe made an immediate pass over the wreckage and saw the pilot in the helicopter on fire, but the aircraft commander had been thrown free about 10 to 20 feet from the aircraft. Under fire from a tree line about 25 meters away, Radcliffe maneuvered his aircraft to within about 20 feet of the downed pilot and his crew chief jumped out to retrieve him. Because of the mud in the crash area, and despite the assistance from a crew chief of a Slick that had landed behind Radcliffe to offer assistance, Captain Radcliffe's crew chief could not move the wounded man fast enough. Hovering just off the ground, Radcliffe maneuvered his aircraft right to the three men, flying so close to the burning aircraft and its exploding ordnance that it singed the hair on his head and face. Once the wounded man was in the aircraft and the Slick had lifted off, Captain Radcliffe directed his crew chief in giving first aid to the wounded pilot while flying back to Tiger Pad to get him medical attention. Once again, Radcliffe had placed his own life in danger in order to save the life of a downed aviator. His actions on April 28, 1972, were originally recognized with the award of a second Silver Star, but it was upgraded in April 1975 to the Distinguished Service Cross, the second highest award the nation has to offer.

Less than a month later, on May 23, 1972, Captain Radcliffe was flying another mission when he was wounded twice. These wounds were of sufficient severity that they forced his evacuation and eventually would lead to his medical retirement on April 1, 1974. Radcliffe was a hero and an excellent pilot, as his recognition as the Michael J. Novosel Aviator of the Year in 1971 clearly shows. His wartime record is enviable to the most seasoned army veteran, indicating that beyond the DSC and Silver Star, he was awarded the Distinguished Flying Cross 6 times, 4 Purple Hearts, 2 Bronze Stars, and 58 awards of the Air Medal.

After his medical retirement, Captain Radcliffe moved with his wife to Houston, Texas, and flew helicopters for the oil companies to offshore rigs. He still resides in Houston and is active with helicopter veteran's organizations and his fellow Vietnam veterans.

James B. Martin

Further Reading

Department of the Army. General Orders No. 10, April 2, 1975. http://www.armypubs/epubs/pdf/go7510.pdf (accessed August 23, 2013).

Westheider, James E. *The African American Experience in Vietnam: Brothers in Arms.* New York: Rowman & Littlefield, 2008.

Westheider, James E. *Fighting on Two Fronts: African Americans and the Vietnam War.* New York: New York University Press, 1997.

Rivers, Ruben

Born: October 31, 1918
Died: November 19, 1944
Home State: Oklahoma
Service: Army
Conflict: World War II
Age at Time of Award: 26

Ruben Rivers was born in Tecumseh, Oklahoma, to Willie and Lillian Rivers on October 31, 1918. He was from a large family of 11 brothers and sisters. Growing up on the farm near Holtuka, Oklahoma, when World War II broke out he was one of three of the brothers who went into military service. His brother Robert served in a supply unit in France and Dewey served in New Guinea in the engineers.

This is an undated photo of Staff Sergeant Ruben Rivers. Rivers was one of seven World War II veterans to become the first black soldiers of that conflict to receive the Medal of Honor, January 13, 1997. (AP Photo/St. Petersburg Times, HO)

Ruben Rivers trained with the 761st Tank Battalion at Camp Hood, Texas, and was the platoon sergeant for A Company. Soon after D-Day, the unit was shipped out to Europe. The "Black Panthers," as the 761st became known, was the first African American armored unit to be deployed. It entered combat on November 8, 1944, with the 26th Infantry Division.

As the tanks advanced toward the town of Moyenvic, France, they ran into a roadblock. Without regard for his personal safety, Staff Sergeant Rivers dismounted from his tank in the face of direct enemy small arms fire, attached a cable to the roadblock, and moved it off the road. For these actions under fire, Rivers was awarded the first Silver Star earned by the Black Panthers. The medal was pinned on his chest in the days that followed by his battalion commander, Lieutenant Colonel Paul Bates. Less than a week later, the unit smashed through the towns of Obreck, Dedeline, and Château Voue. When Rivers was radioed not to advance to the next town, Rivers replied that he had already advanced through that town.

November 16 found Rivers's men spearheading an attack for the 101st Infantry Regiment and ahead of the other 10 tanks in his company. They approached the town of Guebling, and Rivers's tank hit a mine and had its right track sheared off. Rivers himself suffered a serious gash in his leg. His wound was dressed, but he refused to be given a painkiller, fearing this would impair his ability to carry out the responsibilities of command. His captain told him he should be evacuated, but again Rivers refused.

Rivers led the attack the following morning, but by the evening his wound had become infected; again he refused to be evacuated. Throughout the night, the unit was under heavy German fire, and in the morning, the Germans launched a counterattack. Rivers's and his companion tank engaged the enemy armored vehicles to cover the retreating infantry and armor that had been caught by the attack. Though ordered to fall back, Rivers continued to engage the enemy armor with his tank-mounted 76mm cannon until high explosive rounds hit his tank, resulting in Rivers's death and his crew being severely wounded.

About two weeks later, Rivers's mother received the bad news, but might have found some solace in learning that his commanding officer had recommended him for a Medal of Honor to add to the Purple Heart and Silver Star he had already been awarded. Tragically, it took nearly 50 years for his family to receive the award on his behalf. Rivers's Medal of Honor was finally presented to one of his sisters, Grace Woodfork, on January 13, 1997.

That Rivers's actions were recognized with the Medal of Honor was a result of a Shaw University research study to investigate why African American World War II veterans had been overlooked for the Medal of Honor. The study's 272-page report concluded that racism was the reason; it went on to recommend 10 soldiers whose military records warranted the award. In January 1995, the findings were delivered to Washington, D.C., and in April of the following year Congress chose to recognize 7 of the 10 soldiers, all of whom had received less-distinguished awards for their military service or had simply had their recommendations stymied or lost. Only one of the seven nominees, 1st Lieutenant Vernon Baker of Saint Maries, Idaho, was alive to receive the Medal. The process to identify these heroes began with a search for African American recipients of the Distinguished Service Cross in order to see if any should be upgraded. In the case of Staff Sergeant Ruben Rivers, his company commander had made a verbal recommendation for the Medal of Honor for his actions on November 16, 1944. The battalion commander, a temporary replacement for Lieutenant Colonel Bates who had been wounded, indicated it should be put in writing. The company commander did so with the company clerk and the recommendation was forwarded to the battalion commander. While these events were verified by the company commander and company clerk, the temporary battalion commander is reported to have indicated that since Rivers already had a Silver Star he really did not need another medal. The company commander persisted though, and the paperwork was reportedly sent forward. No paperwork for Rivers's recommendation for the Medal of Honor was received in Washington D.C., and no record of it was found in the European Theater. While he was not the only African American soldier to be denied the Medal because of race, he was the only one of those chosen to receive the Medal who had not been officially recommended for any awards for the cited actions. Based on the evidence presented, though Staff Sergeant Rivers was not recommended for the Distinguished Service Cross or any other award for the actions that led to his death, the army determined that he deserved the Medal and sought to correct the errors in his case.

Staff Sergeant Rivers was buried in the Lorraine American Cemetery in Saint Avold, France. The army initially honored Rivers in 1950, by naming the former German post in Giessen, Germany, for him. Rivers Barracks was in active service until September 28, 2007. In September 2012, the Armor Center at Ft. Benning, Georgia, honored Staff Sergeant Rivers once more by naming a barracks after him in the 194th Armored Brigade's new facilities at Harmony Church.

James B. Martin and Jonathan D. Sutherland

Further Reading

Booker, Bryan D. *African Americans in the United States Army in World War II.* Jefferson, NC: McFarland, 2008.

Pfeifer, Kathryn Browne. *The 761st Tank Battalion (African-American Soldiers).* New York: Twenty-First Century Books, 1994.

Wilson, Joe, Jr. *The 761st "Black Panther" Tank Battalion in World War II.* Jefferson, NC: McFarland, 1999.

Roberts, Needham

Born: April 28, 1901
Died: April 18, 1949
Home State: New Jersey

Service: Army
Conflict: World War I
Age at Time of Award: 16

Needham Roberts was born in Trenton, Mercer County, New Jersey, on April 28, 1901. He was the son of Norman and Emma Roberts, a pastor and wife who had moved to Trenton from North Carolina around 1890. He lived at 48 Wilson Street, in Trenton from the time of his birth until he enlisted in the army in 1917. Roberts was only 15 or 16 when he enlisted, but he convinced the recruiting office for the 15th Infantry Regiment of the New York National Guard that he was old enough to serve. After America declared war on Germany in 1917, the 15th New York was made a part of the regular army and redesignated the 369th Infantry Regiment as an all-African American regiment. Because of their geographical origin and their performance during the war, this unit came to be known as the Harlem Hellfighters and became one of the most famous African American units in American history.

The 369th was deployed to France with the main body of the American Expeditionary Force (AEF) in late 1917 and was assigned to the 161st Division of the French Army. This division had been in combat since 1914, and had suffered some of the heaviest losses in the entire French Army. While it would not happen today, it was not unusual for African American units to be attached to the command of allied units during World War I. The U.S. Army was not particularly excited about the prospect of African American combat units and took any opportunity to move them to another sector. The French, for their part, were not as rigid in their prejudice about race and had created racially segregated units from their African colonies for many years. Besides this differing racial outlook, the French Army had taken so many casualties that they could not afford to turn down any offer of assistance, regardless of the form it took.

While other African American units in the U.S. Army were held out of combat as long as possible, the 369th was quickly thrown into combat with the French. They gained combat experience far quicker than any other African American unit and earned a reputation as courageous and hard-nosed fighting soldiers. They were recognized by the French units around them and the senior French leadership for their performance and confused the Germans, who mistakenly believed that they were a Moroccan unit brought in from the French colony.

On May 14, 1918, during a late night patrol with four other members of his unit, Needham Roberts moved to an observation post beyond even the most advanced French positions. They were located there to listen for the movement of German patrols that might signal an attack. The men began to take their turns at the listening duty, with Roberts and the patrol leader, Corporal Henry L. Johnson, taking the first watch. While their three comrades slept, a German attack was launched on the position. Grenades rained on their positions with both Roberts and Johnson being wounded and the other members of the patrol being knocked unconscious. What followed was an attack by a larger force of German soldiers, possibly as many as 24, who attempted to overrun the position before the Americans could regain their composure. Both men fought back fiercely, though they had both sustained significant wounds. Roberts was wounded the worst and could not stand after the first few moments. He sat in the position and threw hand grenades to his partner, who managed to drive off the attackers with a combination of rifle fire, grenades, and hand-to-hand combat. At one point, two German soldiers attempted to drag Roberts away, but Johnson pulled out his curved bolo knife and killed them both. Though Roberts and Johnson were both badly wounded, the ferocity of their resistance convinced the Germans to fall back and not renew their assault on the position.

Both men were hospitalized for their wounds and the regimental commander, Colonel William Hayward, promoted them both to sergeant. Roberts was given the option of returning to his unit or receiving an honorable discharge and he chose to return to New Jersey and leave the war behind him. They were the first heroes in the Harlem Hellfighters and just as they had not given any ground, their regiment became famous for never giving up ground during the war.

Predictably, the American Army ignored the heroics of Roberts and Johnson. While a report was filed on the incident, it did not detail their actions and contained no recommendations for commendations of any sort. They were not even recommended for the Purple Heart, which is presented to all American soldiers who are wounded in a combat zone. The French took a different course and looked closely into the actions of their new American unit. They determined that Roberts and Johnson had acted in a particularly valorous manner and decided to award them the Croix de Guerre, France's highest military honor for bravery in combat. It is the rough equivalent of the American Medal of Honor. These two soldiers became the first Americans, regardless of race, to be honored by the French government with this prestigious award. The French commanding general went so far as to write to General John J. Pershing, commander of the American Expeditionary Force, to tell him of their valor and seek recognition by their own government.

Needham and Johnson became instant heroes in the African American community in New York and New Jersey when their story was told by a journalist in *The Saturday Evening Post*. They provided their community the heroes it had yearned for and were a visible demonstration of the quality and valor of African American soldiers when given the opportunity to serve in combat. African American publications lauded their exploits, while white publications downplayed their actions or liberally sprinkled treatments of their story with racial stereotypes.

After the war, Needham Roberts apparently struggled with his wartime experiences and may have suffered from what today would be termed posttraumatic stress. He received no benefits from the U.S. government, which would not even recognize that he had been wounded in combat. Sometime in 1919, he married Margaret Burrell and they had a daughter named Juanita that same year. While how Roberts made a living is not clear, he did appear in a speaking tour of Ohio that was sponsored by the YMCA in 1920, telling of his exploits during the war. He apparently became depressed and reports have it that he spent time in an asylum. He is reported to have committed suicide, along with Margaret, at their home in Newark on April 18, 1949. He was buried in Fairmount Cemetery in Newark, Essex County, New Jersey. In 1996, 78 years after he was wounded in combat, the U.S. Army finally awarded him the Purple Heart posthumously.

James B. Martin

Further Reading

Scott, Emmett J. "The American Negro in the World War. Washington, D.C., 1919." http://net.lib.byu.edu/estu/wwi/comment/scott/ScottTC.htm (accessed January 26, 2013).

Williams, Chad L. *Torchbearers of Democracy: African American Soldiers in the World War I Era.* Chapel Hill: The University of North Carolina Press, 2010.

Robinson, Roscoe, Jr.

Born: October 11, 1928
Died: July 22, 1993
Home State: Missouri
Service: Army
Conflict: Korean War, Vietnam War
Age at Time of Award: 24

Roscoe Robinson Jr. was born on October 11, 1928, in St. Louis, Missouri. His father was a steel worker from a local mill and was apparently very focused on his son having a better life. When Roscoe thought of working in the mills, his father indicated that it was not the life he wanted for his son and pushed him to focus on getting an education. Robinson graduated from Sumner High School in 1946, and gained acceptance to a quality local institution, St. Louis University. After spending a year as an engineering student at St. Louis, Robinson was presented with the opportunity to attend the U.S. Military Academy at West Point, New York. One of only five African American cadets in the class of 1951, Robinson found that though he was out of the segregated neighborhoods of St. Louis, he still had to deal with a structure which did not treat African Americans as equals. He was commissioned in 1951, and was sent to Ft. Benning, Georgia, to attend his Infantry Officers Basic Course.

Roscoe Robinson Jr., a highly decorated veteran of Korea and Vietnam, was the first African American promoted to four-star general in the U.S. Army. (AP Photo)

Robinson was initially assigned to a segregated unit at Ft. Campbell, Kentucky, but by 1952, he was deployed to Korea as a replacement in the 1st Battalion, 31st Infantry Regiment, 7th Infantry Division. This was an integrated unit and, surprisingly, in just over a month, Robinson was put in command of Charlie Company. With this assignment, he became one of only two African American officers to command infantry companies in the 7th Infantry Division at this time. His tour in Korea was a successful one, including Robinson earning the Bronze Star for valor during the infamous battle for Pork Chop Hill.

After the Korean War, Robinson joined the 11th Airborne Division and a year later was assigned as an instructor in the Airborne Department at Ft. Benning, Georgia. He was promoted to captain in 1957, and in 1960 he joined the 82nd Airborne, rising to company commander of E Company of the 504th Airborne Infantry Regiment. He attended the Army Command and General Staff College at Ft. Leavenworth, Kansas, graduating in 1963. After being awarded a master's degree in 1964 from the University of Pittsburgh, he was assigned to the Office of Personnel Operations with the Department of the Army Staff.

In 1967, Robinson was deployed to the Republic of Vietnam, first serving as a logistics staff officer and then as battalion commander of the 2nd Battalion, 7th Cavalry, 1st Infantry Division. Here, he earned the Distinguished Flying Cross, two Silver Stars, 11 Air Medals, and the Legion of Merit, and added a star to his combat infantryman's badge to identify his second tour as a combat infantryman.

Robinson then attended the National War College. He was promoted to colonel in 1967, and between 1969 and 1972 he served as the executive officer for the chief of staff of the plans directorate at the headquarters of the Pacific Command. He then returned to the 82nd Airborne as the 2nd Brigade's commander in 1972. He was awarded a second Legion of Merit and was then promoted to brigadier general and given the role of deputy commanding general of Okinawa Base command in 1973. He became the commanding general of the garrison in 1975.

Robinson returned to the 82nd Airborne Division in 1976, as its commanding general, becoming the first African American to command the elite paratrooper unit. He then became deputy chief of staff for operations at the U.S. Army headquarters in Europe and later assumed command of the U.S. Army in Japan. In 1982, he was promoted to the rank of general, becoming the first African American to gain this rank in the U.S. Army. Following this promotion, he returned to Europe as the U.S. representative to NATO's Military Committee.

Robinson retired in 1985 after 34 years of commissioned service. He received the Defense Distinguished Service Medal and other awards upon his retirement. After a long bout with cancer, he passed away at Walter Reed Medical Center on July 22, 1993 and was buried at Arlington National Cemetery. Shortly before his death, in May 1993, a cadet review at West Point named him a distinguished graduate, saying, "[his] character, distinguished service and stature draw a wholesome comparison to the qualities for which West Point stands, and is epitomized by its motto–duty, honor, country."

Roscoe Robinson Jr. has been honored in many ways for the work he did for his nation and African Americans in the military service. The army named the Roscoe Robinson Health Clinic at Ft. Bragg, North Carolina, after him. This seems particularly appropriate, as he commanded his brigade and division on the post. At least three of his alma maters have honored his memory. West Point named the main lecture hall in historic Thayer Hall in his honor. The University of Pittsburgh created a distinguished lecture series that bears his name. The Command and General Staff College has erected a bust of General Robinson in the Grove of the Regiments, very close to the Buffalo Soldier Monument.

While he was the first African American four-star general in the army, Robinson downplayed that honor. To a military officer working on an oral history of Robinson's life, he indicated that he had viewed Benjamin O. Davis Sr. and Jr. to be his role models, along with Julius W. Becton Jr. These men had blazed a path as African American military leaders and he used them as guideposts. His career, now part of the army's history, will be a similar guidepost for African Americans who follow him.

James B. Martin and Jonathan D. Sutherland

Further Reading

Haley, Leon L. *The Quiet One: General Roscoe Robinson, Jr.* London: Fortis Publishing, 2010.

Hardesty, Duane E. *General Roscoe Robinson Jr.: He Overcame the Hurdle of Segregation to Become the Army's First Black General.* Carlisle, PA: U.S. Army War College, 1988.

Rogers, Charles Calvin

Born: September 6, 1929
Died: September 21, 1990
Home State: West Virginia
Service: Army
Conflict: Vietnam War
Age at Time of Award: 38

Charles Calvin Rogers was born on September 6, 1929, in Claremont, West Virginia. He was the son of Mr. and Mrs. Clyde Rogers, Sr. who were originally from Indianapolis, Indiana. He attended college at West Virginia State College and graduated with a degree in mathematics. He was in the Army Reserve Officer Training program at West Virginia State College and graduated as a Distinguished Military Graduate. He apparently wanted to be a minister, but that life's goal had to be delayed, as he was commissioned as a second lieutenant after his graduation ceremony on campus at Institute, West Virginia.

Rogers's military career followed a normal trajectory after commissioning, as he attended his Artillery Officer's Basic Course at Ft. Sill, Oklahoma, and, after a tour with an artillery unit, returned to Ft. Sill for his Advanced Course. He had assignments in Korea and the United States prior to the Vietnam War. He also attended the Command and General Staff College before gaining command of the 1st Battalion, 2nd Brigade at Ft. Lewis, Washington. He deployed to Vietnam in 1967.

On November 1, 1968, Lieutenant Colonel Rogers was commanding 1st Battalion, 5th Artillery, 1st Infantry Division in the Republic of Vietnam. His unit was occupying forward Fire Support Base Rita, close to the Fishhook, near the Cambodian border. The Fishhook was a salient in Cambodia about 80 kilometers northwest of Saigon that jutted into the South Vietnamese provinces of Binh Long and Tay Ninh. It was an ending point on the Ho Chi Minh Trail and, as such, was a resting area for large numbers of North Vietnamese Army regulars and Viet Cong warriors. In the early morning hours of November 1, the unit's fire support base came under attack from a massive enemy force. Initially, the unit came under concentrated fires from heavy weapons, such as mortars, rockets, and rocket-propelled grenades. This bombardment was immediately followed by a human wave ground assault, complete with sappers who used explosives to cut through the protective wire at specific points around the camp, and the assault initially penetrated the defensive perimeter of his artillery unit. Ignoring the explosions around him and the danger he placed himself in, Lieutenant Colonel Rogers moved to the endangered areas and directed the fire from his artillerymen to try and stem the human tide. Responding to his leadership and bravery, his men shook off the initial shock of the attack and began to return fire at the enemy. Rogers was knocked off his feet and wounded by an exploding round, but he quickly recovered and moved to personally lead a counterattack force against enemy soldiers who had penetrated a howitzer position and were endangering the camp, driving them off and killing a number of the enemy himself. He was wounded a second time during this counterattack, but refused medical treatment. While a second human wave assault was aimed at another sector of the fire support base, Rogers directed the fire of his artillery unit in that sector to defeat the enemy and led another counterattack to restore the position. Continuing to refuse medical treatment, Rogers moved throughout his unit's position through constant and heavy enemy fire in order to rally his men and direct their fire at the critical points. Yet a third human wave assault was launched at the fire support base and again Lieutenant Colonel Rogers moved to the endangered area and directed fire at the attacking enemy. At this juncture, he saw a howitzer that was not engaged with the enemy because the crew had been badly injured. He moved to help the remaining members of the crew to put the gun back into action and directed its fire against the enemy. As he continued to direct the defensive actions against the enemy formation, he was wounded a third time by a mortar round that exploded very close to him. These wounds were so severe that he could no longer move about the fire support base and he was forced to remain stationary and provide direction and encouragement to his men as they fought off the North Vietnamese. Though wounded multiple times, Lieutenant Colonel Charles Clark Rogers refused medical treatment and stayed at the side of his men, leading them through force of will and bravery to defeat an overwhelming enemy force and save the unit from destruction. For his courage and gallantry, Lieutenant Colonel Rogers received the Medal of Honor.

President Richard M. Nixon presented the Medal of Honor to Lieutenant Colonel Rogers at a White House ceremony on May 14, 1970. He was the highest ranking African American to ever receive the Medal of Honor.

Charles Rogers continued to serve in the U.S. Army until 1984. He served in the United States and Germany during these years, rising to the rank of major general and commanding the VII Corps Artillery in Germany. He also continued his desire to become a minister, pursuing and completing a degree in theology from the University of Munich. In 1988, he became an ordained minister at Heidelberg, Germany, fulfilling a lifelong goal, and spent his remaining years ministering to American soldiers in Germany. He succumbed to cancer on September 21, 1990, and was buried in Section 7-A at Arlington National Cemetery, Arlington, Virginia.

Major General Rogers has been honored in a variety of venues in the military and civilian communities. The Charles C. Rogers Bridge takes West Virginia State Route 16 across the New River near Cotton Hill, West Virginia. The Carlisle Barracks chapter of the ROCKS, Inc.—a professional military officer association largely made up of African American officers—is named for him.

James B. Martin

Further Reading

Hanna, Charles W. *African American Recipients of the Medal of Honor: A Biographical Dictionary, Civil War through Vietnam War.* Jefferson, NC: McFarland, 2002.

Murphy, Edward F. *Vietnam Medal of Honor Heroes.* New York: Ballantine Books, 2005.

Reef, Catherine. *African Americans in the Military.* New York: Facts on File, 2010.

Westheider, James E. *The African American Experience in Vietnam: Brothers in Arms.* New York: Rowman & Littlefield, 2008.

Salem, Peter

Born: circa 1750
Died: August 16, 1816
Home State: Massachusetts
Service: Army
Conflict: American Revolution
Age at Time of Award: N/A

Little is known of Salem's early life. He was born a slave in Framingham, Massachusetts, around 1750. His owner was Jeremiah Belknap, who most likely named him after his hometown of Salem, Massachusetts. At some point, Belknap sold Salem to Maj. Lawson Buckminster (also of Framingham), who granted him his freedom in exchange for his enlistment in the colonial militia; this event most likely occurred in the spring of 1775.

Like his fellow townsmen, Salem walked to Concord, Massachusetts, in the early morning hours of April 19 in a company led by the town militia's Capt. Simon Edgel. Framingham had received word that British forces were marching on Concord to seize one of the province's secret stashes of military supplies, gathered by the colonists during the preceding winter in light of mounting tensions between themselves and the British authorities. Salem did not fight at the North Bridge but participated in harassing the British retreat back to Boston, a maneuver that cost the British dearly. A week later, Salem enlisted in Col. John Nixon's 5th Massachusetts Regiment, which spent the next two months in Cambridge, Massachusetts, laying siege to the British forces holed up in Boston.

On the night of June 16, 1775, Salem and his compatriots secretly mounted a hill in neighboring Charlestown that provided a perfect vantage point from which to bombard the British in Boston. The hill in question was actually called Breed's Hill, although at the time the colonists mistakenly thought they were on Bunker Hill, which gave its name to the battle that followed. Working with remarkable speed and silence, the American troops hastily erected fortifications that caused the British severe alarm when they awoke the next morning to see their position

Peter Salem, an African American who fought at the Battle of Bunker Hill, is depicted here shooting British Major Pitcairn. (Bettmann/Corbis)

in Boston compromised. Determined to remove the Americans from the hill, the British quickly organized an assault. Before the morning was out, three successive waves of British troops had hurled themselves at the American positions. Salem and his companions in the 5th Massachusetts were positioned on the right side of the American redoubt, and in the third assault, during which the Americans were finally forced to retreat, Salem is reputed to have fired the shot that killed British Maj. John Pitcairn, who had earned fame for leading the advance troops at the Battles of Lexington and Concord two months earlier. Suffering tremendous losses, the British pressed on and seized the American position but at a horrific cost of lives. Pitcairn's demise did little to slow the overall British effort, but it held great symbolic significance for the Americans, who rejoiced that the leader of the British troops at the Battle of Lexington had been brought to justice for his involvement in what amounted to a massacre of eight colonists.

Like other African American militiamen, Salem's position within the colonial military was tenuous at best in the months following Bunker Hill. When newly appointed commander in chief of the Continental Army George Washington arrived in Cambridge in early July, he declared that blacks would not be enlisted in the army, although those already serving were allowed to complete their terms of enlistment (but could not reenlist). The Continental Congress supported Washington's position by passing legislation to that effect in November of that year. The same month, though, the British governor of Virginia Lord Dunmore issued a proclamation inviting all bondsmen (slaves and indentured servants) to join the British ranks in exchange for their freedom. This move prompted colonial officials to rethink their policy on African Americans, and they eventually grudgingly allowed them to serve in the Continental Army, but only if they were already free.

Salem reenlisted in January 1776, and fought at the battles leading up to the British surrender at Saratoga in October 1777, after which point the theater of operations shifted to the southern colonies and active fighting in the north drew to a close. Many New England soldiers returned to their homes at this time, although there is no record to indicate whether Salem did so or if he journeyed south to fight with the army there. Most likely, he went home.

After the war, the details of Salem's life are even more obscure. He apparently married a free black woman named Katy Benson and moved with her to Leicester, Massachusetts, where he built a log cabin. His profession was either a cane weaver or a furniture maker, although he does not appear to have been successful in his chosen line of work. He outlived his wife and died in a poorhouse in Framingham on August 16, 1816. He was buried in an unmarked grave in the Old Burying Ground in Framingham. The town of Framingham erected a monument for Salem in 1882.

Jonathan D. Sutherland

Further Reading

Brooks, Victor. *The Boston Campaign: April 1775–March 1776. Great Campaigns.* Conshohocken, PA: Combined Publishing, 1999.

Davis, Lenwood, and George Hill, eds. *Blacks in the American Armed Forces, 1776–1983.* Westport, CT: Greenwood Press, 1985.

Sandel, Edward. *Black Soldiers in the Colonial Militia: Documents from 1639 to 1780.* Baton Rouge, LA: Tabor Lucas Publications, 1994.

Tourtellot, Arthur Bernon. *Lexington and Concord: The Beginning of the War of the American Revolution.* New York: W.W. Norton, 1963.

Sargent, Ruppert Leon

Born: January 6, 1938
Died: March 15, 1967
Home State: Virginia
Service: Army
Conflict: Vietnam War
Age at Time of Award: 29

Ruppert Leon Sargent was born in Hampton, Virginia, on January 6, 1938. He attended public schools in Hampton and then went on to college at Virginia State College and the Hampton Institute. He was raised a Jehovah's Witness and because of this background would not have been expected to enter the service. Apparently the call of the army was too great and, in direct conflict with his wife and his mother, he entered service at Richmond, Virginia, on January 8, 1959, without finishing college. Sargent served for six years as an enlisted soldier and then went to officer's candidate school, completing the course and gaining his commission as a 2nd Lieutenant of Infantry at Ft. Benning, Georgia, on October 15, 1965. He deployed to the Republic of Vietnam in 1966, and served as a lieutenant in Company B, 4th Battalion, 9th Infantry Regiment of the 25th Infantry Division. He sacrificed his life to save his fellow soldiers in action near Củ Chi, in Hậu Nghĩa Province, on March 15, 1967.

Now 1st Lieutenant, Sargent was leading his platoon on a mission to investigate a possible Viet Cong meeting house and a nearby weapons cache. The area around Củ Chi was well known for its tunnel complex and he identified one of these tunnels, noticing that the entrance was booby-trapped. He attempted to clear the booby trap himself but was not successful in the initial attempt. He and his explosives expert then moved to try to clear the tunnel entrance again but were surprised when a Viet Cong rushed from the tunnel area. Luckily, Sargent's platoon sergeant was in an overwatch position and killed the Viet Cong soldier before he could do any harm. With this danger out of the way, Sargent, the platoon sergeant, and their forward observer once again began to move toward the tunnel entrance. This time they were not as lucky, as another Viet Cong was flushed from the tunnel, but before he could be killed, he threw two hand grenades into the trio of American soldiers. Lieutenant Sargent shot the Viet Cong soldier, killing him, but knew that the grenades would kill all three men. He dove on the two hand grenades, pulling them to his body and absorbing the blast. Lieutenant Sargent was mortally wounded by the grenade blasts but he sacrificed his life to save his fellow soldiers. The platoon sergeant and observer would most certainly have been killed and a number of other members of the platoon were close enough to have been seriously wounded by the blasts. 1st Lieutenant Ruppert Leon Sargent exhibited rare bravery and self-sacrifice that day near Củ Chi and to recognize his courage he received the Medal of Honor.

Lieutenant Sargent's family had not been supportive of his joining the military because his religion called for an allegiance to God only and not to any government. His wife and mother declined to receive the Medal on his behalf, though the military continued to negotiate with them. Eventually, Mrs. Sargent agreed to accept the Medal in a private ceremony at her home. On March 7, 1969, General Donley P. Bolton presented Lieutenant Sargent's Medal of Honor to his wife at her home in Hampton, Virginia. Lieutenant Sargent was not the first African American officer to receive the Medal of Honor, largely owing to the delay in presentation. The actions that led to him receiving the Medal of Honor occurred earlier than any other commissioned officer's, but the various delays caused his Medal to be presented many months later. Ruppert Leon Sargent was buried in Hampton National Cemetery, in Hampton, Virginia. He is memorialized on the Vietnam Memorial on Panel 16E, Row 86.

After Sargent's death, his company commander, who had recommended him for the Medal of Honor, sent a letter to a city official in Hampton, Virginia, with money orders asking him to place a wreath on Lieutenant Sargent's grave once he was buried. The official was a veteran and was affected by what the company commander had to say about Sargent in the letter. While he made sure the commander's wishes were fulfilled, he began a campaign to honor Hampton's only Medal of Honor recipient. Eventually, after considerable time spent explaining the importance of the kind of courage and bravery exhibited by Sargent, the official had his opening. With the planning of a new administrative building for the city of Hampton, he was able to convince the city council to name the facility after Hampton's greatest military hero. The Ruppert Leon Sargent Memorial City Administration Building in Hampton, Virginia, was officially dedicated on October 5, 2002. Sargent's company commander, along with a number of his comrades, and Ruppert Sargent's family, was present to see his friend honored.

James B. Martin

Further Reading

Hanna, Charles W. *African American Recipients of the Medal of Honor: A Biographical Dictionary, Civil War through Vietnam War*. Jefferson, NC: McFarland, 2002.

Manchu Web Page: http://www.manchu.org/linage/sargent.htm (accessed September 12, 2013).

Murphy, Edward F. *Vietnam Medal of Honor Heroes*. New York: Ballantine Books, 2005.

Sasser, Clarence Eugene

Born: September 2, 1947
Home State: Texas
Service: Army
Conflict: Vietnam War
Age at Time of Award: 20

Clarence Eugene Sasser was born on September 2, 1947, in Chenango, Texas. He was drafted after losing his college deferment at the University of Houston, but because of his education he was trained as a combat medic. Sasser's tour of duty in Vietnam with Headquarters Company, 3rd Battalion, 60th Infantry Regiment, 9th Infantry Division, lasted only 51 days.

On January 10, 1968, Sasser was attached to the 3rd Battalion's Company A, which was part of a "reconnaissance in force" being inserted into an area of reported Viet Cong (VC) activity. As the Americans approached the landing zone (LZ), the lead helicopter was heavily damaged by enemy small arms fire and crashed. The remaining helicopters quickly disgorged the company's other soldiers, not realizing that the enemy occupied fortified positions on three sides of the LZ and that the single American company was facing an entire VC regiment. The American soldiers came under fire from VC small arms, mortar, and rocket fire, and, in less than five minutes, more than 30 American soldiers were wounded.

Sasser immediately began to aid the wounded soldiers around him. He crawled in the muck of rice paddies from soldier to soldier through enemy fire. As he carried a comrade

Clarence Sasser received the Medal of Honor for valor during the Vietnam War. His actions that led to the Medal saved the lives of many of his comrades and he noted his pride in receiving the Medal for saving lives rather than taking them. (U.S. Army Medical Department Regiment)

to safety, shrapnel from a VC mortar wounded Sasser in the left shoulder and side. Refusing assistance, he bandaged himself and returned to the rice paddy to assist more wounded soldiers. VC machine gun fire subsequently wounded him in both legs. Despite this injury, he pulled himself through the mud 100 meters with his hands to help another soldier. Then, peering over the top of the dike that separated him from a neighboring rice paddy, Sasser received a glancing blow on the head from a VC sniper. Bleeding from his scalp, he lay unconscious for some time before more mortar rounds woke him.

Despite the pain and loss of blood from his wounds, Sasser not only continued to treat wounded Americans but also encouraged others in the fight against the VC. Finding a group of soldiers pinned down by enemy fire 200 meters from the main American element, he convinced them to make their way back to the rest of the Americans. "I felt that if I could get the guys up and fighting," he said later, "we might all get out of there somehow." Despite the best efforts of American higher command, the main support lent to the trapped company was airpower. "All we got was air support from the [U.S. Air Force F-4] Phantoms. My respect for the

Phantoms went up immediately," he said. "Man they were dropping napalm on the wood lines, laying it in there so close that a lot of times you'd think the pilot was going to get his tail caught in it when he pulled up, it was that close."

After returning to the American lines, Sasser continued to treat the wounded for five hours until they were safely evacuated. In the course of that day, 34 Americans were killed and 59 wounded—and doubtless more Americans would have died had it not been for his efforts. Sasser took pride in saving American lives, telling an interviewer,

> I am particularly proud that my medal was for saving lives, rather than destroying lives. That's not to say anything against the guys that were combat soldiers, or whatever, that killed people, and of course received the medal. I do not mean to insult or belittle their accomplishment. Of course, in war, war is just what it says; someone has to die and so on. And of course if someone dies someone has to kill them. I don't begrudge anything like that. I have no compunctions whatsoever about that. It's just that I'm particularly proud that mine was for being a medic, and was for saving lives, rather than taking lives. It's a source of pleasure with me to have received it for that.

After three months in a hospital at Camp Zama, Japan, the army initially intended to return Sasser to combat in Vietnam. Thankfully, an army doctor arranged for him to be reassigned to the camp dispensary. While still at Camp Zama, Sasser was informed that he would receive the Medal of Honor.

On March 7, 1969, in a ceremony held at the White House, President Richard Nixon presented Sasser and two others with the Medal of Honor. President Nixon remarked during the ceremony that presenting these medals was the greatest honor of his young presidency, as these were the first Medals of Honor he had bestowed.

After leaving the army, Clarence Sasser attended Texas A&M University to study chemistry but left after he married. After working for Dow Chemical Company and Amoco for five years, he began working for the Veterans Administration, where he still works at the time of the writing.

Alexander M. Bielakowski

Further Reading

Collier, Peter, and Nick Del Calzo. *Medal of Honor: Portraits of Valor beyond the Call of Duty.* New York: Artisan, 2006.

Oral History Interview with SP5 Clarence G. Sasser, U.S. Army Medical Department. http://ameddregiment.amedd.army.mil/moh/bios/sasserInt.html (accessed November 12, 2012).

Smith, Larry. *Beyond Glory: Medal of Honor Heroes in Their Own Words—Extraordinary Stories of Courage from World War II to Vietnam.* New York: W.W. Norton, 2003.

Sims, Clifford Chester

Born: June 18, 1942
Died: February 21, 1968
Home State: Florida
Service: Army
Conflict: Vietnam War
Age at Time of Award: 25

Clifford Chester Sims was born in Port St. Joe, Florida, on June 18, 1942. Newspaper reports indicate that Sims never knew his biological father and his mother was killed when he was an infant. His stepfather was killed in the Korean War and at age three or four, he became an orphan. He was raised for a short time by relatives, but eventually found himself on the streets of Panama City, Florida, as a homeless youth. He returned to Port St. Joe at age 13 and was adopted by James and Irene Sims. He graduated from Washington High School in Port St. Joe and shortly after graduation joined the U.S. Army on October 31, 1961. He went through basic training at Ft. Jackson, South Carolina, on his way to becoming a career soldier. He married his wife, Mary, and they had a daughter named Gina. Sims was stationed with the 101st Airborne Division at Ft. Campbell, Kentucky, and was deployed with the division to the Republic of Vietnam.

On February 21, 1968, Staff Sergeant Sims was now a rifle squad leader with Company D, 2nd Battalion (Airborne), 501st Infantry Regiment, 101st Airborne Division and operating to the northwest of the South Vietnamese city of Hue. The Tet Offensive was three weeks old at this point and the 2/501st was one of the army units given the mission of assisting the marines and South Vietnamese Army units with retaking the city of Hue from the Viet Cong. Six days earlier, Staff Sergeant Sims had performed well in combat; in fact, he was posthumously awarded the Silver Star for his actions on February 15, 1968. On February 21, his unit was engaged in heavy fighting against Viet Cong forces. His squad from 2nd Platoon was the company reserve and he was providing covering fire for the headquarters element, when the company commander gave orders for his squad to close a gap that had been created between the 1st and 3rd Platoons. Sims moved his squad into the small village through which the company was fighting to regain contact with the two platoons, but caught sight of a building filled with ammunition that was on fire. He moved his squad back and warned the headquarters element, just as the building exploded. Once the air had cleared of debris, Staff Sergeant Sims once again moved his squad into the breach between the two platoons, attempting to make contact with each and close the potentially dangerous gap in the company's lines. His Medal of Honor citation indicates that a booby trap went off just in front of his squad position, though some reports from members of Company D indicate it was a hand grenade. Whatever the source of the explosive device, Sims recognized the danger his squad was in and reacted immediately. He jumped onto the explosive device and absorbed the blast with his body, suffering mortal wounds and saving numerous members of his platoon. For the second time in less than a week, Staff Sergeant Clifford Chester Sims had proven to be a hero and his courage and self-sacrifice resulted in a recommendation for the Medal of Honor.

This action by Company D, 2/501st was one in which numerous heroes and their actions came to light and were recognized. Staff Sergeant Sims's Medal of Honor was not the only one received by a member of Company D for actions on February 21, 1968, as Staff Sergeant Joe Ronnie Hooper also received America's highest award for valor for his actions that day. In addition, Sergeant Dale Urban received the Distinguished Service Cross and, by all accounts, probably deserved the Medal of Honor along with Sims and Hooper. Obviously, Clifford Sims was a hero amid a group of heroes that day. No one unit action resulted in two Medals of Honor for a single unit again until the 1993 rescue efforts in Mogadishu, Somalia, that have been immortalized by the movie *Black Hawk Down*. In the action involving Company D during the Battle of Hue, the number could easily have been three Medals of Honor.

Staff Sergeant Clifford Sims's family gathered in Washington, D.C., on December 2, 1969, for the presentation of his Medal of Honor by Vice President Spiro T. Agnew. His Medal was handed to his wife, Mary, who was there along with his daughter Gina and Sims's parents, James and Irene. Staff Sergeant Sims was buried in Barrancas National Cemetery in Pensacola, Florida, at Section 29, Grave 546. He is memorialized on the Vietnam Memorial at Panel 40E, Row 56.

Sims was honored by his home state of Florida on August 21, 2003, when Florida governor Jeb Bush presided over the dedication ceremony of Florida's 4th Veterans' Nursing Home as it was named in his honor in Springfield, Florida.

James B. Martin

Further Reading

Hanna, Charles W. *African American Recipients of the Medal of Honor: A Biographical Dictionary, Civil War through Vietnam War.* Jefferson, NC: McFarland, 2002.

Jones, Maxine D., and Kevin M. McCarthy. *African Americans in Florida.* Sarasota, FL: Pineapple Press, 1993.

Maslowski, Peter, and Don Winslow. *Looking for a Hero: Staff Sergeant Joe Ronnie Hooper.* Lincoln: University of Nebraska Press, 2004.

Murphy, Edward F. *Vietnam Medal of Honor Heroes.* New York: Ballantine Books, 2005.

"Nursing Home for Veteran's Named after Combat Hero." Lakeland Ledger,. http://news.google.com/newspapers?nid=1346&dat=20030822&id=nwcwAAAAIBAJ&sjid=-P0DAAAAIBAJ&pg=6170,750687, posted August 22, 2003 (accessed August 30, 2013).

"Wife Gets Sims' Medal of Honor." *The Evening Independent.* http://news.google.com/newspapers?nid=950&dat=19691205&id=YUtQAAAAIBAJ&sjid=i1cDAAAAIBAJ&pg=7068,1301786, posted December 5, 1969 (accessed August 30, 2013).

Smalls, Robert

Born: April 5, 1839
Died: February 23, 1915
Home State: South Carolina
Service: Navy
Conflict: Civil War
Age at Time of Award: N/A

Smalls was born in Beaufort, South Carolina, on April 5, 1839; his mother, Lydia, was a slave, and his father may have been her master, John McKee. When John McKee died in 1848, Smalls and his mother became the property of Henry McKee, with whom they moved to Charleston in 1851. In Charleston, Smalls met Hannah Jones, a hotel maid 14 years his senior, whom he married on December 24, 1856. The couple had two daughters, Elizabeth Lydia (b. 1858) and Sarah Voorhees (b. 1863), and a son Robert Jr. (b. 1861), who died at the age of three. Smalls took any employment he could find in Charleston, striving to buy his family's freedom. He worked as a waiter at the Planter's Hotel, as a lamplighter for the city, and as a rigger and sail-maker.

As a trusted slave, at the outbreak of the Civil War, Smalls had been employed as a sailor on the steamer *Planter* and had gained familiarity with the local waterways. When the *Planter* was rented by the Confederate government for use as a troop ship, together with other members of the African American crew, Smalls planned an escape, hoping to slip from the ship's mooring and sail to the safety of the Union blockade fleet just outside Charleston harbor.

On the night of May 13, 1862, the opportunity arose when Gen. Roswell Ripley and other white Confederate officers of the *Planter* went ashore to attend a party. The families of the African American crew

Robert Smalls won acclaim for his valor in escaping Charleston Harbor with the Confederate steamer *Planter* and turning it over to the Union. He went on to serve 15 years in the House of Representatives after the war. (Library of Congress)

(including Smalls's wife and daughters) had been hiding in other vessels nearby. Once they had quickly and quietly jumped aboard the steamship, Smalls, who had actually been acting as pilot, although as a slave he was not given the title, got the vessel underway. Donning the absent captain's clothing, Smalls ordered the hoisting of the Confederate and South Carolina flags and sounded the departure signal as he backed the *Planter* from its mooring. The knowledge he had gained while aboard the *Planter* stood him in good stead for sailing the vessel out of Charleston harbor, through the Helena Sound, down the Beaufort River. His mimicking of the actions and gestures of the captain of the steamship helped allay any suspicion the port authorities might have had about the ship's sailing. The African American crewmembers and their families hoisted the white flag of surrender as they approached the USS *Onward*, a Union blockade runner, and they handed the valuable vessel over to the enemy of the Confederates, along with information about mines and code signals.

The daring escape was reported in newspapers worldwide. A $4,000 reward for his capture was offered by the Confederate government. In the north, Smalls was hailed as a war hero, and his story influenced the debates raging over the continued existence of slavery and the use of African Americans as soldiers. The commander of the Union's Department of the South, Gen. David Hunter, sent Smalls to Washington, D.C., to discuss the formation of black regiments with the president and Secretary of State Edwin Stanton; as a result, Stanton authorized Hunter to recruit 5,000 African American volunteers in South Carolina.

Commissioned as a second lieutenant and attached to Company B, 33rd Regiment, U.S. Colored Troops, Smalls remained as pilot on the *Planter* with only a short break during service on the *Keokuk*. In November 1863, the *Planter* was involved in an engagement in which Smalls took command of the vessel while its captain hid in the coal bin. Smalls was then promoted to the rank of captain in the U.S. Navy, the first and only African American to be so promoted during the war.

During the remainder of the war, Smalls worked as a recruiter of African American troops for the Union Army. He later became a respected South Carolina politician and purchased his former owner's home in Beaufort. After winning promotion to the rank of major general in the South Carolina Militia and being elected to the South Carolina Constitutional Convention, Smalls assisted in the drafting of documents that eventually helped the black suffrage movement and contributed to the purchase of a school for African American children. He was elected to five terms (1875–1887) in the U.S. House of Representatives and became paramount in the introduction of legislation to protect the rights of children.

In 1883, Hannah Smalls died in their Beaufort, South Carolina, home. Smalls had been trying unsuccessfully to collect a pension from the U.S. Navy. Eventually he was awarded $30 a month and, in 1900, he was awarded $5,000 for his role in the capture of the *Planter*. In 1890, he had remarried, to Annie Wigg, with whom he had a son, William Robert Smalls (b. 1892).

The Honorable Robert Smalls died on February 23, 1915, after a long illness. He was buried at the Tabernacle Baptist Church, and a memorial bust of him was erected in front of the African Baptist Church, also in Beaufort. His former home is listed on the National Register of Historic Places.

Jonathan D. Sutherland

Further Reading

Astor, Gerald. *The Right to Fight: A History of African Americans in the Military.* Novato, CA: Presidio Press, 1998.

Cohn, Michael. *Black Men of the Sea.* New York: Dodd Mead, 1978.

Cooper, Michael L. *From Slave to Civil War Hero: The Life and Times of Robert Smalls.* New York: Lodestar Books, 1994.

Nalty, Bernard C. *Strength for the Fight.* New York: Free Press, 1986.

Uya, Okon Edet. *From Slavery to Public Service: Robert Smalls, 1839–1915.* New York: Oxford University Press, 1971.

Smith, Andrew Jackson

Born: September 3, 1842
Died: March 4, 1932
Home State: Kentucky
Service: Army
Conflict: Civil War
Age at Time of Award: 21

Andrew Jackson Smith was born into slavery on or about September 3, 1842. His mother, Susan, was a slave, and his father was Elijah Smith, a slave owner. When he was 10 years old, his owner assigned him to run a ferry transporting people and supplies across the Cumberland River. He continued this task for almost eight years, becoming an accomplished boatman in the process.

When the Civil War broke out, Andrew's father and owner, Elijah Smith, immediately enlisted in the Confederate Army. After a year's absence, he returned home on leave and indicated that he planned to take Andrew back with him. When Andrew, 19 at the time, overheard the plans, he and another slave decided to run away.

They made their way 25 miles through a freezing rain to seek protection from a Union Army regiment, the 41st Illinois Infantry, near Smithland, Kentucky. Andrew became a servant to Maj. John Warner. The two agreed that if Warner fell in battle, Jackson would take his belongings to Warner's home in Clinton, Illinois. The regiment moved on to battle at Ft. Henry, where the Union forces captured

Confederate general Lloyd Tillingham. The regiment then moved on to Ft. Donelson, where it lost 200 soldiers during the heavy fighting there.

In March 1862, Smith's regiment moved to Pittsburg Landing and participated in the Battle of Shiloh in April. During the battle, Major Warner had two horses shot out from under him, and Smith provided him fresh mounts. During the course of the battle, Smith was struck with a Confederate minie ball that entered his left temple, rolled just under the skin, and stopped in the middle of his forehead. The ball was removed by the regimental surgeon, leaving Smith with only a scar.

After the battle, Major Warner, accompanied by Smith, returned to Clinton, Illinois. Smith was there when he heard that President Abraham Lincoln had authorized black troops to join the Union forces to fight for their freedom.

Smith left Illinois to enroll in the Massachusetts Colored Volunteers. On May 16, 1863, he and 55 other Illinois volunteers were mustered into Company B of the 55th Regiment. After the 54th Regiment of Colored Volunteers, the sister regiment of the 55th, fought at Ft. Wagner, South Carolina, it was joined by the 55th Regiment, and they fought five major engagements together over the next two years.

In the late afternoon of November 30, 1864, the 54th and 55th regiments were involved in a bloody battle to take Honey Hill, near Boyd's Landing in South Carolina. The Confederates, in fortified entrenchments, occupied an elevated position on a rise fronted by swampy ground. As the Union troops advanced through the swamp, they came under withering fire from the Confederates. When the lead Union forces were thrown back, the 55th Regiment was ordered forward into the furious fight. Forced into a narrow gorge in the face of the enemy position, the Union troops took heavy casualties. The 55th regimental color sergeant was killed by an exploding shell, and Smith, now a corporal, took the state and federal flags from his hand and carried them forward through the heavy canister and rifle fire.

Although one-half the officers and a third of the enlisted men in his unit were killed or wounded, Corporal Smith continued to expose himself to enemy fire by carrying the colors throughout the battle. As the color-bearer, he presented a conspicuous target to the Confederates, but he pressed forward, disregarding his own safety and inspiring his fellow soldiers in the attack.

Smith was promoted to color sergeant soon after the battle at Honey Hill. He was discharged on August 29, 1865, and was sent to Boston on the steamer *Karnac* for his formal mustering out. After the war, he went back to Clinton, Illinois, for a short period of time but returned to Kentucky, where he lived out his days as a leader in the local community. He died at age 89 on March 4, 1932, and was buried in Mount Pleasant Cemetery in Grand Rivers, Kentucky.

Andrew Smith was nominated for the Medal of Honor in 1916, but the army denied the nomination, citing a lack of official records documenting the case. It was not until January 16, 2001, 137 years after the fact, that Smith's valor at Honey Hill was finally recognized; on that day, President Bill Clinton presented the Medal of

Honor to several of Smith's descendants, including his 93-year-old daughter, during a White House ceremony. Smith's Medal of Honor set a record for the longest period between a soldier's valorous act and the official recognition of that act by presentation of the medal. Also during that ceremony, the president presented the Medal of Honor posthumously to the relatives of former president Theodore Roosevelt for his action during the Spanish-American War.

James H. Willbanks

54TH MASSACHUSETTS INFANTRY REGIMENT

African Americans had been forbidden to serve in the American military in 1792 and were not allowed to enlist in the Union Army until after the Emancipation Proclamation. With the announcement of the proclamation freeing African Americans in the states in rebellion, President Lincoln had opened up enlistment to African Americans in the northern forces. In March 1863, the governor of Massachusetts, John A. Andrew, called for the formation of an African American unit to serve under the flag of Massachusetts during the conflict. African Americans were recruited from a number of New England states by prominent abolitions and formed into a unit in the city of Boston. White officers were handpicked by the governor to lead the unit and the regimental command was given to Colonel Robert Gould Shaw, the son of prominent abolitionists in Boston. Shaw had left his education at Harvard to serve in the Union Army and had been wounded during combat at the Battle of Antietam in 1862. Shaw and his officers formed the unit and moved it to Camp Meigs, just outside of Boston. Here, Colonel Shaw and his officers trained the unit in drill and marksmanship to prepare it for the combat they hoped would come. Shaw's officers were an experienced group with the vast majority of the 29 officers being combat veterans. They were also a determined group, as evidenced by their continued service leading the 54th in light of the announcement by the Confederate government that any white officer found leading African American troops would be put to death.

Departing from the Boston Commons on May 28, 1863, Shaw and the 54th Massachusetts traveled to Beaufort, South Carolina, to join the Union forces as part of the Department of the South. After an initial mission that was not militarily relevant, Colonel Shaw asked for the honor of leading the assault in the next major operation that the Department of the South would launch. The unit was afforded that privilege on July 18, 1863, at Ft. Wagner, near Charleston, South Carolina. The new commander of the Department of the South, Brigadier General George C. Strong, placed the 54th in the van of his assault on this heavily fortified Confederate position. Ft. Wagner was a relatively small fortification, but was well situated and manned by nearly 1,600 Confederate soldiers. After a long artillery barrage on the Confederate position, Colonel Shaw led the 54th across the sand and into the teeth of the enemy's defense. The shelling had not been as effective as Brigadier General Strong had anticipated and Ft. Wagner held more Confederate soldiers than his intelligence had indicated. The result was the 54th attacking a determined force, made even more determined by the presence of an African American unit in the attack. The 54th fought valiantly and pressed the attack to the fullest. The national and state colors they carried had to be repeatedly retrieved by members of the regiment, as the color bearers were hit and fell among the dead and wounded. Eyewitness recounts of the battle indicated that Colonel Shaw was shot in the chest as he mounted the parapet of the fortification and encouraged the 54th to follow him in the attack. He and many of his soldiers were killed and even more were wounded or captured. In all, of the 600 men who attacked Ft. Wagner, 54 died, 15 were captured, 149 were wounded, and 52 were listed as missing in action. This total of 272 "killed, wounded, or captured" was the highest loss the 54th would suffer during the entire Civil War. With Colonel Shaw's death, Lieutenant Colonel Edward Needles Hallowell, the regimental second in command, was promoted to Colonel of the Regiment and commanded the 54th for the remainder of the war.

The 54th Massachusetts continued to serve in the Department of the South until the war's end and added battle streamers to its flag for actions at Olustee, Honey Hill, and Boykin's Mill to accompany those of Grimball's Landing and Ft. Wagner. One member of the 54th, Sergeant William Harvey Carney, received the Medal of Honor for his efforts at Ft. Wagner. Colonel Shaw and the African American soldiers who died with him were buried in a mass grave in an attempt to desecrate the colonel's burial. In later years, his family would chose to have his remains stay buried in honor with the brave soldiers who had died with him at Ft. Wagner.

The 54th Massachusetts is only the best known of the African American units that fought for the Union Army during the Civil War. They have been immortalized in film and honored with monuments in their home state. The award-winning film, *Glory*, was based on the story of the 54th Massachusetts. In 1897, a monument was erected to the colonel and his regiment at the spot from which they departed the Boston Commons for service with the Union Army. The monument, a bronze piece depicting the 54th marching off to war, was designed and crafted by Augustus Saint-Gaudens. In addition to these honors, the 54th Massachusetts was remembered in poem and literature by the people of New England often over the years since the Civil War.

Of the approximately 180,000 African American soldiers who fought for the Union Army during the Civil War, about 40,000 died from wounds or disease. This total of African American soldiers represents approximately 10 percent of all soldiers who served in the Union Army during the war. These soldiers fought the same enemy that white soldiers did but also had to fight the hatred and prejudice present in both gray and blue uniforms. As in every conflict in American history, African American soldiers and sailors performed admirably. In the Civil War, unlike World War I, African Americans were recognized for their bravery during the conduct of the war. In addition to Sergeant Carney from the 54th Massachusetts, 24 more African Americans from the army and the navy received the Medal of Honor for their bravery and sacrifice. The segregated 54th Massachusetts set the model for segregated units in the U.S. Army that would last nearly until the conclusion of the Korean War.

James B. Martin

Further Reading

Gomez-Granger, Julissa. *CRS Report for Congress: Medal of Honor Recipients: 1979–2008.* Washington, DC: Congressional Research Service, RL 30011, June 4, 2008.

Hanna, Charles W. *African American Recipients of the Medal of Honor: A Biographical Dictionary, Civil War through Vietnam War.* Jefferson, NC: McFarland, 2002.

Reef, Catherine. *African Americans in the Military.* New York: Facts on File, 2004.

Stance, Emanuel (Edmund)

Born: circa 1847
Died: December 25, 1887
Home State: Louisiana
Service: Army
Conflict: Indian Wars
Age at Time of Award: approximately 23

Emanuel Stance was born into slavery in Carroll Parish, Louisiana, around 1847, although the exact date of his birth is unknown and few details of his early life were recorded.

It is clear, however, that Stance could read and write by October 2, 1866, when he joined the newly formed African American 9th Cavalry at Lake Providence, Louisiana. His age at the time was recorded as 19 and he was listed as a farmer, but Stance was so short (a little over five feet tall) that the African American enlistment officer, Lt. John Maroney, was not certain he was suitable for one of the new African American regiments, which later collectively became known as the Buffalo Soldiers.

Stance, nevertheless, succeeded in enlisting as a member of Company F of the 9th Cavalry, and he began his six-month training course. By February 1867, he had been promoted to corporal and was based in Carrolton, Louisiana. The following month, the 9th Cavalry was transferred to San Antonio, Texas, on frontier duty. He remained there until June 1867, when he was moved to Ft. Davis, Texas. In July of the same year, he was promoted to sergeant, and during the following two years, he was involved in five different encounters with hostile Native Americans.

In December 1868, Stance's Company F was involved in an attack by a 100 Mescalero Indians. The Buffalo Soldiers managed to hold off the attack, losing very few men. The company moved to Camp Quitman (later to be called Ft. Quitman), where it suffered 16 different Native American attacks, all successfully repelled. In September 1868, as part of the 9th Cavalry, Company F members managed to spring a surprise attack on 200 Native Americans camped close to Horsehead Hills. They killed 25 and wounded and captured many more. Only one of the Buffalo Soldiers was killed in this attack.

A group of men from Stance's Company F was transferred to Ft. McKavett, Texas. There, in early 1870, they were involved in a skirmish with 200 Comanche and Kiowa Indians close to the Brazos River. They chased the Indians for eight miles; the Native American warriors suffered 25 casualties, and three men from Company F were wounded.

On May 20, 1870, at Kickapoo Springs, Texas, Stance rode out from Ft. McKavett with 12 other members of Company F in search of Kickapoo Indians who had been raiding the local settlements and who had captured two white children, brothers, from a farm 40 miles from the fort. Stance's orders from Capt. Henry Carroll were "to endeavor to the utmost to intercept the Indians that stole the two children of Phillip Buckmeier of Loyal Valley" (Schubert 1997, 19).

During their search for the children, the soldiers came across a band of Native Americans who were herding stolen horses. Stance immediately gave the order to charge, which forced the warriors to scatter and allowed Company F to retrieve the horses. The next day, Stance and his troops encountered another band of Native Americans, who were attempting to ambush government wagons. Again Stance and his men drove off the Indians and recaptured the horses. Despite an Indian counterattack later in the day, Stance and his troops managed to successfully recover the younger of the two children they had been searching for. The older boy, however, was not to return home for another eight years.

For his heroism and gallantry at Kickapoo Springs, Stance was recommended for and received the Medal of Honor, the first African American to win the award since the Civil War (awarded July 9, 1870). Captain Carroll wrote of Stance's actions, "The gallantry displayed by the sergeant and his party as well as good judgment used on both occasions, deserves much praise" (quoted in Schubert 1997, 21). Stance said of his Medal of Honor, "I will cherish the gift, as a thing of priceless value and endeavor by my future conduct to merit the high honor conferred upon me" (quoted in Schubert 1997, 21).

However, Stance's conduct did not always meet the standard set by the army, and by April 1871, his rank had been reduced to private, probably as a result of either drinking, fighting, or not showing up for duty. He was promoted again to sergeant at least four times before 1880, but each time he was again reduced to private. He was always keen to reinvent his identity, and on one occasion, he changed his name to Edmund Stance before reenlisting.

In 1882, approaching the age of 40 and having served for 16 years, Stance reenlisted in Company F, still under Captain Carroll, and was promoted to sergeant for the fifth time. But by the time Company F was transferred to Ft. Robinson in 1885, Stance's behavior had still not improved; he was often involved in brawls with the other men and was accused of bullying his men. His treatment of his troops was often described as outdated.

Stance was found shot dead on Christmas morning 1887. The evidence gathered at the time implicated members of Stance's own regiment. One member of Company F, Pvt. Miller Milds, was charged with the murder, but he was later released for lack of evidence, and the killing remains unsolved.

Jonathan D. Sutherland

Further Reading

Leckie, William H. *The Buffalo Soldiers: A Narrative of the Negro Cavalry in the West.* Norman: University of Oklahoma Press, 1967.

Miller, Robert. *Buffalo Soldiers: The Story of Emanuel Stance.* Morristown, NJ: Silver Press, 1995.

Rickey, Don, Jr. *Forty Miles a Day on Beans and Hay: The Enlisted Soldier Fighting the Indian Wars.* Norman: University of Oklahoma Press, 1963.

Schubert, Frank N. *Black Valor: Buffalo Soldiers and the Medal of Honor, 1870–1898.* Wilmington, DE: Scholarly Resources, 1997.

Schubert, Frank N. "The Violent World of Emmanuel Stance, Fort Robinson, 1887." *Nebraska History* 55 (Summer 1974): 203–219.

Utley, Robert M. *Frontier Regulars: The United States Army and the Indian, 1866–1890.* New York: Macmillan, 1973.

Stowers, Freddie

Born: January 12, 1896
Died: September 28, 1918
Home State: South Carolina
Service: Army
Conflict: World War I
Age at Time of Award: 22

The grandson of a slave, Freddie Stowers was born on January 12, 1896, and raised on a farm in Sandy Springs, South Carolina. Drafted in 1917, he was inducted in the newly formed 1st Provisional Infantry Regiment (Colored) at Camp Jackson, South Carolina. In December 1917, the 1st Provisional Infantry Regiment (Colored) was redesignated the 371st Infantry and assigned to the 186th Infantry Brigade (Colored) of the 93rd Division (Provisional). The division was composed of four African American regiments, three from the National Guard and the 371st composed of draftees from the National Army.

At Camp Jackson, the 93rd spent many long days drilling and training basic soldier skills. British officers and noncommissioned officers arrived to train the men on trench warfare tactics, along with rifle practice, bayonet drill, grenade throwing, and even training on foreign mortars and machine guns. The 371st deployed with the division on April 5, 1918, arriving at their final destination of Vaubecourt, France, by the end of the month. Although part of the American Expeditionary Force, upon reaching France, all four African American regiments of the 93rd were permanently assigned to different French divisions. The 371st Infantry Regiment became a permanent unit of the French 157th "Red Hand" Division under the command of Gen. Mariano Goybet. The men of the 371st Infantry Regiment exchanged their American equipment for all French equipment except the U.S.-issued brown woolen uniform. General Goybet even reorganized the 371st to the structure of a French infantry regiment.

By early June 1918, the men of the 371st were in the trenches in the Verrières sector between the Aire and Meuse rivers. Throughout the rest of the summer, the

The headstone honoring Freddie Stowers, the only African American to receive the Medal of Honor during World War I. (Reuters/Corbis)

371st made numerous raids on German positions, some small and some large, but all bloody. During this fighting, Stowers was recognized early on for his initiative and leadership abilities. Promoted to corporal and squad leader in Company C of the 1st Battalion, his leadership qualities would soon be put to the ultimate test in one of the largest battles of the war.

On September 28, 1918, the 371st jumped off in the Champagne-Marne sector as part of the immense Meuse-Argonne Offensive. Attacking across a front of 500 meters, the objective was Hill 188, a heavily fortified defense, including massive barbed wire entanglements. Under intense machine gun and artillery fire, Stowers's company penetrated the barbed wire and were closing in on the German positions. Suddenly, the Germans ceased fire and crawled out of their positions with their hands in the air. As the Americans moved forward to take prisoners, the Germans jumped back into their trenches and opened fire. Exposed in the open approximately 100 meters from the German positions, C Company was devastated by a withering fire from interlocking machine guns and mortars. Corporal Stowers's platoon lost all of its leaders within seconds, and he immediately took charge by reorganizing the survivors in order to continue the attack. With complete disregard for his own safety, Stowers crawled forward toward a machine gun nest that was causing heavy casualties to his company. After destroying the machine gun nest, Stowers continued to lead his men forward to take the German positions. Stowers was struck by machine gun fire, and although mortally wounded, he continued to lead and encourage his fellow soldiers onward through heavy fire. Because of his extraordinary and inspirational courage, Stowers and his men captured the German trenches and all the machine gun positions. Stowers collapsed while organizing defensive positions to prepare for the inevitable enemy counterattack. He later died of his wounds.

Recommended by Stowers's company commander for the Medal of Honor, the paperwork was lost for over 70 years. Found among army records in 1990, the army dispatched a team to France to investigate Freddie Stowers's actions. As a result of this investigation, the Army Decorations Board approved the only African American to be awarded the Medal of Honor in World War I. On April 24, 1991, in a White House ceremony, President George Bush presented the Medal of Honor to Stowers's surviving sisters, Georgina Palmer and Mary Bowens. Corporal Stowers was buried in the Meuse-Argonne American Cemetery and Memorial east of the village of Romagne-sous-Montfaucon in France.

Scott A. Porter

Further Reading

Aster, Gerald. *The Right to Fight: A History of African Americans in the Military.* Cambridge, MA: Da Capo Press, 1998.

Franklin, John Hope, and Alfred A. Moss Jr. *From Slavery to Freedom: A History of African Americans.* 8th ed., 2 vols in one. New York: Random House, 2004.

Lengel, Edward G. *To Conquer Hell: The Meuse-Argonne, 1918: The Epic Battle That Ended the First World War.* New York: Henry Holt, 2008.

Roberts, Frank E. *The American Foreign Legion: Black Soldiers of the 93d in World War I.* Annapolis, MD: Naval Institute Press, 2004.

Thomas, Charles L.

Born: April 17, 1920
Died: February 15, 1980
Home State: Michigan
Service: Army
Conflict: World War II
Age at Time of Award: 24

Thomas was born in Birmingham, Alabama, on April 17, 1920. As a child, he moved with his family from Alabama to Detroit and graduated from Cass Technical High School in 1938. He then worked with his father at the Ford Motor Company River Rouge factory as a molder and metal pourer, at the same time enrolling at Wayne State University. He was drafted into the U.S. Army on January 20, 1942, as a private who was assigned to the 614th Tank Destroyer Battalion and sent to Tank Destroyer Officer Candidate School at Camp Wolters, Texas. He was commissioned as a second lieutenant in March 1943, and was then deployed with the 614th to Metz, France, in August 1944, to join Patton's Third Army.

Thomas's C Company was lead element of a task force of the 614th assigned to capture the enemy-held French town of Climbach, five miles from the Siegfried Line. The available accounts of exactly what happened as Thomas led his unit toward Climbach differ, as they often do, but his actions were those of a true leader and hero. His scout car was disabled by enemy artillery and small arms fire. Though he was wounded by the initial engagement, Lieutenant Thomas halted the column and provided assistance to the crew of the scout car, though he himself was badly injured. As he left the protection of the wrecked vehicle, Thomas was repeatedly hit by enemy fire, resulting in wounds to his chest, legs, and left arm. Though severely wounded, Lieutenant Thomas continued to command his unit, supervising the emplacement of two antitank guns. These weapons were used with great accuracy by his soldiers and within moments were suppressing the enemy fire. Recognizing that his wounds would soon leave in a state unable to effectively command, he called for the platoon leader to join him. Only after he had thoroughly prepared the junior officer concerning the disposition of the enemy and his own unit, and was convinced he was in full control of the situation, did Lieutenant Thomas allow himself to be evacuated for medical care.

Later Thomas explained why he had not allowed himself to be evacuated immediately: "This was hardly the place to . . . I knew what had to be done. They say men under stress can do unusual. . . . I know I hung onto one thought, deploy the guns and start firing or we're dead" (quoted in Cohen 2003).

For five hours Thomas's command continued, despite severe casualties, to hold and return fire, allowing other U.S. troops to approach the town and overrun the German positions. Thomas himself was evacuated to England and from there to the Percy Jones Hospital (Battle Creek). Meanwhile, the 614th drove on into Germany and Austria.

Lt. Col. John Blackshear, a white commander, recommended Thomas for the Distinguished Service Cross. Thomas was promoted to captain and received the award in March 1945, in a ceremony in Detroit. In response to the accolade, he said: "I was just trying to stay alive out there" (quoted in Cohen 2003).

The engagement also led to the 614th becoming the first African American formation to be awarded a Distinguished Unit Citation. In addition to this collective honor and Thomas's Distinguished Service Cross, his Third Platoon received other accolades for their combat outside of Climbach. In all, the other members of the Third Platoon received four Silver Stars and nine Bronze Stars for their actions during this engagement. Collectively, for engagements throughout the entire war, the 614th received 8 Silver Stars, 28 Bronze Stars, and 79 Purple Hearts.

Thomas was officially discharged from the army in 1947 (by which time he had been promoted to major). He never recovered full use of his right hand and continued to receive disability payments until he died. Thomas married in July 1949 and had two children; he worked at Selfridge Field as a technician and later as a computer programmer for the Internal Revenue Service.

For many years after the war, old comrades in arms who happened to meet him could not believe that Thomas had survived his wounds at Climbach and were amazed that he was still alive. Thomas was a modest man who never asked for recognition of what he had done; in fact, while being honored by Detroit civic leaders in March 1945, he shared that "I was just trying to stay alive out there."

In 1993, the U.S. Army commissioned a study to determine why no African Americans had been awarded the Medal of Honor during World War II. The study found widespread racism, and army records revealed a number of Medal of Honor recommendations that had been downgraded to the DSC. On the basis of this evidence, seven African Americans awarded the Silver Star or DSC during World War II had their awards upgraded to the Medal of Honor. In 1995, Thomas became one of the seven African Americans to have the recognition of their contributions and bravery upgraded to Medal of Honor status. Unfortunately, the ceremony, which took place on January 13, 1997, at the White House, came 17 years too late for Thomas, who had died on February 15, 1980. He was buried in Westlawn Cemetery in Wayne County, Michigan.

Jonathan D. Sutherland

Further Reading

Bruning, John Robert, Jr. *Elusive Glory: African-American Heroes of World War II.* Greensboro, NC: Avisson Press, Inc., 2001.

Cohen, Warren. "Recognizing Valor." *Michigan History Magazine*, January/February 1997. http://wjcohen.home.mindspring.com/otherclips/thomas.htm (accessed July 16, 2003).

Converse, Elliott, III, Daniel K. Gibran, John A. Cash, Robert K. Griffith, Jr., and Richard H. Kohn. *The Exclusion of Black Soldiers from the Medal of Honor in World War II: The Study Commissioned by the United States Army to Investigate Racial Bias in the Awarding of the Nation's Highest Military Decoration.* Jefferson, NC: McFarland, 1997.

Motley, Mary Penick, ed. *The Invisible Soldier: The Experience of the Black Soldier, World War II.* Detroit: Wayne State University Press, 1975.

Thompson, William Henry

Born: August 16, 1927
Died: August 6, 1950
Home State: New York
Service: Army
Conflict: Korean War
Age at Time of Award: 22

William Thompson was born in New York and lived a tough life split between his grandmother's care and a center for homeless boys in the Bronx. He entered service in the Bronx and was initially assigned to a unit in Adak, Alaska. Transferred to Korea, he was eventually assigned to Company M, 24th Infantry Regiment, part of the 25th Infantry Division. His unit was attacked during the North Korean push on the Pusan Perimeter and Thompson stood his ground to protect his retreating comrades. He became the first African American to be awarded the Medal of Honor since the Spanish-American War.

On August 6, 1950, elements of Company M were reorganizing under the cover of darkness in preparation for another attack from North Korean forces. The attack came as an overwhelming number of the enemy converged on the unit in a surprise attack. Recognizing the imminent danger to his unit, Private First Class Thompson established a hasty defensive position with his machine gun and began to slow the assault with a witheringly accurate fire. Though he was able to only slow the assault and pin down the attacking North Koreans for moments, his actions allowed the rest of his unit to withdraw to a more defensible position and prepare to accept the attack. During his stand against the North Korean forces, Thompson was repeatedly hit by enemy fire and hand grenade shrapnel but he refused to withdraw from his advantageous position. Private First Class Thompson continued to pour accurate fire into the enemy elements until a hand grenade finally left him mortally wounded.

The thinly explained reorganization under the cover of darkness alludes to the fact that it was believed at the time that the 24th ran from the enemy assaults in the area near Haman, Korea, on August 6, 1950. The army's own historian's account of the actions of the 24th Infantry Regiment is sharply disputed by members of the unit, a number of the battalion and regimental commanders, and more modern historians removed from the racially contentious times of the midcentury. Indeed, Thompson's own commanding officer, Lieutenant Colonel Melvin Blair, who was later relieved of his command by the Regimental Commander, initially tried to block the application for the Medal of Honor. Eventually, Blair became the biggest advocate for the award of Thompson's Medal of Honor and a supporter of the fighting spirit of the 24th Infantry Regiment. The actions of Private First Class Thompson bring the historical accounts of the 24th Infantry Regiment breaking and running into question, as his actions are not indicative of a broken unit or African American soldiers who were afraid to fight.

The situation at the time was that the North Koreans were driving on Pusan from the west along the Chinju-Masan corridor. This had forced Lt. Gen. Walton H. Walker, Eighth Army commander, to concentrate his troops in this area. Reinforcements were arriving in the form of the 5th Regimental Combat Team and the 1st Provisional Marine Brigade (some six battalions of infantry, supported by tanks and artillery). Walker planned to counterattack where he was already the strongest. It seemed that the best option was to order the Eighth Army to mount an attack in the Chinju-Masan area between August 5 and 10, and then to launch a general offensive in the middle of the month and drive west to Yosu. The army would then head north on the Sunch'on-Chonju-Nonsan axis toward the Kum River.

It was decided that there were insufficient resources to mount the second phase of the operation, but the initial attacks would go ahead. This would, at least, relieve enemy pressure against the perimeter in the Taegu area by forcing the diversion of some North Korean units southward. The Fifth Air Force, over August 5–6, interdicted all enemy movement in the proposed area of operations, and on August 6, Walker approved the launching of ground operations (by the units collectively known as Task Force Kean, after Maj. Gen. William Kean of the 25th Division). The offensive was intended to get under way at 06:30 AM on August 7; collectively some 20,000 men were to be involved in the operations.

The situation had, however, taken a different turn on August 6, when the North Koreans ambushed Companies I and L of the 24th Infantry west of Haman. Most of the men fled before the enemy attack, and the whole of the 3rd Battalion retreated to the rear. But not all had fled; Pfc. William Thompson of the Heavy Weapons Company set up his machine gun in the face of the onslaught and fired at the enemy until he was killed by grenades. His efforts permitted the remainder of his platoon to withdraw to a safer position.

Thompson was buried in Long Island National Cemetery in Farmingdale, New York. His mother, Mary Henderson, received William's Medal of Honor from General of the Armies Omar Bradley on June 21, 1951. In 2011, on the 84th anniversary of his death, PFC Thompson and the other African American Medal of Honor recipient from the Korean War, Cornelius Charlton, were honored by the citizens of the Bronx through the creation of the Charlton Thompson Memorial Garden. This garden honors the two hometown heroes who are also the only African American Medal of Honor recipients from the Bronx.

James B. Martin and Jonathan D. Sutherland

A PROBLEM OF LEADERSHIP

One of the keys to success in combat is leadership. The segregated units in the U.S. Army were normally led by white officers—often individuals who did not want to be there and had no respect for their African American troops. This lack of respect shown through in their actions and attitudes and normally led to poor morale and inadequate training. Well-led troops perform well in stressful situations, regardless of their race. The histories of three segregated units show the impact of leadership and morale.

The 369th Infantry Regiment's history is detailed elsewhere in this volume, but it is included here as a comparison of a segregated unit's performance when it was not constrained by the leadership of uninterested white officers within the shackles of the U.S. Army's racial bias at the time. Assigned to a French division, the unit was given responsibilities equivalent to those given to French regiments without any preconceived notion of their performance. The French were in dire straits and did not have the time for the social aspects of race to interrupt their combat power. The 369th was very successful during World War I, largely because they were able to receive the same training as their French counterparts and then maintain a level of trust between the leader and the led that resulted in high morale. The 369th proved that African American soldiers with proper training and good leadership could perform as well as any white soldier in combat.

The 92nd Infantry Division was the only segregated African American infantry division to see combat in World War II. It was commanded by a white southern general officer who saw race as most of his contemporaries did at the time. Most of the white officers who led the division at all levels were dismissive of their African American soldiers and did nothing to build morale in the unit. These leaders allowed or supported racial discrimination in the United States before the unit was deployed to Europe and created an environment in Italy that showed their disdain for African Americans in general. It was a standing order in the division that no African American officer would be allowed to command or be on staff at the battalion level or higher. Policies like this were illustrative of how the senior leadership viewed African Americans and only served to create a negative atmosphere in the division. The history of the division in World War II has two sides, that told by Major General Ned Almond, the division commanding general and that told by veterans of the division and their company, battalion, and regimental leaders who were more accepting of the African American race. The division was eventually broken up by General George Marshall, the army chief of staff, based on Almond's recommendation. Almond did not believe that African American soldiers could be effective combat soldiers and indicated that on more than one occasion. The history of the division, from an individual soldier's perspective, was not unlike the more successful 369th Infantry Regiment. According to one historian of the division, African American soldiers serving in the unit received three Distinguished Service Crosses (two of which were later upgraded to Medals of Honor), 102 Silver Stars, 753 Bronze Stars, and 1,910 Purple Hearts during nine months of combat. During those nine months, the division lost 518 killed in action, 2,242 wounded in action, 67 who later died of wounds, and 21 soldiers captured. As with the 369th, numerous individual soldiers performed bravely and proved that race was not a factor in the quality of a combat soldier. The difference between the two units came down to leadership, mainly the problems incurred by white senior officers who did not respect the men serving under them and subsequently could not bring themselves to build the best possible combat unit.

No story in the U.S. Army's history better illustrates the inherent difficulty that African American soldiers faced in trying to prove their worth and get their bravery recognized by the white military establishment than that of the 24th Infantry Regiment during the Korean War. In the United States, African American soldiers were regularly denigrated by white officers and the white civilian society around them. Positive actions by African American soldiers were ignored or downplayed, while any negative actions were highly publicized and often identified as a consequence of their race. The environment in Korea was little different and resulted in a unit that performed well at times and horribly at others. This description could apply to many units in the early weeks and months of the Korean War, but the 24th Infantry Regiment was placed under a microscope. Major General William Dean, commanding general of the

25th Infantry Division in Korea, recommended the dissolution of the regiment to Lieutenant General Matthew Ridgway. Ridgway eventually accepted the recommendation and sought to integrate all of the units in the Korean War Theater as a way to improve combat effectiveness. Dean based his recommendations on his perception that the soldiers of the 24th would not stand and fight, a perception tinged with the racial bias that African American soldiers were not of adequate quality. Dean never uttered or wrote those words, but of all the disorganized and underperforming units in the Korean War (of which there were many), the only unit singled out for dissolution was the segregated 24th Infantry Regiment. An unbiased observer looking at the unit's history can easily ascertain that when the unit was well led, it performed well. Examining the various histories that have been written on the regiment's performance shows instances of failure and others of success. In almost every case, the leadership exhibited by the regimental commander and the senior officers was normally the influencing factor. Under the command of Lieutenant Colonel John T. Corley, an officer who spent much time in the forward positions with his soldiers and was highly regarded by the vast majority of the regiment, the unit performed well and had few continuing discipline problems. The same is true for the last commander of the regiment, Colonel Thomas D. Gillis. These officers are singled out by veterans of the regiment for their leadership and the improvement in morale that occurred during their tenure. They both informed the division commander that the problem in the regiment was leadership and took actions to correct it by relieving underperforming officers. Corley spoke positively in the press about the heroic actions of members of the regiment and undoubtedly hurt his career in doing so. The individual soldiers of the 24th, like those in the other two segregated units examined here, showed courage that was rewarded by medals for heroism. Two members of the regiment, Sergeant Cornelius H. Charlton and Private First Class William Henry Thompson, received the Medal of Honor posthumously for their actions in Korea. Numerous other soldiers in the regiment received awards, including Distinguished Service Crosses and Silver Stars.

These three units took different paths during their combat histories, but the common threads were twofold: when well led, these segregated units could perform on a level with a similar all-white army unit and no matter the theater of war or the enemy they faced, individual soldiers acquitted themselves as true heroes and proved the race had no bearing on bravery or sacrifice.

James B. Martin

Further Reading

Bowers, William T., William M. Hammond, and George L. MacGarrigle. *Black Soldier, White Army: The 24th Infantry Regiment in Korea.* Washington, DC: Center of Military History, U.S. Army, 1996.

Reef, Catherine. *African Americans in the Military.* New York: Facts on File, 2010.

Williams, Albert E. *Black Warriors: The Korean War.* Haverford, PA: Infinity, 2004.

Tubman, Harriet

Born: circa 1820
Died: March 10, 1913
Home State: Maryland
Service: Army
Conflict: Civil War
Age at Time of Award: N/A

Tubman was born in 1820 or 1821 into slavery in Bucktown, Dorchester County, Maryland. She was abused repeatedly while a slave and escaped at the age of 25 via the Underground Railroad set up by abolitionists and former slaves to help slaves flee to the North and sometimes on to Canada. The so-called railroad was actually a string of safe houses and hiding places in the South that slaves could use on their journey north.

A former slave, Harriet Tubman courageously served the Union Army as a scout and spy during the Civil War. She was recognized for her valor by British Queen Victoria, but never by her own government. (Library of Congress)

Once in the North, it was not long before Tubman had become actively involved in an abolitionist group in Philadelphia. When Congress enacted the Fugitive Slave Act in 1850, it became illegal to help a runaway slave, but such legislation did little to deter Tubman from helping her fellow bondsmen. The following year, she embarked on her first mission with the Underground Railroad.

Over the next decade, Tubman became the most famous "conductor" on the Underground Railroad, gaining the moniker "Moses of her people." Undeterred by a $40,000 reward placed on her head, Tubman returned to the South 19 times during the 1850s, guiding over 300 slaves to Canada and freedom.

In the years before the Civil War, Tubman was a defiant opponent of the Fugitive Slave Law, not only laboring for the Underground Railroad but also snatching runaway slaves from the authorities in New York. If circumstances had not prevented her, she would have joined John Brown's raid on the arsenal and armory at Harpers Ferry on October 16, 1859, and she was greatly disappointed at not being able to take part.

During the war, Tubman continued her rescue efforts across enemy lines and also worked as a nurse, scout, and spy. In 1862, Massachusetts governor John Andrew helped arrange for her to work in Beaufort, South Carolina, as a nurse for the Union Army and among the recently freed slaves on the Carolina Sea Islands. Tubman recalled her nursing experiences to her biographer Sarah Bradford:

> Well, Missus, I'd go to de hospital, I would, early eb'ry mornin'. I'd get a big chunk of ice, I would, and put it in a basin, and fill it with water; den I'd take a sponge and begin. Furst man I'd come to, I'd thrash away de flies, an' dey'd rise, dey would, like bees roun' a hive. Den I'd begin to bathe der wounds, an' by de time I'd bathed off three or four, de fire and heat would have melted de ice and made de water warm, as' it would be as red as clar blood. Den I'd go an' git more ice, I would, an' by de time I got to de nex' ones, de flies would be roun' de fust ones, black an' thick as eber." In this way she worked, day after day, till late at night; then she went home to her little cabin, and made about fifty pies, a great quantity of ginger-bread, and two casks of root beer. These she would hire some contraband to sell for her through the camps, and thus she would provide her support for another day; for this woman never received pay or pension, and never drew for herself but twenty days' rations during the four years of her labors. (quoted in Bradford 1869, 97–98)

By early 1863, Tubman had begun the dangerous duties of scout and spy for the Union forces in South Carolina. Employing former slaves from the area, Tubman organized a network of spies and reported the gathered intelligence to Col. James Montgomery, commander of the 2nd South Carolina Colored Infantry, a unit made up entirely of former slaves. In her own missions, Tubman often adopted the disguise of a field hand or a poor farmer's wife.

In late May 1863, Gen. David Hunter requested Tubman's assistance to personally guide a raiding party up the Combahee River. In the gathering dusk on June 2, Tubman led Montgomery and 150 soldiers in gunboats past Confederate picket lines and up the river. The raid was a success and destroyed significant amounts of Confederate supplies while bringing back over 700 slaves. After the expedition, Gen. Rufus Saxton reported to Secretary of War Edwin Stanton: "This is the only military command in American history wherein a woman, black or white, led the raid and under whose inspiration it was originated and conducted" (quoted in Lewis 2003). Tubman was also present at Ft. Wagner to see the unfortunate yet glorious demise of Col. Robert Gould Shaw and harrowing experiences of the all-African American 54th Massachusetts Infantry.

Tubman received glowing testimonials from a number of Union generals for her exploits during the war and received a medal from Britain's Queen Victoria. On the other hand, she was never paid her back pay, and the U.S. War Department adamantly refused to pay her a pension, despite the fact that her claim was supported by Secretary of State William Seward, Col. Thomas Wentworth Higginson, and Saxton.

After the war ended, Tubman returned to her home in Auburn, New York, where she had settled with her parents and some of the rest of her family. Although still an active campaigner for African American civil rights, she also joined the women's rights movement and the temperance crusade. Tubman died in New York on March 10, 1913, at the approximate age of 93.

Jonathan D. Sutherland

Further Reading

Bradford, Sarah E. *Harriet: The Moses of Her People.* 1901. New York: J.J. Little & Co.

Bradford, Sarah E. *Scenes in the Life of Harriet Tubman.* 1869. Reprint, Salem, NH: Ayer, 1986.

Lewis, Jone Johnson. "Harriet Tubman: Fugitive Slave, Underground Railroad Conductor, Civil War Nurse and Soldier, Women's Rights Advocate and Social Reformer." http://womenshistory.about.com/library/weekly/aa020419c.htm (accessed July 17, 2003).

Rose, P.K. "Black Dispatches: Black American Contributions to Union Intelligence during the Civil War." http://www.cia.gov/cia/publications/dispatches/dispatch.html

Walley, Augustus

Born: March 10, 1856
Died: April 9, 1938
Home State: Maryland
Service: Army
Conflict: Indian Wars, Spanish-American War
Age at Time of Award: 25

Augustus Walley was born in Reistertown, Baltimore County, Maryland, on March 10, 1856. He was born into slavery, but became a free man after the end of the Civil War. He worked as a laborer around his hometown until he enlisted in the army on November 26, 1878, to join the famous 9th Cavalry (Buffalo Soldiers) and served initially in Troop I of the 9th.

Walley was serving with this same unit on August 16, 1881, part of an element that was in pursuit of the Apache chief Nana and his renegade group of warriors.

They were resting after a lengthy chase of the Indians, when a local man burst into camp to report that Nana had hit a settlement just two miles from where the troopers were resting. The farm belonging to Mr. Chavez had been attacked and everyone living there had been killed. The troop commander, Lieutenant Valois, directed one of his officers, Lieutenant Burnett, to take a small detachment of 12 troopers and give immediate chase to Nana's band. Valois and the remainder of the troop would follow as soon as they were made ready. When they arrived at the ranch, Burnett and his small detachment found the local citizen's account to be accurate and set out after Nana, now accompanied by a large group of armed local citizens for assistance. They found Nana in the foothills of the Cuchillo Negro Mountains, New Mexico, and proceeded to engage his band in a running battle, successively attacking Nana's positions on each of the ridgelines as he retreated deeper into the mountains. At numerous points during this running battle, Walley was mentioned as staying with Burnett and providing covering fire whenever someone was in danger. Burnett later wrote that he was "always to the front" throughout the engagement. Eventually, Lieutenant Valois and the remainder of Troop I caught up with Burnett's detachment, but as they did both organizations found themselves caught in a trap set by Nana. Valois called for both units to retreat, with Burnett, Sergeant Moses Williams, and Private Walley providing covering fire for all of the 9th Cavalry troopers. Just as this trio of heroes was about to withdraw, they heard voices coming from their front asking for help. Three troopers from Valois contingent had been left behind as they sought cover behind some prairie dog mounds. Now situated between the enemy and the troopers, they needed help to survive. Burnett, Moses, and Walley stayed put to continue covering fire and two of the troopers crawled to their position and safety. The third trooper, named Burton, had been wounded and was unable to accompany his comrades as they withdrew under the covering fire. Private Walley volunteered to make a rescue attempt and Lieutenant Burnett consented. Riding his horse so that he was low in the saddle away from the enemy fire, Walley made it safely through the hail of bullets to Burton's position. Hoisting the wounded man into the saddle, Walley mounted behind him and spurred the horse to safety, covered by the fire of Burnett and Moses. Private Walley's courage and sacrifice saved the life of one of his comrades and kept him from falling into the hands of Nana's Apaches. All three men, Burnett, Moses, and Walley received the Medal of Honor, with Walley also receiving a Certificate of Merit. This was an important thing for a Buffalo Soldier, because the certificate meant another few dollars in his monthly pay.

Private Augustus Walley's Medal of Honor was issued on October 1, 1890, but he was not done with his heroism. He was transferred to Troop I, 10th Cavalry after 15 years in the 9th and was with this troop during the famous charge-up San Juan Hill in Cuba during the Spanish-American War. He was again cited for gallantry during this action, as he saved the life of Major James M. Bell of the 1st Cavalry by carrying him off the field of battle under constant, deadly enemy fire. Captain Charles G. Ayers, who was with Walley during this action, recommended him for a second Medal of Honor, but this award was denied and Walley received another Certificate of Merit. Some historians have claimed that Walley's case was reexamined after World War I and his certificate was upgraded to the new Silver Star Medal, but official confirmation is unavailable.

Augustus Walley continued to serve with the 10th Cavalry, including time spent in the Philippines participating in the Philippine Insurrection, until his retirement at Ft. Washakie, Wyoming, in 1907. By this time, he had served with the Buffalo Soldiers for 30 years, been promoted to First Sergeant of Troop E, and had received the Medal of Honor and two Certificates of Merit. He was old as Buffalo Soldiers went in those days, as life as a private soldier on the frontier was very hard on a man. He left Ft. Washakie and moved to Butte, Montana, but left to live in Prague, Oklahoma, and Cleveland, Ohio, before returning to the town of his birth, Reisterstown, Maryland. In 1918, First Sergeant Walley was called to active duty with the beginning of World War I, though historians disagree as to whether or not he was allowed to serve at his advanced age. Whether on active duty or not, Walley spent the war at Camp Beauregard, Louisiana, helping with the war effort.

First Sergeant Augustus Walley died on April 9, 1938, at his home on Etting Avenue in Baltimore, Maryland. He had been a hero as a member of the Buffalo Soldiers and led a long life by their standards—seeing his country in three different wars. He was buried in the cemetery of St. Luke's Methodist Church in Reistertown, Maryland, and the small road next to the church was renamed Augustus Walley Way in his honor. In 1995, the publication of the Medal of Honor Historical Society indicated that Augustus Walley Day had been held in Baltimore County to honor a local hero. Walley's actions in Cuba were immortalized in the work of noted military artist, Don Stivers, when he was chosen as the central figure in Stivers's 1998 print *A Day of Honor*.

James B. Martin

Further Reading

"Apache Campaigns: Victorio." *Huachua Illustrated: A Magazine of the Fort Huachuca Museum*, 6 (1999): 45–75.

Beer, W. F., and O. F. Keyed. *Deeds of Valor: How America's Heroes Won the Medal of Honor*. Detroit: Perrien-Keydel, 1903.

Hanna, Charles W. *African American Recipients of the Medal of Honor: A Biographical Dictionary, Civil War through Vietnam War*. Jefferson, NC: McFarland, 2002.

Leckie, William H. *The Buffalo Soldiers: A Narrative of the Negro Cavalry in the West.* Norman: University of Oklahoma Press, 1967.

Schubert, Frank N. *Black Valor: Buffalo Soldiers and the Medal of Honor, 1870–1898.* Wilmington, DE: Scholarly Resources, 1997.

Wanton, George Henry

Born: May 15, 1868
Died: November 27, 1940
Home State: New Jersey
Service: Army
Conflict: Spanish-American War
Age at Time of Award: 30

George Wanton was born in Paterson, New Jersey, on May 15, 1868. As a very young man, he joined the navy, but left sea service after a nearly five-year enlistment. He enlisted in the army in 1889, joining the 10th Cavalry as a Buffalo Soldier. His early career with the 10th was not distinguished, as he was constantly in and out of trouble, some of which resulted in a number of court martial convictions. By 1898, when he deployed to Cuba with Troop M of the 10th Cavalry, he had apparently begun to mature and had earned back his corporal stripes.

Wanton and a number of other Buffalo Soldiers were assigned to a mission led by Lieutenant Carter P. Johnson, a former enlisted man with over two decades of experience in the army. The unit was given the task of resupplying and reinforcing Cuban rebels operating behind Spanish lines. After an abortive attempt to land the nearly 400 Cuban insurgents at an initial location, Johnson settled on landing near the small settlement of Tayabacoa. On June 30, 1898, a landing party of 300 insurgents and 28 American troopers attempted to land in the face of a blockhouse at the mouth of the Tayabacoa River. They were met with intense fire, despite supporting fires from a gunboat accompanying the naval landing vessels. The attacking force never seized a beachhead and they were forced to withdraw at night, but lacked the necessary boats to transport everyone, having lost at least two boats to Spanish cannon fire. Two wounded Americans and a number of wounded Cuban insurgents were stranded in the water at the shoreline.

The Cuban insurgent forces attempted to rescue the trapped men, only to have four successive rescue missions fail in the face of Spanish defensive fire. At the urging of his 10th Cavalry Troopers, Johnson eventually agreed to allow one additional attempt to rescue the stranded men. Five Americans, including Corporal Wanton, were selected to carry out the rescue. Moving their landing boat through the water as quietly as possible, because the Spanish garrison was still on high alert for such a rescue mission, the five men made it to the wounded men and pulled them into the boat. As the Spanish positions poured fire into the ocean, the party successfully rescued the stranded men and returned to the *Florida* safely. Lieutenant Johnson is quoted as saying that the "rescue was pronounced by all who witnessed it, as a brave and gallant deed, and deserving of reward."

In early 1899, Lieutenant Johnson would petition the War Department for proper acknowledgment of the heroic actions of the five troopers at Tayabacoa. The War Department made the decision quickly and determined that the four Buffalo Soldiers deserved the Medal of Honor. This is very interesting in hindsight, as these would be the last Medals of Honor awarded to black soldiers until well after World War II. No black soldiers were awarded the Medal of Honor during World War I or World War II, apparently due to the pervasive racism in the military during the intervening years. A number of black soldiers would be belatedly honored in the 1990s for their actions during the two world wars.

Wanton received his Medal of Honor on June 23, 1899, and left the army shortly thereafter. He returned to Paterson, New Jersey, but was unable to find consistent work in the civilian world. Though ambivalent toward the military, he reenlisted in the army in 1902 in order to find a more stable living. His second enlistment only lasted until 1904, when he again tried his hand at civilian life. Five years later, in 1909, he reenlisted once again and stayed in the army this time until his retirement as a Master Sergeant in 1925. Though his career in the service was interrupted a number of times, in the end, Wanton appears to have become a fine noncommission officer by his retirement. Because of his Medal of Honor, he was well treated, relative to most retired Buffalo Soldiers. He was given the opportunity, in 1921, to serve as an honorary pallbearer during the burial of the Unknown Soldier at Arlington National Cemetery. He was later honored by President Hoover and the American Legion at gatherings for Medal of Honor recipients. He died in Washington, D.C. on November 27, 1940, and was buried in Section 4 at Arlington National Cemetery.

James B. Martin

Further Reading

Fletcher, Marvin. *The Black Soldier and Officer in the United States Army, 1891–1917.* Columbia: University of Missouri Press, 1974.

Hanna, Charles W. *African American Recipients of the Medal of Honor: A Biographical Dictionary, Civil War through Vietnam War.* Jefferson, NC: McFarland, 2002.

Schubert, Frank N. *Black Valor: Buffalo Soldiers and the Medal of Honor, 1870–1898.* Wilmington, DE: Scholarly Resources, 1997.

Warren, John E., Jr.

Born: November 16, 1946
Died: January 14, 1969
Home State: New York
Service: Army
Conflict: Vietnam War
Age at Time of Award: 22

John Earl Warren Jr. was born in Brooklyn, Kings County, New York, on November 16, 1946. He apparently lived in New York his entire life, as he enlisted in the U.S. Army from New York City. He went to officer candidate school and was a first lieutenant when he was deployed to the Republic of Vietnam on September 8, 1968.

Warren was a platoon leader in Company C, 2nd Battalion (Mechanized), 22nd Infantry Regiment, 25th Infantry Division. His unit was operating in Tay Ninh Province on the Cambodian border in January 1969. On January 14, 1969, 1st Lieutenant Warren's company was moving in a convoy to reinforce another unit from their battalion. As they passed through a rubber plantation, the convoy came under intense enemy fire from heavily fortified and well-hidden enemy positions. 1st Lieutenant Warren immediately dismounted his vehicle and began to move to engage the enemy positions, deploying the men of his platoon as he fired his weapon. Reaching a point just a few feet from one of the enemy bunkers, Warren pulled a grenade from his harness and was about to throw it into the bunker. Before he could do so, a North Vietnamese hand grenade was thrown from the bunker, endangering the small force, and Warren saw it immediately. With no concern for his own safety, focused only on saving the lives of his platoon members, 1st Lieutenant John Warren dove on the hand grenade and absorbed the blast with his body. His wounds proved to be fatal, but he saved at least three members of his platoon from certain death. For his courage and self-sacrifice, 1st Lieutenant John Earl Warren Jr. received the Medal of Honor.

1st Lieutenant Warren's Medal of Honor ceremony was held at the White House and officiated by President Richard M. Nixon on April 7, 1970. President Nixon presented Warren's family with his Medal and thanked them for their son's service and sacrifice. Lieutenant John Earl Warren Jr. was buried in Long Island National Cemetery in Farmingdale, New York, at Section O, Grave 33144. He is memorialized on the Vietnam Memorial at Panel 34W, Row 3.

James B. Martin

Further Reading

Hanna, Charles W. *African American Recipients of the Medal of Honor: A Biographical Dictionary, Civil War through Vietnam War.* Jefferson, NC: McFarland, 2002.

Westheider, James E. *The African American Experience in Vietnam: Brothers in Arms.* New York: Rowman & Littlefield, 2008.

Westheider, James E. *Fighting on Two Fronts: African Americans and the Vietnam War.* New York: New York University Press, 1997.

Watson, George

Born: March 14, 1914
Died: March 8, 1943
Home State: Colorado
Service: Army
Conflict: World War II
Age at Time of Award: 28

George Watson was born in Birmingham, Alabama, on March 14, 1914. Raised in Birmingham, Watson graduated from Colorado A&M College (now known as Colorado State University) in 1942 and was drafted on September 1, 1942. Despite his university education, Watson—an African American—was assigned as a private to the U.S. Army's 2nd Battalion, 29th Quartermaster Regiment.

On March 8, 1943, Watson was aboard the transport USAT *Jacob* near Porlock Harbor, New Guinea, when Japanese aircraft attacked the ship. With the vessel sinking and still under attack by the Japanese, the order was given to abandon ship. In the chaos that followed, Watson, rather than saving himself, assisted many soldiers who could not swim into the life rafts. Swimming back and forth from the sinking ship to the life rafts, he continued to rescue his comrades until he himself was so exhausted that he was pulled down by the tow of the sinking ship. It is believed that Watson drowned since his body was never recovered.

Watson was the first African American to earn the Distinguished Service Cross (DSC) during World War II. In the late 1990s, the army conducted a three-year review of the records of 10 African Americans heroes to determine if they met the standards for award of the Medal of Honor. Of these, seven names were submitted to Congress and the president. On January 13, 1997, in a crowded White House ceremony, President Bill Clinton awarded the Medal of Honor to these seven African American veterans of World War II. Only one of the men, 77-year-old Vernon Baker, who had been a platoon leader with the 92nd Infantry Division, was alive and present for the ceremony. The others, including Watson, were awarded the Medal of Honor posthumously. While some of the other departed were represented by next of kin, Watson's wife had passed away by this time and no other living next of kin could be found.

When Watson's DSC was upgraded to the Medal of Honor, he became the only African American to earn the medal while serving in the Pacific Theater. He has been memorialized at the Manila American Cemetery in the Philippines and by the George Watson Memorial Field at Ft. Benning, Georgia. In addition, in 1997, the U.S. Navy named USNS *Watson* (T-AKR-310) in Private Watson's honor. The *Watson* is the lead ship of a class of large, medium-speed, roll-on roll-off (LMSR) ships.

George Watson's Medal of Honor now resides in the U.S. Army Quartermaster Museum at Ft. Lee, Virginia.

Alexander M. Bielakowski

Further Reading

Bruning, John R., Jr. *Elusive Glory: African-American Heroes of World War II*. Greensboro, NC: Avisson Press, 2001.

Converse, Elliott, III, Daniel K. Gibran, John A. Cash, Robert K. Griffith, Jr., and Richard H. Kohn. *The Exclusion of Black Soldiers from the Medal of Honor in World War II: The Study Commissioned by the United States Army to Investigate Racial Bias in the Awarding of the Nation's Highest Military Decoration*. Jefferson, NC: McFarland, 1997.

Hanna, Charles W. *African American Recipients of the Medal of Honor: A Biographical Dictionary, Civil War through Vietnam War*. Jefferson, NC: McFarland, 2002.

Moore, Christopher. *Fighting for America: Black Soldiers—The Unsung Heroes of World War II*. New York: Presidio Press, 2005.

Williams, Moses

Born: October 10, 1845
Died: August 23, 1899
Home State: Louisiana
Service: Army
Conflict: Indian Wars
Age at Time of Award: 25

Moses Williams was born in Carrollton, Louisiana, on October 10, 1845. He was born into slavery and freed after the Civil War ended, living in East Carroll Parish. On October 1, 1866, Williams enlisted in the newly formed 9th Cavalry Regiment at Lake Providence, Louisiana, and began a 30-year career with the famed Buffalo Soldiers. Though he apparently could not read in 1866, as he signed his enlistment papers with an X, he obviously had natural leadership characteristics, because in a very short period of time he was promoted to first sergeant in his unit, Troop F, 9th Cavalry, and moved to west Texas to serve on the border. His unit spent its time guarding mail and stage routes and Williams served successively as the first sergeant of Troop F, Troop K, and Troop I of the 9th Cavalry. With his reenlistment and assignment to Troop I in 1876, Williams and his unit moved to New Mexico and were there when the problems began with the Warm Springs Apaches. He participated in campaigns against two major Apache leaders, Victorio and Nana, earning respect in both but glory in the latter.

Moses Williams was serving as first sergeant of Troop I on August 16, 1881, part of an element that was in pursuit of the Apache chief Nana and his renegade group of warriors. They were resting after a lengthy chase of the Indians, when a local man burst into camp to report that Nana had hit a settlement just two miles from where the troopers were resting. The farm belonging to Mr. Chavez had been attacked and everyone living there had been killed. The troop commander, Lieutenant Valois, directed one of his officers, Lieutenant Burnett, to take a small detachment of 12 troopers and give immediate chase to Nana's band. Valois and the remainder of the troop would follow as soon as they were made ready. When they arrived at the ranch, Burnett and his small detachment found the local citizen's account to be accurate and set out after Nana, now accompanied by a large group of armed local citizens for assistance. They found Nana in the foothills of the Cuchillo Negro Mountains, New Mexico, and proceeded to engage his band in a running battle, successively attacking Nana's positions on each of the ridgelines as he retreated deeper into the mountains. Williams was at Burnett's side throughout much of the engagement, providing covering fire when necessary and leading troops when called upon. He was given control of the right flank of the unit for a large part of the three- or four-hour fight and performed with courage and professionalism. At one point, Burnett's horse was shot at while they were dismounted, causing it to run, and the detachment thought he was dead. A cry of "they got the lieutenant" went up and the men began to retreat. Williams moved quickly to reorganize the men and get them back into line, though they were under heavy fire the entire time from an enemy with commanding positions above them. He rapidly seized control of the situation and brought the detachment back into the fight. Eventually, Lieutenant Valois and the remainder of Troop I caught up with Burnett's detachment, but as they did both organizations found themselves caught in a trap set by Nana. Valois called for both units to retreat, with Burnett, Williams, and Private Walley providing covering fire for all of the 9th Cavalry troopers. Just as this trio of heroes was about to withdraw, they heard voices coming from their front asking for help. Three troopers from Valois's contingent had been left behind as they sought cover behind some prairie dog mounds. Now situated between the enemy and the troopers, they needed help to survive. Burnett, Moses, and Walley stayed put to continue covering fire and two of the troopers crawled to their position and safety. The third trooper, named Burton, had been wounded and was unable to accompany his comrades as they withdrew under the covering fire. Private Walley volunteered to make a rescue attempt and Lieutenant Burnett consented. Riding his horse so that he was low in the saddle away from the enemy fire, Walley made it safely through the hail of bullets to Burton's position. Hoisting the wounded man into the saddle, Walley mounted behind him and spurred the horse to safety, covered by the fire of Burnett and Moses who had risen from their concealed position to draw the Apaches' fire.

Lieutenant Burnett later wrote about Moses Williams and praised him for his "coolness, bravery, and unflinching devotion to duty" during the running fight with Nana that day. In his report to the army's adjutant general, Burnett cited Williams for "standing by me in an open exposed position under heavy fire from a large party of Indians, at a comparatively short range." These actions were directly responsible for saving three men's lives and were eventually recognized when Williams received the Medal of Honor on November 12, 1896. Burnett and Walley also received the Medal of Honor for their actions in the fight at Cuchillo Negro Mountains.

After the Apache Wars of 1880–1881 ended, Williams continued to serve with the 9th Cavalry Regiment until 1886. He had learned to read and write and sought to become an ordnance sergeant. This required specific minimum service time, a physical examination, and a written examination by a board of officers. Moses Williams became an ordnance sergeant in 1886, and has been identified by the U.S. Army's Ordnance Corps history as the first African American to attain this rank. He served initially in North Dakota in this capacity and was eventually transferred to Ft. Stevens, near the mouth of the Columbia River, in 1895. New 10-inch seacoast guns were being emplaced to guard the river's opening and Williams was sent to be the caretaker of the guns and the fort. Poor health caused Moses Williams to retire to Ft. Vancouver, Washington, in 1898; he had served his country for 32 years and had received its highest award for valor. He died at Ft. Vancouver from heart problems on August 23, 1899, and was buried in the Ft. Vancouver Military Cemetery.

Williams was in the first group of African American professional soldiers who paved the way for others to follow them into careers of service with the U.S. Army. The backbone of a great army is the noncommissioned officers who lead soldiers on a day-to-day basis, and Moses Williams's history shows that he was just such a backbone for the men of the 9th Cavalry. In 2005, over 100 years after his death, he was honored by induction into the U.S. Army's Ordnance Corps Hall of Fame.

James B. Martin

THE BUFFALO SOLDIERS

The name, Buffalo Soldiers, is widely believed to have originated during the Indian Wars, as the American Indians likened the coarse hair of the African American soldiers to that of the omnipresent buffalo. The first known report of this name came from an army wife who was living on the frontier with her husband. While in this instance the name is focused on the African American regiments that were created in the aftermath of the American Civil War, the term has been used by historians and authors widely to identify African American segregated units prior to the integration of the armed forces.

Approximately 180,000 African Americans fought for the Union Army during the Civil War. At the conclusion of that conflict, it was only natural that some opportunities in the American military establishment opened to the continued service of these brave men. On July 28, 1866, President Andrew Johnson signed a bill authorizing the raising of two regiments of cavalry and four regiments of infantry to be manned exclusively by African American soldiers. While such a bill would have been impossible in the years before the Civil War, and equally impossible in the years following the Spanish-American War, the timing of the process made the creation of the 9th and 10th Cavalry and the 38th, 39th, 40th, and 41st Infantry a reality. The states which had been in rebellion during the Civil War were not represented in the U.S. Congress in 1866, and the House and Senate were controlled by politicians who wanted to raise the stature and opportunities of African Americans, punish the rebellious states, or both.

All of these units compiled valorous records over the next two decades during combat and security operations on the western frontier. The 10th Cavalry was recruited and formed at Ft. Leavenworth, Kansas, with Colonel Benjamin Grierson appointed to command the regiment. Grierson's posting as the commander of the regiment would last for 22 years, from 1866 to 1888. Although initially serving at Ft. Leavenworth, the regiment was transferred to Ft. Riley, Kansas, and stationed there for service in the western theater. The 9th Cavalry was recruited from the southern states and was formed in 1866 in New Orleans, Louisiana. It was initially commanded by Colonel Edward Hatch and posted to San Antonio, Texas, to patrol that portion of the western frontier. As the army reduced the number of infantry regiments in 1869, the African American infantry regiments were consolidated, with the 38th and 41th Regiments being consolidated into the 24th and the 39th and 40th being consolidated into the 25th.

These regiments spent the latter portion of the 19th century patrolling the western frontier, providing protection for forts, wagon trails, and white settlers. They fought and controlled the American Indian population from Ft. Leavenworth to the Pacific Ocean and performed admirably in unpleasant and dangerous conditions. Long periods of tedious boredom and poor living conditions were interrupted by dangerous campaigning and even worse living conditions. During their service in the west, the Buffalo Soldiers fought in over 125 engagements against various American Indian tribes. The regiments encountered hostiles from the Cheyenne, Apache, Kiowa, Ute, Comanche, and Sioux tribes and were often required to shepherd these tribes to reservations and supervise their imprisonment there. Often broken up into troop-sized units, living on isolated frontier posts, they made a life for themselves in the army for the hefty sum of $13.00 a month and room and board.

Although making up nearly 20 percent of the army's cavalry and 10 percent of the army overall, these four regiments faced not only the enemy outside their cantonments but also the racial prejudice of the whites inside. These units were employed almost exclusively on the western frontier due to the racial problems still overtly visible in American society, but proved time and again that African American soldiers were capable of service at the same level as their white counterparts, if not better. From the outset, the bill that created the regiments did not allow for African American officers, with the regiments being formed and commanded by white officers. While these men, such as Grierson and Hatch, proved to able leaders who valued their African

American soldiers, the private soldiers still lacked leaders of their own race to look up to and emulate. The first African American officer to be assigned to one of the regiments was Lieutenant Henry O. Flipper, the first African American to graduate from the U.S. Military Academy at West Point. Flipper was followed by the next two African American graduates from West Point, Lieutenants John Hanks Alexander and Charles Young. While Flipper and Alexander's careers were shortened by scandal or illness, Charles Young served until 1922, having led soldiers in both the 9th and 10th Cavalry. At the time of his death, he was a full colonel and the military attaché in Nigeria.

All four of the regiments would be called into duty for the Spanish-American War, with two of them actively engaged in Cuba alongside the much more famous Rough Riders, commanded by future president Theodore Roosevelt. During the Battle of San Juan Heights (often called San Juan Hill), the 24th Infantry fought alongside white units in the initial assault and were among the first to reach the summit of the heights. Nearby, the Rough Riders and the 10th Cavalry were among the units that attacked Kettle Hill and seized the high ground there. While the Rough Riders are credited with taking the position, based on statements from white officers, such as later general of the Armies John J. (Blackjack) Pershing (then an officer in the 10th Cavalry), the first man to the top of Kettle Hill was Sergeant George Berry of the 10th Cavalry. While the public record affords this honor to Thomas Rynning of the Rough Riders, the historical confusion can be explained through the lens of racial discrimination and politics in the years following the war.

Between the creation of the Buffalo Soldier regiments in 1866 and the end of the Spanish-American War, the members of the Buffalo Soldiers proved themselves to be reliable and brave soldiers, the equal of any in the U.S. Army. The four regiments served admirably in the west and overseas during the war, with 23 members of the Buffalo Soldiers receiving the Medal of Honor during that time. Twenty-one of these honors were received for bravery during the Indian Wars and two were received for actions during the Spanish-American War. The history of these regiments is the story of brave soldiers who fought against adversaries and fellow soldiers alike for respect and honor.

The regiments have been honored in a variety of ways throughout the years since they were disbanded or integrated. The Buffalo Soldier Monument at Ft. Leavenworth, Kansas, was built through the support of General Colin Powell and recognizes the service of the 9th and 10th Cavalry in the west. The Command and General Staff College at Ft. Leavenworth presents an award from the Buffalo Soldiers Association to one of the top students of its graduating class every year. The Buffalo Soldiers are part of the legends of the U.S. Army today and are proudly honored and remembered for their service and perseverance.

James B. Martin

Further Reading

Leckie, William H. *The Buffalo Soldiers: A Narrative of the Negro Cavalry in the West.* Norman: University of Oklahoma Press, 1967.

Rickey, Don, Jr. *Forty Miles a Day on Beans and Hay: The Enlisted Soldier Fighting the Indian Wars.* Norman: University of Oklahoma Press, 1963.

Schubert, Frank N. *Black Valor: Buffalo Soldiers and the Medal of Honor, 1870–1898*. Wilmington, DE: Scholarly Resources, 1997.

"Sergeant Moses Williams: Medal of Honor Recipient." Ordnance Corps Hall of Fame Statement. http://www.goordnance.army.mil/hof/2000/2005/williams.html (accessed September 1, 2013).

Utley, Robert M. *Frontier Regulars: The United States Army and the Indian, 1866–1890*. New York: Macmillan, 1973.

Wilson, William Othello

Born: September 16, 1867
Died: January 18, 1928
Home State: Maryland
Service: Army
Conflict: Indian Wars
Age at Time of Award: 23

Wilson enlisted on August 21, 1889, at the age of 21. He had been born in Hagerstown in western Maryland and was promoted to the rank of corporal in December 1890, with a reputation for being one of the best marksmen in his unit. He also had a reputation for wearing a long, black leather coat, a broad-brimmed, white hat, and a large pair of spurs on his boots. His flamboyant appearance seems to have been accepted by his officers.

On December 30, 1890, a day after the massacre at Wounded Knee Creek, Wilson was with Troops D, F, I, and K of the 9th Cavalry protecting a supply train. Shortly after first light, a large band of Sioux attacked the troops. The cavalry, under Capt. John S. Loud, formed a circle with the wagons and decided to send a rider to seek reinforcements. Wilson offered to carry the dispatch, and as he sped out of the encampment he was pursued by 8 or 10 warriors. He outran them with help from his fellow cavalrymen, who opened fire on his pursuers from the encampment, and found Maj. Guy V. Henry, who saddled up his men and rode off to relieve the besieged wagon train. After a brief skirmish, the Sioux broke off, and the wagons were successfully driven to their destination.

On New Year's Day, acting on the orders of Major Henry, his adjutant described Wilson's ride as "one involving much risk as the Indians knowing what was intended would endeavor to intercept the messenger, and overwhelmed by numbers certain death would follow" (quoted in Schubert 1997, 126). A copy was sent to Regimental Headquarters at Ft. Robinson.

Wilson stayed with the regiment in Pine Ridge throughout the freezing winter until March 1891. A few days before the regiment was due to leave, Wilson decided to head to Chadron, Nebraska, where he stayed in a hotel. He was immediately recognized, and the army had him arrested for desertion. He was also charged with the theft of a rifle and the forgery of a civilian name on checks in the amount of $200. Wilson denied the desertion charge and said: "My reason for being in Chadron was a drinking spell and while I was under the influence of drink I found myself in Chadron having been constantly on duty for about four months as acting commissary sergeant at Pine Ridge Agency and Battalion 9th Cavalry in the field which was the most mental strain to which I have been subjected to in my life" (quoted in Schubert 1997, 127).

Wilson was locked up at Ft. Robinson, and in May, a court martial was convened. In the event, he was found guilty only of absence without leave and check forgery. He was sentenced to four years' hard labor and forfeiture of pay, and he lost his corporal's stripes. But because the reviewing authority, Gen. John R. Brooke, did not believe the forgery charge to be accurate, the sentence was rejected except for the demotion in rank.

Rather than being daunted by this setback, Wilson asked to be awarded the Medal of Honor, and his officers were still prepared to support him. Lt. Powell wrote: "It is with pleasure that I commend the very gallant conduct of the within named applicant and invoke the bestowal upon him of a Medal of Honor to which in my judgement he is unquestionably entitled" (quoted in Schubert 1997, 129). Within a month the Medal of Honor was on its way to Wilson.

In August 1893, as a private in H Troop based at Ft. Duchesne, Wilson set off for Bellevue near Omaha, Nebraska, to represent the regiment in the annual marksmanship contest. He attended, but he only made it back as far as Denver. He claimed that he had lost his train fare and asked for a duplicate ticket and money to pay for his meals. It was at that point that Wilson disappeared with his carbine and revolver. Wilson made no attempt to hide; he went back to his native Hagerstown, where he married, had seven children, and worked as a teacher, a cook, and a carpenter. The army never seemed to be interested in dragging him before a court martial again, and he remained in Hagerstown until he died in Washington County Hospital on January 18, 1928, the only known deserter to have received the Medal of Honor. He was buried in Rose Hill Cemetery in Hagerstown. It was only after his death that it became public knowledge that he had won the Medal of Honor, as he had never spoken of it since he had made his decision to desert the army. On Armed Forces Day in 1990, his hometown of Hagerstown honored this American hero by dedicating a small park named Medal of Honor Triangle.

Jonathan D. Sutherland

Further Reading

Hanna, Charles W. *African American Recipients of the Medal of Honor: A Biographical Dictionary, Civil War through Vietnam War*. Jefferson, NC: McFarland, 2002.

Schubert, Frank N. *Black Valor: Buffalo Soldiers and the Medal of Honor, 1870–1898*. Wilmington, DE: Scholarly Resources, 1997.

BIBLIOGRAPHY

Abdul-Jabbar, Kareem, and Anthony Walton. *Brothers in Arms: The Epic Story of the 761st Tank Battalion, WWII's Forgotten Heroes*. New York: Broadway Books, 2004.

Adams, Virginia Matzke, ed. *On the Altar of Freedom: A Black Soldier's Civil War Letters from the Front, Corporal James Henry Gooding*. Amherst: University of Massachusetts Press, 1991.

African American Publications. 2001. "Frank Petersen, Jr." http://www.africanpubs.com/Apps/bios/1075PetersenFrank.asp?pic=none.

"American Hero: William Henry Johnson, New York National Guard." *StrategyWorld.com*: http://www.strategypage.com/respect/articles/20020321.asp.

Amos, Preston E. *Above and beyond in the West: Black Medal of Honor Winners, 1870–1890*. Washington, DC: Potomac Corral, Westerners, 1974.

"Apache Campaigns: Victorio." *Huachuca Illustrated: A Magazine of the Fort Huachuca Museum* 6 (1999): 45–75.

Appleman, Roy. *South to Naktong, North to the Yalu*. Washington, DC: U.S. Army Center for Military History, 1961.

Arnold, Thomas St. John. *Buffalo Soldiers: The 92nd Infantry Division and Reinforcements in World War II, 1942–1945*. Manhattan, KS: Sunflower University Press, 1999.

Astor, Gerald. *The Right to Fight: A History of African Americans in the Military*. Cambridge, MA: Da Capo Press, 1998.

Beer, W. F., and O. F. Keyed. *Deeds of Valor: How America's Heroes Won the Medal of Honor*. Detroit: Perrien-Keydel, 1903.

Bielakowski, Alexander. *African American Troops in World War II*. Oxford, UK: Osprey Publishing, 2007.

Blatt, Martin H., Thomas J. Brown, and Donald Yacovone, eds. *Hope & Glory: Essays on the Legacy of the Fifty-Fourth Massachusetts Regiment*. Amherst: University of Massachusetts Press, 2001.

Booker, Bryan D. *African Americans in the United States Army in World War II*. Jefferson, NC: McFarland, 2008.

Bowers, William T., William M. Hammond, and George L. MacGarrigle. *Black Soldier, White Army: The 24th Infantry Regiment in Korea*. Washington, DC: Center for Military History, U.S. Army, 1996.

Bradford, Sarah E. *Harriet: The Moses of Her People*. New York: J. J. Little & Co, 1901.

Bradford, Sarah E. *Scenes in the Life of Harriet Tubman*. 1869. Reprint, Salem, NH: Ayer, 1986.

Brooks, Victor. *The Boston Campaign: April 1775–March 1776. Great Campaigns*. Conshohocken, PA: Combined Publishing, 1999.

Bruning, John Robert, Jr. *Elusive Glory: African-American Heroes of World War II*. Greensboro, NC: Avisson Press, Inc., 2001.

Buckley, Gail. *American Patriots: The Story of Blacks in the Military from the Revolution to Desert Storm*. New York: Random House, 2001.

Burchard, Peter. *We'll Stand By the Union: Robert Gould Shaw and the Black 54th Massachusetts Regiment*. New York: Facts on File, 1993.

Bussey, Charles M. *Firefight at Yechon: Courage & Racism in the Korean War*. Washington, DC: Brassey's, 1991.

Carter, Allene G., and Robert L. Allen. *Honoring Sergeant Carter: Redeeming a Black World War II Hero's Legacy*. New York: HarperCollins Press, 2003.

Cash, John A. *Seven Firefights in Vietnam*. Washington, DC: Office of the Chief of Military History, United States Army, 1985.

Claxton, Melvin, and Mark Puls. *Uncommon Valor: A Story of Race, Patriotism, and Glory in the Final Battles of the Civil War*. Hoboken, NJ: John Wiley and Sons, 2006.

Cohen, Warren. "Recognizing Valor." *Michigan History Magazine*. http://wjcohen.home .mindspring.com/otherclips/thomas.htm, posted January/February 1997 (accessed July 16, 2003).

Cohen, William S. Speech. http://www.defenselink.mil/speeches/1998/c19981209-secdef .html, posted December 9, 1998 (accessed August 2, 2003).

Cohn, Michael. *Black Men of the Sea*. New York: Dodd Mead, 1978.

Colley, David P. *The Road to Victory: The Untold Story of World War II's Red Ball Express*. New York: Grand Central Publishing, 2001.

Collier, Peter, and Nick Del Calzo. *Medal of Honor: Portraits of Valor beyond the Call of Duty*. New York: Artisan, 2006.

Converse, Elliott, III, Daniel K. Gibran, John A. Cash, Robert K. Griffith, Jr., and Richard H. Kohn. *The Exclusion of Black Soldiers from the Medal of Honor in World War II: The Study Commissioned by the United States Army to Investigate Racial Bias in the Awarding of the Nation's Highest Military Decoration*. Jefferson, NC: McFarland, 1997.

"Cook Third Class Doris Miller USN." Washington, DC: Naval History and Heritage Command. http://www.history.navy.mil/faq57-4.htm (accessed August 25, 2013).

Cooper, Michael L. *From Slave to Civil War Hero: The Life and Times of Robert Smalls*. New York: Lodestar Books, 1994.

Crenshaw, Wayne. "Marine Recalls Heroic Act of Medal of Honor Recipient Rodney Davis." Macon.com. http://www.macon.com/2012/11/10/2244622/new-memorial-un veiled-for-medal.html, posted November 10, 2012 (accessed August 18, 2013).

Custer, Elizabeth B. *"Boots and Saddles": Or, Life in Dakota with General Custer*. Norman: University of Oklahoma Press, 1961.

Davis, Benjamin O., Jr. *Benjamin O. Davis, Jr., American: An Autobiography*. Washington, DC: Smithsonian Institution Press, 1991.

Davis, Burke. *Black Heroes of the American Revolution*. San Diego: Harcourt Brace Jovanovich, 1991.

Davis, Lenwood, and George Hill, eds. *Blacks in the American Armed Forces, 1776–1983*. Westport, CT: Greenwood Press, 1985.

Dye, Julia. *Backbone: History, Traditions, and Leadership Lessons of Marine Corps NCOs*. New York: Open Road Media, 2013.

Emilio, Luis F. *A Brave Black Regiment: History of the Fifty-Fourth Regiment of Massachusetts Volunteer Infantry, 1863–1865*. New York: Bantam Books, 1992.

Fletcher, Marvin. *The Black Soldier and Officer in the United States Army, 1891–1917*. Columbia: University of Missouri Press, 1974.

Francis, Charles E., and Adolph Caso. *The Tuskegee Airmen: The Men Who Changed a Nation*. Boston: Branden Publishing, 1997.

Franklin, John Hope, and Alfred A. Moss Jr. *From Slavery to Freedom: A History of African Americans*. 8th ed. 2 vols in one. New York: Random House, 2004.

Gibran, Daniel. K. *The 92nd Infantry Division and the Italian Campaign in World War II*. Jefferson, NC: McFarland, 2001.

Gomez-Granger, Julissa. *CRS Report for Congress: Medal of Honor Recipients: 1979–2008*. Washington, DC: Congressional Research Service, RL 30011, 2008.

Goodwin, Doris Kearns. *No Ordinary Time*. New York: Simon and Schuster, 1994.

Green, Michael Cullen. *Black Yanks in the Pacific: Race in the Making of American Empire after World War II*. Ithaca, NY: Cornell University Press, 2010.

Gubert, Betty Kaplan, Miriam Sawyer, and Caroline M. Fannin. *Distinguished African Americans in Aviation and Space Science*. Westport, CT: Oryx Press, 2002.

Haley, Leon L. *The Quiet One: General Roscoe Robinson, Jr.* London: Fortis Publishing, 2010.

Hanna, Charles W. *African American Recipients of the Medal of Honor: A Biographical Dictionary, Civil War through Vietnam War*. Jefferson, NC: McFarland, 2002.

Hargrove, Hondon B. *Buffalo Soldiers in Italy: Black Americans in World War II*. Jefferson, NC: McFarland, 1985.

Harrison, Eric. "A Tribute to American's 'Buffalo Soldiers' Military: Gen. Colin L. Powell Breaks Ground for a Memorial to the Black Fighting Units That 'Have Served This Nation Over Its Long History.'" *Los Angeles Times*, July 29, 1990, p. 18.

Haulman, Daniel L. "Tuskegee Airmen-Escorted Bombers Lost to Enemy Aircraft." Maxwell Air Force Base, AL: U.S. Air Force Historical Research Agency, 2009.

Hollis, John. "Medal of Honor Recipient Sgt. Rodney M. Davis to Be Honored in Macon." *AtlantaBlackstar.*http://atlantablackstar.com/2012/11/09/medal-of-honor-recipient-sgt-rodney-m-davis-to-be-honored-in-macon/, posted November 9, 2012 (accessed August 18, 2013).

Houston, Ivan J. *Black Warriors: The Buffalo Soldiers of World War II Memories of the Only Negro Infantry Division in World War II*. Bloomington, IN: iUniverse Star, 2011.

Johnson, Edward A. *History of Negro Soldiers in the Spanish-American War and Other Items of Interest.* Raleigh, NC: Capital Printing Company, 1899.

Johnson, Tisha. "NCOs Inducted into Fort Leavenworth Hall of Fame." *Fort Leavenworth Lamp.* http://www.army.mil/article/21394/ (accessed September 1, 2013).

Jones, Maxine D., and Kevin M. McCarthy. *African Americans in Florida.* Sarasota, FL: Pineapple Press, 1993.

Kaplan, Sidney, and Emma Nogrady Kaplan. *The Black Presence in the Era of the American Revolution.* Amherst: University of Massachusetts Press, 1989.

Kingseed, Cole C. *Old Glory Stories: American Combat Leadership in World War II.* Annapolis, MD: Naval Institute Press, 2006.

Kingseed, Cole C. "The Saga of Vernon J. Baker." *Army Magazine*, February 2008, 37–4.

"Laggard Draft Boards." *Baltimore Afro-American*, January 20, 1966.

Leckie, William H. *The Buffalo Soldiers: A Narrative of the Negro Cavalry in the West.* Norman: University of Oklahoma Press, 1967.

Lengel, Edward G. *To Conquer Hell: The Meuse-Argonne, 1918: The Epic Battle That Ended the First World War.* New York: Henry Holt, 2008.

Lewis, Jone Johnson. "Harriet Tubman: Fugitive Slave, Underground Railroad Conductor, Civil War Nurse and Soldier, Women's Rights Advocate and Social Reformer." http://womenshistory.about.com/library/weekly/aa020419c.htm (accessed July 17, 2003).

Little, Arthur W. *From Harlem to the Rhine: The Story of New York's Colored Volunteers.* New York: Haskell House, 1974.

Lopez, Todd. "Pioneering Tuskegee Airman Laid to Rest in Arlington." http://www.defenselink.mil/news/Jul2002/n07172002_200207174.html, posted July 17, 2002 (accessed August 2, 2003).

Lowry, Richard S. *New Dawn: The Battles for Fallujah.* Havertown, PA: Casemate Publishing, 2010.

MacGregor, Morris J., Jr. *Integration of the Armed Forces, 1940–1965.* Washington, DC: Center for Military History, 1985.

Manchu Web Page: http://www.manchu.org/linage/sargent.htm (accessed September 12, 2013).

Mapp, Zoey. "Elaine Matlow: DNA Spectrum Hung the Moon." DNA Spectrum Website. http://highlights.dnaspectrum.com/elaine-matlow-dna-spectrum-hung-the-moon/, posted April 3, 2013 (accessed August 24, 2013).

Maslowski, Peter, and Don Winslow. *Looking for a Hero: Staff Sergeant Joe Ronnie Hooper.* Lincoln: University of Nebraska Press, 2004.

McConnell, Roland. "Isaiah Dorman and the Custer Expedition." *The Journal of Negro History* 33(3) (July 1948): 344–52.

McLaurin, Melton A. *The Marines of Montford Point.* Chapel Hill: The University of North Carolina Press, 2007.

Miller, Robert. *Buffalo Soldiers: The Story of Emanuel Stance.* Morristown, NJ: Silver Press, 1995.

Moore, Christopher Paul. *Fighting for America: Black Soldiers—The Unsung Heroes of World War II.* New York: Ballantine Books, 2005.

Moore, Harold G., and Joseph L. Galloway. *We Were Soldiers Once . . . and Young: Ia Drang—The Battle That Changed the War in Vietnam*. New York: Random House, 1992.

Motley, Mary Penick, ed. *The Invisible Soldier: The Experience of the Black Soldier, World War II*. Detroit: Wayne State University Press, 1975.

Moye, J. Todd. *Freedom Flyers: The Tuskegee Airmen of World War II*. New York: Oxford University Press, 2010.

Murphy, Edward F. *Vietnam Medal of Honor Heroes*. New York: Ballantine Books, 2005.

Nalty, Bernard C. *The Right to Fight: African-American Marines in World War II*. Washington, DC: Marine Corps History and Museums, World War II Commemorative Series, 1995.

Nalty, Bernard C. *Strength for the Fight*. New York: Free Press, 1986.

Navy Office of Information. "Navy Secretary Names Destroyer to Honor World War II African American Hero." Press release. http://www.pinckney.navy.mil/PR.htm, posted February 2000 (accessed August 29, 2013).

Nawrozki, Joe. "Honoring the men of Ia Drang." *The Baltimore Sun*, November 11, 2003. http://articles.baltimoresun.com/.../0311110242_1_drang-valley-ia-drang-forrest (accessed November 24, 2013).

Nelson, Peter N. *A More Unbending Battle: The Harlem Hellfighters' Struggle for Freedom in WWI and Equality at Home*. New York: BasicCivitas Books, 2009.

"Nursing Home for Veteran's Named after Combat Hero." *Lakeland Ledger*. http://news.google.com/newspapers?nid=1346&dat=20030822&id=nwcwAAAAIBAJ&sjid=-P0DAAAAIBAJ&pg=6170,750687, posted August 22, 2003 (accessed August 30, 2013).

O'Neal, Bill. *Doris Miller: Hero of Pearl Harbor*. Waco, TX: Eakin Press, 2007.

Oral History Interview with SP5 Clarence G. Sasser, U.S. Army Medical Department. http://ameddregiment.amedd.army.mil/moh/bios/sasserInt.html (accessed November 12, 2012).

Osur, Alan M. *Blacks in the Army Air Forces during World War II: The Problem of Race Relations*. Washington, DC: Office of Air Force History, 1977.

Petersen, Frank E. *Into the Tiger's Jaw: America's First Black Marine Aviator—The Autobiography of Lieutenant General Frank E. Petersen*. Novato, CA: Presidio Press, 1998.

Pfeifer, Kathryn Browne. *The 761st Tank Battalion (African-American Soldiers)*. New York: Twenty-First Century Books, 1994.

Ploski, Harry A., and James Williams. *The Negro Almanac: A Reference Work on the African American*. New York: Bellwether, 1983.

Potter, Lou, William Miles, and Nina Rosenblum. *Liberators: Fighting on Two Fronts in World War II*. New York: Harcourt Brace Jovanonich, Publishers, 1992.

Press Releases from Gov. George Pataki's Office, "Governor Pataki Honors WWI Hero Sgt. Henry Johnson." http://www.state.ny.us/governor/press/year02/jan10_1_02.htm, posted January 10, 2002; and "Governor Urges Awarding Medal of Honor to Henry Johnson." http://www.state.ny.us/governor/press/year01/feb12_2_01.htm, posted February 12, 2001.

Price, James S. *The Battle of New Market Heights: Freedom Will Be Theirs by the Sword*. Charleston, SC: The History Press, 2011.

Quarles, Benjamin. *The Negro in the American Revolution.* Chapel Hill: University of North Carolina Press, 1961.

Reef, Catherine, *African Americans in the Military,* New York: Facts on File, 2010.

Reef, Catherine. *Benjamin Davis, Jr.* New York: Scholastic, 1992.

"The Richard K. Sorenson Award." www.fightingfourth.com (accessed January 27, 2013).

Rickey, Don, Jr. *Forty Miles a Day on Beans and Hay: The Enlisted Soldier Fighting the Indian Wars.* Norman: University of Oklahoma Press, 1963.

Roberts, Frank E. *The American Foreign Legion: Black Soldiers of the 93d in World War I.* Annapolis, MD: Naval Institute Press, 2004.

Rogers, Bernard William. *Vietnam Studies Cedar Falls—Junction City: A Turning Point.* Washington, DC: Department of the Army, 1989.

"Ronald Radcliffe." http://www.myblackhistory.net/Ronald_Radcliffe.htm (accessed November 24, 2013).

Rose, P. K. "Black Dispatches: Black American Contributions to Union Intelligence during the Civil War." http://www.cia.gov/cia/publications/dispatches/dispatch.html.

Sandel, Edward. *Black Soldiers in the Colonial Militia: Documents from 1639 to 1780.* Baton Rouge, LA: Tabor Lucas Publications, 1994.

Schubert, Frank N. *Black Valor: Buffalo Soldiers and the Medal of Honor, 1870–1898.* Wilmington, DE: Scholarly Resources, 1997.

Schubert, Frank N. "Buffalo Soldiers at San Juan Hill." 1998 Conference of Army Historians. http://www.history.army.mil/documents/spanam/BSSJH/Shbrt-BSSJH.htm (accessed September 1, 2013).

Schubert, Frank N. "The Violent World of Emmanuel Stance, Fort Robinson, 1887." *Nebraska History* 55 (Summer 1974): 203–19.

Scott, Emmett J. "The American Negro in the World War." Washington, DC, 1919. http://net.lib.byu.edu/estu/wwi/comment/scott/ScottTC.htm (accessed January 26, 2013).

"Sergeant Moses Williams: Medal of Honor Recipient." Ordnance Corps Hall of Fame Statement. http://www.goordnance.army.mil/hof/2000/2005/williams.html (accessed September 1, 2013).

Shaw, Henry I. Jr., and Ralph W. Donnelly. *Blacks in the Marine Corps.* Washington DC: History and Museum Division, Headquarters United States Marine Corps, 1975.

Smith, Charles R. *U.S. Marines in Vietnam: High Mobility and Standdown, 1969.* Washington, DC: Headquarters United States Marine Corps, Marine Corps in Vietnam Series, 2002.

Smith, Larry. *Beyond Glory: Medal of Honor Heroes in Their Own Words—Extraordinary Stories of Courage from World War II to Vietnam.* New York: W. W. Norton, 2003.

Smithsonian National Air and Space Museum. http://www.nasm.si.edu/features/black wings/hstudent/bio_davis.cfm (accessed August 2, 2003).

Stentiford, Barry M. *Tuskegee Airmen.* Santa Barbara, CA: Greenwood, 2012.

Tillman, Barrett. *Heroes: U.S. Army Medal of Honor Recipients.* New York: Berkley, 2006.

Tourtellot, Arthur Bernon. *Lexington and Concord: The Beginning of the War of the American Revolution.* New York: W. W. Norton, 1963.

Trice, Craig A. "The Men That Served with Distinction: The 761st Tank Battalion." Unpublished Master's Thesis, U.S. Army Command and General Staff College, 1997.

United States Navy. USS *Pinckney*. http://www.public.navy.mil/surfor/ddg91/Pages/our ship.aspx#.Uh-MAxbJAlI (accessed August 29, 2013).

Utley, Robert M. *Frontier Regulars: The United States Army and the Indian, 1866–1890*. New York: Macmillan, 1973.

Uya, Okon Edet. *From Slavery to Public Service: Robert Smalls, 1839–1915*. New York: Oxford University Press, 1971.

Washburn, Patrick S. *A Question of Sedition*. New York: Oxford University Press, 1986.

Westheider, James E. *The African American Experience in Vietnam: Brothers in Arms*. New York: Rowman & Littlefield, 2008.

Westheider, James E. *Fighting on Two Fronts: African Americans and the Vietnam War*. New York: New York University Press, 1997.

"Wife Gets Sims' Medal of Honor." *The Evening Independent*, December 5, 1969. http://news.google.com/newspapers?nid=950&dat=19691205&id=YUtQAAAAIBAJ&sjid=i1 cDAAAAIBAJ&pg=7068,1301786 (accessed August 30, 2013).

Willbanks, James H., ed. *America's Heroes: Medal of Honor Recipients from the Civil War to Afghanistan*. Santa Barbara, CA: ABC-CLIO, 2001.

Williams, Albert E. *Black Warriors: The Korean War*. Haverford, PA: Infinity, 2004.

Williams, Chad L. *Torchbearers of Democracy: African American Soldiers in the World War I Era*. Chapel Hill: The University of North Carolina Press, 2010.

Williams, Michael W. *The African-American Encyclopedia*. New York: Marshall Cavendish, 1993.

Wilmer, L. Allison, J. H. Jarrett, and George W. F. Vernon. *History and Roster of Maryland Volunteers, War of 1861–5*. Baltimore, MD: Guggenheimer, Weil & Co., 1899.

Wilson, Joe, Jr. *The 761st "Black Panther" Tank Battalion in World War II*. Jefferson, NC: McFarland, 1999.

Wilson, Kimberly. "Lance Cpl. Todd Corbin." www.beliefnet.com (accessed January 27, 2013).

Work, David. "United States Colored Troops in Texas during Reconstruction, 1865–1867." *The Southwestern Historical Quarterly* 109(3) (January 2006): 337–58.

"WWI 'Harlem Hellfighter' Posthumously Nominated for Medal." National Guard Web site. http://www.ngb.army.mil/news/2001/02/12/johnson.shtml, posted February 12, 2001.

Yacovone, Donald, ed. *A Voice of Thunder: The Civil War Letters of George E. Stephens*. Urbana: University of Illinois Press, 1997.

Zimmerman, Beth. "Marines Brave "Hell" in Haditha." *Marine Corps Times*, September 18, 2006.

INDEX

Note: Page numbers in **boldface** reflect main entries in the book.

ABOUT THE EDITOR

James B. Martin, PhD, is associate dean of academics at the U.S. Army Command and General Staff College at Ft. Leavenworth, Kansas. His published works include *Third War: Irregular Warfare on the Western Border, 1861–1865—Leavenworth Papers No. 23* (2013). Martin holds a BA in political science from the University of Kentucky and an MA and PhD in history from The University of Texas at Austin.

CONTRIBUTORS

Alexander M. Bielakowski, PhD
Department of Military History
U.S. Army Command and General
    Staff College

James B. Martin, PhD
Associate Dean
U.S. Army Command and General
    Staff College

Scott A. Porter
Department of Command and
    Leadership
U.S. Army Command and General
    Staff College

Jonathan D. Sutherland
Independent Scholar

Christopher S. Trobridge
Department of History
Texas Tech University

James H. Willbanks, PhD
Director
Department of Military History
U.S. Army Command and General
    Staff College